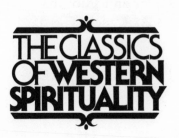

THE CLASSICS
OF WESTERN
SPIRITUALITY

Bonaventure

THE SOUL'S JOURNEY INTO GOD •
THE TREE OF LIFE • THE LIFE OF ST. FRANCIS

TRANSLATION AND INTRODUCTION
BY
EWERT COUSINS

PREFACE
BY
IGNATIUS BRADY, O.F.M.

PAULIST PRESS
NEW YORK • RAMSEY • TORONTO

Cover Art:
The artist Ruth Anaya was born in Canada and now lives in Larchmont, New York. She was educated in Montreal at McGill University and Sir George Williams College, exhibits nation-wide and is the recipient of very many awards. Her work can be found in prominent international collections. Of her cover painting she says:
"One should not portray St. Bonaventure as a simple friar. yet the simplicity of his spirit commands it. Though he was a leading intellectual of his day who later became a cardinal, he always retained the spiritual values of the teachings of St. Francis. To portray the true feelings of St. Bonaventure I gave a simple friar a bishop's crozier, a saintly halo, and an aura containing Bonaventure's spiritual father, Saint Francis."

Design: Barbini Pesce & Noble, Inc.

Copyright © 1978 by The Missionary Society
of St. Paul the Apostle
in the State of New York

Library of Congress
Catalog Card Number: 78-60723

ISBN: 0-8091-0240-4 (cloth)
ISBN: 0-8091-2121-2 (paper)

Published by Paulist Press
Editorial Office: 1865 Broadway, New York, N.Y. 10023
Business Office: 545 Island Road, Ramsey, N.J. 07446

Printed and bound in the
United States of America

CONTENTS

Author of the Preface

IGNATIUS BRADY, O.F.M., one of the world's leading authorities on Bonaventure and early Franciscan spirituality, is Prefect of the Theology Section of the Franciscan research center Collegio S. Bonaventura at Grottaferrata near Rome. Father Ignatius was assigned to this post in 1961, when the center was located at Quaracchi in Florence. It was at this center that the critical text of Bonaventure's work was edited and published from 1882 to 1902. Following in the distinguished tradition of the Quaracchi editors, Father Ignatius has produced as his major scholarly achievement the critical text of *The Sentences of Peter Lombard* and has written important articles on the authenticity and textual status of works of Bonaventure. Born in Detroit in 1911, he entered the Order of Friars Minor, receiving the Franciscan habit in 1929, and was ordained a priest in 1937. From the Pontifical Institute of Medieval Studies, Toronto, he received a licentiate in medieval studies in 1941; and from the University of Toronto, a master of arts degree in 1940, and a doctorate in philosophy in 1948. He has taught at Duns Scotus College, Detroit; the Franciscan Institute of St. Bonaventure University; the Catholic University of America; and the Antonianum, the international university of the Friars Minor at Rome. In 1962 the Friars Minor conferred upon him the title Lector Jubilatus, the highest recognition afforded to their teachers. A recognized authority on Franciscanism, he has attended General Chapters of his Order, has been appointed a member of pre-General Chapter committees and was assigned as theological consultant to the Union of Major Superiors. He has been increasingly in demand in many parts of the world to conduct Franciscan study weeks and retreats and to give conferences on Franciscan spirituality: especially in the Far East, Italy, England, Ireland and the United States. In addition to his textual work, he has translated a number of books and has published numerous articles for journals and encyclopedias on early Franciscan history, philosophy, theology and spirituality.

Editor of this Volume

EWERT COUSINS was born in 1927 in New Orleans. He holds a licentiate in sacred theology from St. Louis University and a Ph.D. in philosophy from Fordham University. From 1960 to 1963 he taught in the Classics Department of Fordham University and since 1963 has been a member of Fordham's Theology Department, where he presently has the rank of professor. For ten years he also taught in Fordham's graduate school of religious education and for the last three years has been director of the graduate program in spirituality of Fordham's Theology Department. He has been visiting professor at Columbia University and has taught and lectured at a number of colleges and universities in the New York area. A specialist in Bonaventure, he was a member of the International Bonaventure Commission, which published five volumes of scholarly studies to commemorate the seventh centenary of Bonaventure's death in 1974. He was also active in organizing national and international conferences for the Bonaventure centenary. Over the last ten years, he has done research in Italy, France and England on early Franciscan spirituality and in 1972–1973 was a resident scholar at the Ecumenical Institute for Advanced Theological Studies in Jerusalem, exploring the Muslim background of medieval Christian theology. Active in the dialogue of world religions, he is a consultant to the Vatican Secretariat for Non-Christians. Specializing also in contemporary theology and spirituality, he has worked in the area of religion and culture, was president of the American Teilhard Association and edited *Process Theology* and *Hope and the Future of Man*. The author of numerous articles on Bonaventure in scholarly journals, he has written a book entitled *Bonaventure and the Coincidence of Opposites*, which will be published soon by Franciscan Herald Press. He is editorial consultant for the present series The Classics of Western Spirituality. A Catholic layman formally affiliated with the Holy Name Province of the Order of Friars Minor, he resides in Bethlehem, Connecticut, with his wife Kathryn and their three children, Hilary, Sara and Emily.

ACKNOWLEDGMENTS

It is impossible to express here my gratitude to all who have contributed to my work in Bonaventure through the years. I must, therefore, limit my acknowledgments to those who have assisted in the present volume. I am grateful to Father Kevin Lynch, C.S.P., President of Paulist Press, for his vision in inaugurating the series of which this book is a part and for his gracious leadership throughout the project. I owe an enormous debt of gratitude to Richard Payne, Associate Editor of Paulist Press and Editor-in-Chief of The Classics of Western Spirituality, for his personal friendship and his professional guidance at every step of the way. Not least among his many contributions was his suggestion to set the text in sense lines. It is an honor to have the preface written by the eminent Franciscan scholar Father Ignatius Brady, O.F.M., who through the years has generously shared with me his vast knowledge of Bonaventure and early Franciscan spirituality. My understanding of Bonaventure's biography of Francis has been greatly influenced by the research of Father Regis Armstrong, O.F.M. Cap. whose recent dissertation may well usher in a new phase of interpretation of the work. Father Armstrong also read my translation of the biography and my introduction, and made many valuable suggestions. My work could not have reached its present state without the tireless efforts of Jaime Vidal, who painstakingly checked the translation and introduction, suggesting many improvements in the light of his linguistic skill and historical erudition. I am grateful to my wife Kathryn for her constant support in the project and for her professional assistance both in editing my manuscript and in producing the index, a task she is performing for all of the volumes in the series. For typing the manuscript I am indebted to Carolyn Gonzales, who, in spite of the complexities of the sense lines, maintained her usual high level of precision. I owe a special debt of gratitude to my friends in Bethlehem, Connecticut, who generously helped in checking the proofs.

PREFACE

"How wholesome it is, always to meditate on the Cross of Christ": *Optimum est semper in cruce meditari*" (St. Bonaventure, Sermon 11 on Good Friday, vol. IX, 265).

Long before John Gerson (d. 1429) gave Bonaventure the title of Seraphic Doctor (as it would appear), he was known throughout Christendom as the *Doctor Devotus*, the Devout Teacher, by reason of the unction, in the true sense of the word, manifested in his writings and sermons. To grow in the things of the Spirit, he would say, love must go hand in hand with learning; nay, at a certain point it must leave study to dally behind while the heart runs ahead with inner joy to the gift that is God himself.[1] In the Prologue of the *Itinerarium*, he invites the reader of the work to enter upon it with deep longing, with prayerfulness, with groanings of the inner man, "so that he not believe that reading is sufficient without unction, speculation without devotion, investigation without wonder, observation without joy . . . knowledge without love . . . or reflection . . . without divinely inspired wisdom."[2]

The three works here published by Professor Ewert Cousins bear witness of Bonaventure's adherence to such principles of the spirit. The *Itinerarium mentis in Deum*, the journey of the inner man inward and upward to God, one of the best known works of the Seraphic Doctor, is a deeply theological and mystical study of man's soaring quest for the Triune God and the steps he must take to arrive at the Good and the Beautiful and enter into the Cloud of the Unknowing, which is itself perhaps the most perfect knowing here below of the One in Three.

The *Lignum vitae*, *The Tree of Life*, may not at first sight seem to soar to such heights in its delightful series of meditations on the role of Christ in the plan of God. Nonetheless, it is a quest

---

1. Cf. *The Soul's Journey into God*, VII, 5, pp. 113-115.
2. *Ibid.*, prol., 4, pp. 55-56.

for the tree of knowledge (since to know Christ is to live), a quest for wisdom, the wisdom to be found in the Tree of Life which is Christ, and itself a prayer that we may eat of that Tree and thus find Life and obtain salvation from the Lord.

The *Legenda maior, The Life of St. Francis,* is not without its place in this trilogy, since it portrays in vivid colors the inner life of the Seraph of Assisi, his own Journey to God in the strength of the fruit plucked from the Tree of Life. How wholesome, how enriching in the things of God is it always to meditate on, as Francis did, and shape one's life in union with the Cross of Christ!

Hence it is not too extravagant to suggest that it is the figure of Saint Francis which gives this book its inner unity and ultimate inspiration. Even more, it is the great and deep love of Francis for the Crucified, as shown in the *Legenda,* which motivates Bonaventure to undertake the Journey of the Soul to God and, en route, to gather the fruits that grow on the Tree of Life to sustain him on that Journey. We do not hereby imply, be it added, that we thus establish the chronology of these works. It is well known that the *Legenda* was undertaken at the request of the Chapter of Narbonne (1260), whereas the *Itinerarium* is the fruit of Bonaventure's meditations on La Verna in late 1259. The *Lignum vitae,* I believe, cannot be dated with any precision.

At the Chapter, the friars had requested Bonaventure to reduce the trilogy of Thomas of Celano (the First Life, the Second Life and the treatise on the Miracles of Francis) to "one good legend."[3] Though indeed factually and often verbally dependent on the earlier texts, Bonaventure's Legend or Life of Saint Francis is far more than that. The theologian and mystic enters into its composition, to put in bold relief the mysteries of the Cross in the life of Francis, whom Bonaventure in the *Legenda minor* calls the *insignis sectator crucifixi Iesu,* the outstanding

---

3. On the meaning of *legenda* or *legend* in the Middle Ages, cf. pp. 37-38.

follower of Jesus Crucified.[4] Later in the same work[5] he was to characterize the virtues of the Poverello as so many ways in which he was made like to Christ, and thus as so many steps which prepared him for the reception of the stigmata. And then, in the last hours of his life, as he urges his sons to follow poverty and peace as the only riches he can leave them, Francis bids them keep heart and mind fixed on the footprints of the Crucified and walk in them always.[6] The signs of the Passion which marked him within and without, Francis seems to say, should be impressed on their very souls and made evident by their total conformity to the Crucified.

This is clearly Bonaventure's vision of Francis which pervades the whole of the *Legenda maior*. No matter what some modern writers since Paul Sabatier have said about this work, to the point of accusing Bonaventure of betraying the ideals of Francis, a careful, prayerful reading will show both Saints: the real Francis (if without the host of incidents recounted by Celano) and the true Bonaventure devoted from childhood onward to his Seraphic Father in very deed and very truth. For there is about Bonaventure a great spirit of reverence for Saint Francis and the workings of the Spirit in him and through him, a reverence and love manifested on other occasions too, in the truly remarkable sermons he preached on Francis (not often known to those who criticize Bonaventure) and a profound grasp of the Gospel perfection which Francis sought to make his rule of life and the Rule of the Lesser Brothers the Lord gave him.

There is one aspect, too, of the *Legenda maior* which we should not forget: that by Bonaventure's time the Order had become largely a clerical community in which many, if not the majority, possessed a considerable theological training. What they needed perhaps was not a collection of stories or incidents

---

4. *Legenda minor*, III, 1.
5. *Ibid.*, VI, 9.
6. *Ibid.*, VII, 4.

in the life of Francis, but a greater knowledge of and insight into the inner life of the Poverello, the workings of the Spirit and grace in him, a portrait based primarily on a theological interpretation of the historical facts. Hence the emphasis on the role of grace in Francis, how he grew in grace and virtue, in knowledge of the things of the Spirit, in wisdom and likeness to Christ, and so became, for his age and for all centuries since, the true leader of those who with him would follow the wisdom of the Cross.

We thus grasp the deep significance of the mission God gave Francis to the men of his day and ours, a mission so vividly set forth by Bonaventure in the prologue to the Life: to be a new leader and herald of the Gospel and its demands, to be himself a living Gospel in deed and in truth, and to call men of his day and ours, whether they join his Order or not, to mourning and weeping, to sackcloth and penance, to the Cross and the sign of the Tau on their foreheads, as men who would follow him who is the Way and the Truth and the Life.

Thus to know Christ and him crucified is a gift of the Spirit: a gift however which can be fostered within a man by frequent nourishment at the *Tree of Life*, by constant meditation on him who is himself that Tree in his life, his teachings, his death, his glorification. To this end Bonaventure composed, likely some time after the *Legenda maior*, the *Lignum vitae* and accompanied the text with an original design of the Tree, perhaps in as simple a form as that found in a late thirteenth-century manuscript.[7] The opuscule is, quite evidently, a highly original work. Apart from frequent anonymous use of the meditations once ascribed to Saint Anselm, it reveals no dependence on other writers and little or none on Bonaventure's sermons or other treatises, save perhaps some use of his gloss on Saint Luke.

That the *Lignum vitae* proved immensely popular is more than evident from the great number of handwritten copies still to be found, usually preceded by the figure of the Tree, and from

---

7. *Vatic. lat.* 1058, f. 28v.

the pieces of art which it inspired in many a Franciscan church or refectory, and in at least one cathedral, that of Saint-Nazaire at Carcassonne.

Again it is Saint Francis who inspired the greatest piece perhaps that Bonaventure ever wrote: the *Itinerarium*, the ascent of the inner man into the mystery of the Triune God in loving contemplation and union.

The heart of Bonaventure on La Verna, the mountain of the stigmata, is revealed in part in the letter he wrote to the Poor Clares of Assisi on hearing from Brother Leo, then at La Verna, of their love of Christ crucified after the example of their most blessed Mother Clare.[8] But his own love of the Crucified was led to new heights when Leo spoke to him and others of Francis' mystical experiences in the vision of the Crucified Seraph on that holy mountain.[9]

Such experiences Bonaventure sought to penetrate and analyze in the masterpiece he was to write later, the *Itinerarium mentis in Deum*, itself a mirror of his own thoughts and intuitions, of his own wrestling with the Spirit, and of his own desire to die to self and enter the darkness of the mountain, to pass over with Christ crucified from this world to the Father. His language may be that of Pseudo-Dionysius the Areopagite; it may borrow from the school of Saint Bernard of Clairvaux and the tradition of the Victorines at Paris; but his pursuit of Wisdom is that of the Seraph of La Verna, his father Saint Francis.

Of Francis himself Thomas of Celano, his first biographer, had remarked that he was always new, always fresh, always eager to begin again.[10] That freshness of spirit he has passed on to us as a precious heritage to be shared and imitated. If Christians seek to follow Christ in newness of spirit, if they would obey his injunction: "Whoever wishes to be my follower, must deny himself, take up his cross daily and follow in my steps"

---

8. *Epistolae officiales*, 7 (VIII, 473-474).
9. Cf. *The Soul's Journey into God*, VII, 3, p. 112.
10. 1 Cel., 103.

(Matt. 16:24), they shall find in Francis the model to follow. The penance of the Cross must be ever new and fresh, such as we witness in Francis, who even on his deathbed urged his brothers: "Let us begin and go forward, for till now we have done little to heed and obey these words of the Lord."[11]

Need we add that the three writings of Saint Bonaventure here presented are so many ways in which he sought to understand and to nourish in himself and in others the love needed to heed that invitation of the Master?

Ignatius Brady O.F.M.
Collegio S. Bonaventura
Grottaferrata, Rome, Italy
Easter 1978

---

11. Bonaventure, *Commentarius in Evangelium S. Lucae*, IX, v. 23, no. 38 (VII, 228); cf. *Legenda maior*, XIV, 1, p. 315.

FOREWORD

This volume contains translations from Latin of three works of St. Bonaventure (1217-1274), theologian and minister general of the Franciscan Order. The first, *The Soul's Journey into God (Itinerarium mentis in Deum)*, is a speculative mystical treatise whose central theme came to Bonaventure in 1259 while he was meditating at Mount La Verna in Tuscany on the vision of the six-winged Seraph in the form of the Crucified, which St. Francis of Assisi had at that very spot in 1224. The six wings symbolized for Bonaventure the six stages of contemplation by which the soul ascends into God: through a twofold consideration of nature, of the soul and of God himself. Considered Bonaventure's masterpiece, this work contains a technical statement of his theological vision, in which God is seen reflected, in characteristic Franciscan fashion, throughout the created universe.

The second work, *The Tree of Life (Lignum vitae)*, is a meditation on the life of Christ, based on the Gospel accounts of his birth, public ministry, passion, death, resurrection and glorification. Christ is seen as the Tree of Life on whose branches blossom such virtues as humility, piety, patience, constancy, and justice. Christ's virtues are models for the Christian to meditate upon and imitate. Written after *The Soul's Journey*, *The Tree of Life* presupposes the theological vision of the former treatise, but evokes a more simple and direct devotional response to the humanity of Christ that became characteristic of Franciscan religious sensibility as it developed in the later Middle Ages.

The third work, *The Life of St. Francis (Legenda maior)*, was commissioned by the General Chapter of the Friars Minor held at Narbonne in 1260. After doing research among Francis' early companions, Bonaventure completed his biography by 1263. It was adopted as the official biography of the Franciscan Order, thus assuring its widespread dissemination and influence in subsequent centuries. The work is chiefly a compilation from the earlier biographies of Francis written by Thomas of Celano and Julian of Speyer. Although Bonaventure does add some new historical material, his distinctive contribution lies in the sphere of spirituality, for he shapes the historical material into a spiritual treatise on the life of the virtues with Francis presented as the ideal of Gospel perfection. Our translation of the *Legenda maior* in this volume does not include Bonaventure's lengthy account of miracles attributed to Francis after his death.

Taken together, the three selections offer a comprehensive picture of Bonaventure's Franciscan spirituality. The person of Francis, in the concrete events of his life, leads to meditation on the humanity of Christ and imitation of his virtues which, in turn, energize the soul on its journey into God, as it is drawn along the stages of the ascent by the reflection of God throughout creation. This spiritual vision is articulated by Bonaventure with a remarkable combination of speculative penetration, symbolic power and poetic sensibility. As explained in our introduction, in order to capture some of the complexity of Bonaventure's style, we have broken the text into sense lines where this seemed appropriate.

A Note on the Use of Scripture

The scriptural passages in this book are translated directly from the Latin Vulgate, which was the text used by Bonaventure and other Western Christians throughout the Middle Ages. In certain passages our version will therefore differ from modern Bibles, which are translated from the Hebrew or Greek originals. The numbering of the Psalms is also different; from Psalm 10 to Psalm 147 the modern editions add one number to that of the Vulgate. Thus our reference to Psalm 50 would be to Psalm 51 of most modern translations.

Ewert Cousins
Fordham University
New York

INTRODUCTION

In the history of Western spirituality, Bonaventure holds a central and pivotal position. The 13th-century friar, professor at the University of Paris, minister general of the Franciscan Order, cardinal and adviser to popes, played a major role in the spiritual ferment of the high Middle Ages. Viewed within the religious context of the Middle Ages as a whole—when Islamic, Jewish and Christian spirituality were flourishing—he produced one of the richest syntheses of Christian spirituality. Although cosmic in its scope, it was distinctively Christian in its content, grounded on the doctrine of the Trinity and devotion to the humanity of Christ. Within Christianity he achieved a striking integration of Eastern and Western elements. Living at a time when the rift between the Greek East and the Latin West was not yet so radical, he integrated the distinctively Greek spirituality of the Pseudo-Dionysius with the emerging Franciscan devotion to the humanity and passion of Christ, which was to give a decisive direction to the spirituality of Western Europe for centuries.

In the Western Middle Ages, which saw successive monastic reforms and the emergence of new religious orders, Bonaventure played a significant role in the evolution of forms of religious life. When controversy arose over the new mendicant orders, the Franciscans and the Dominicans, Bonaventure and his Dominican contemporary Thomas Aquinas defended the mendicant life-style against the attacks launched by the secular masters of the University of Paris. Within the Franciscan Order, Bonaventure is considered its second founder and the chief architect of its spirituality. As minister general of the Friars Minor for seventeen years at a crucial period in their history, he attempted to integrate the ideal of Francis of Assisi into the cumulative traditions of Christian spirituality and to shape that ideal into institutional forms which have survived to this day.

In the 13th century he flourished during that brief period

1

when spirituality and speculation were not yet separated. It was still possible for him to produce a speculative system with spirituality at its core and a spiritual synthesis enhanced by theoretical reflection. With 13th-century genius for speculative synthesis, he produced a type of spiritual *summa* that integrates psychology, philosophy and theology. Grounding himself in Augustine and drawing from Anselm, he brought together the cosmic vision of the Pseudo-Dionysius with the psychological acumen of Bernard of Clairvaux and Richard of St. Victor. And he balanced a richness of Biblical symbolism with abstract philosophical speculation. In no other medieval Christian spiritual writer were such diverse elements present in such depth and abundance and within such an organic systematic structure. In a certain sense, Bonaventure achieved for spirituality what Thomas did for theology and Dante for medieval culture as a whole.

BONAVENTURE'S LIFE

Bonaventure was born in Bagnoregio, a small town in central Italy, situated in the Etruscan country about sixty miles north of Rome, between Viterbo and Orvieto.[1] The date of his birth is not certain; until recently it was considered to be 1221, but now is generally accepted by specialists to be 1217.[2] Bonaventure, then, was born at the period when the new Franciscan Order was reaching a peak in its early development. It

---

1. The definitive biography of Bonaventure has not yet been written; for recent studies of his life, cf. Jacques Guy Bougerol, *Saint Bonaventure: un maître de sagesse* (Paris: Editions franciscaines, 1966); Ignatius Brady in *New Catholic Encyclopaedia*, vol. II, s.v. "Bonaventure, St.," pp. 658-664; John Quinn in *The New Encyclopaedia Britannica: Macropaedia*, vol. III, s.v. "Bonaventure, Saint," p. 17.

2. Cf. Giuseppe Abate, "Per la storia e la cronologia di S. Bonaventura, O. Min.," *Miscellanea francescana* 49 (1949): 534-568; 50 (1950): 97-130; for dating Bonaventure's works and the major events of his life, I am indebted to the recent research of Jacques Guy Bougerol, John Quinn and Ignatius Brady: cf. the chronology in *S. Bonaventura 1274-1974*, ed. Jacques Guy Bougerol, vol. II (Grottaferrata: Collegio S. Bonaventura, 1973), pp. 11-16; John F. Quinn, "Chronology of St. Bonaventure (1217-1257)," *Franciscan Studies* 32 (1972): 168-186; idem, "Bonaventure, Saint"; Ignatius Brady, "Bonaventure, St."

was in 1205 that Francis heard the crucifix in the church of San Damiano speak to him and direct him on a path that was to lead to his founding a new religious order. Within four years Francis had obtained the approval of Pope Innocent III for his rule of life based on the Gospel. The young Franciscan Order grew with surprising rapidity, attracting followers from all walks of life and spreading geographically over central Europe, soon extending to Spain, England and to foreign missions in Africa and the Middle East. A sign of the rapid growth of the Order was the celebrated "Chapter of the Mats," held in 1221 at the Portiuncula near Assisi. The chapter was attended by some three thousand friars (five thousand according to other estimates), whose numbers were too great to be accommodated by the houses prepared there by the town of Assisi. As a result many had to sleep in the open air or in huts of woven boughs or mats.[3] The rapid spread of the Franciscans reached Bagnoregio, where a friary was established in the early 13th century, at which Bonaventure is said to have received his preliminary education.[4]

While Bonaventure was still a boy, Francis died in 1226, venerated as a saint and acclaimed for the gift of the stigmata, which he had received two years before. As the fame of Francis's sanctity spread, the Order continued to grow. Only two years after his death, when Bonaventure was only eleven years old, Francis was canonized by Pope Gregory IX, his personal friend and former protector of the Order.

It is unlikely that Bonaventure ever met Francis. Although it is possible that Francis visited Bagnoregio during Bonaventure's childhood on one of his many preaching tours, Bonaventure makes no mention of having seen Francis personally. However, he does give clear testimony of having been cured of a

---

3. Cf. *Compilatio Assisiensis*, 18, ed. Marino Bigaroni (Santa Maria degli Angeli: Tipografia Porziuncola, 1975), p. 54.

4. In his brief of October 14, 1482, to the Franciscan convent at Bagnoregio, on the occasion of Bonaventure's canonization, Sixtus IV stated that Bonaventure "in dicta domo educatus exstitit"; *Bullarium franciscanum*, III, 838.

serious illness through Francis while still a boy. In his major biography of Francis, he states: "When I was a boy, as I still vividly remember, I was snatched from the jaws of death by his [Francis's] invocation and merits. So if I remained silent and did not sing his praises, I fear that I would be rightly accused of the crime of ingratitude. I recognize that God saved my life through him, and I realize that I have experienced his power in my very person."[5] In his shorter biography of Francis, Bonaventure states in greater detail: "God's numberless favors granted through Francis in various parts of the world do not cease to abound, as I myself who have written this life have verified through my own personal experience. For as I lay seriously ill while still a child, I was snatched from the very jaws of death and restored to perfect health owing to a vow made by my mother to the blessed Father Francis."[6] A tradition developed that Francis performed this cure personally on a visit to Bagnoregio; however, recent scholarship claims that the cure did not take place until after Francis's death and canonization, perhaps between 1228-1231, when Bonaventure was between eleven and fourteen years of age.[7] Whatever the circumstances of the cure, it is clear that it made a lifelong impression on Bonaventure, establishing a close bond between him and Francis.

Of the facts of Bonaventure's childhood, little is known. His father was John di Fidanza, who seems to have been a physician and a man of some means; his mother was Maria di Ritello. Baptized John, he received the name Bonaventure only on his entry into the Franciscan Order.

About 1234, when he was seventeen years of age, he went to study at the University of Paris in the faculty of arts. At Paris he came in contact with the Franciscans, who had gone to France first in 1217. Francis himself had intended to bring the Order to

---

5. *Legenda maior*, prol., 3 cf. our translation, p. 182.
6. *Legenda minor*, de transitu mortis, 8 (VIII, 579).
7. Cf. Bougerol, *Saint Bonaventure: un maître de sagesse*, pp. 8-11.

France personally; but when his plans were interrupted, he sent Brother Pacificus in his place with a small band of friars.[8] After settling first at Saint-Denis, they eventually were given the use of some property within the city walls, where in 1240 they began construction on what would become the major house of studies in the Order, where the great Franciscan masters were to teach: Alexander of Hales, Bonaventure and Duns Scotus.[9] Shortly after Bonaventure's arrival in Paris, the most illustrious professor of the university, the Englishman Alexander of Hales, entered the Franciscan Order. This was a decisive event in Franciscan history, for Alexander brought his doctoral chair to the Franciscan house, thus establishing the school of the Friars Minor as officially part of the University of Paris and launching the great Franciscan intellectual tradition, which would stand in tension with the simplicity of Assisi.

In 1243 Bonaventure entered the Franciscan Order and studied theology under Alexander of Hales and John of La Rochelle until their deaths in 1245, when he continued under Eudes Rigaud and William of Middleton. Bonaventure was greatly devoted to and much influenced by Alexander, who recognized his talent and admired his virtue, as is attested to by the following statement of Sixtus IV in his bull of canonization: "Bonaventure was great in learning, but no less great in humility and holiness. His innocence and dove-like simplicity were such that Alexander of Hales, the renowned doctor whose disciple Saint Bonaventure became, used to say of him that it seemed as though Adam had never sinned in him."[10] It was not merely the learning of Alexander and the other scholars of the Franciscan

---

8. Cf. *Legenda maior*, IV, 9; cf. our translation, p. 213-214.

9. On the history of the Franciscan establishment at Paris, cf. Christian Eugène, "Saint Bonaventure et le grand couvent des cordeliers de Paris," in *Etudes franciscaines* 18 (Supplément annuel, 1968): 167-182.

10. Sixtus IV, Bull of Canonization, in *Doctoris Seraphici S. Bonaventurae Opera Omnia*, vol. I, xl (Quaracchi: Collegium S. Bonaventurae, 1882); for sources of the remark of Alexander, cf. the chronicle attributed to Bernard of Bessa, Bonaventure's secretary, in *Analecta franciscana*, III, 699; also *Chronica XXIV generalium, ibid.*, 324.

5

school that attracted Bonaventure, but also the simplicity of Francis. Although Bonaventure was and remained an intellectual of the Paris tradition, he was drawn by the simplicity of Assisi, as he later described:

> Do not be upset that in the beginning the Friars were simple and unlettered. This ought rather to strengthen your faith in the Order. For I acknowledge before God that what made me love the life of blessed Francis so much was the fact that it resembled the beginning and growth of the Church. As the Church began with simple fishermen and afterwards developed to include renowned and skilled doctors, so you will see it to be the case in the Order of Blessed Francis. In this way God shows that it was not founded by the prudence of men but by Christ.[11]

In 1248 Bonaventure was licensed as a bachelor of Scripture and lectured on the Bible for the next two years; from 1250 to 1252 he lectured on the *Sentences* of Peter Lombard and produced his *Commentary on the Sentences.* In 1253 or 1254 he became a master in theology, taking over the leadership of the Franciscan school in Paris, where he taught until 1257, when he was elected minister general of the Order. In 1256, when a controversy broke out at the University of Paris over the new mendicant orders, he defended their ideal of poverty against the attack of William of Saint-Amour.[12]

Not long after its founding, tensions arose in the Order between those who wanted to follow the ideals of Francis in stark simplicity and those who favored adaptation as the Order expanded. The situation became complicated by the fact that the Spirituals, as the first group was called, began to interpret their position in the light of the eschatology of Joachim of Fiore, who had prophesied that an age of the Spirit would begin in 1260

---

11. *Epistola de tribus quaestionibus,* 13 (VIII, 336).
12. On this controversy, cf. Decima Douie, *The Conflict between the Seculars and the Mendicants at the University of Paris in the 13th Century* (London: Blackfriars, 1954); "St. Bonaventura's Part in the Conflict between Seculars and Mendicants at Paris," in *S. Bonaventura 1274-1974,* II, pp. 585-612.

and last until the end of the world.[13] As some interpreted Joachim, in this age Church institutions would be superseded by a free life in the Spirit. Joachim further prophesied that this age would be ushered in by a new religious order of contemplative and spiritual men. The Spirituals saw the fulfillment of this prophecy in Francis and in themselves. In 1257 the situation reached a head when John of Parma, the minister general of the Order, was secretly ordered by Pope Alexander IV to resign because of his leanings toward Joachimism. At the suggestion of John, Bonaventure was chosen as his successor by a general chapter held in Rome.[14] This inaugurated for Bonaventure an intense and fruitful career as minister general that lasted for seventeen years.

During the years of his generalate he had to deal with a variety of problems in the growing Order. In his policies he favored a moderate position, attempting to be faithful to the ideals of Francis while developing the Order along institutional lines.[15] In his interpretation of poverty, he allowed for adaptation and evolution as the Order expanded. An intellectual himself and a trained theologian of the University of Paris, he saw no radical conflict between learning and Franciscan simplicity; hence he encouraged learning and cultivated centers of study. Through his personal holiness, the respect he commanded and his gifts of reconciliation, he was able to give form and direction to the moderate position, thus meriting to be called the Second Founder of the Order.

In this busy time as general of the Order, he did not cease to write, but managed to produce a number of spiritual treatises,

---

13. On Joachim and his influence, cf. Marjorie Reeves, *The Influence of Prophecy in the Later Middle Ages: A Study of Joachimism* (Oxford: Clarendon, 1969), pp. 3-228.

14. Cf. Salimbene, *Cronica fratris Salimbene de Adam ordinis minorum*, in *Monumenta Germaniae historica: Scriptorum*, vol. XXXII, ed. O. Holder-Egger (Hanoverae et Lipsiae: Impensis Bibliopolii Hahniani, 1905-1913), pp. 309-310; cf. Quinn, "Chronology of St. Bonaventure (1217-1257)," pp. 174-176.

15. Cf. John Moorman, *A History of the Franciscan Order: From its Origins to the Year 1517* (Oxford: Clarendon, 1968), pp. 140-154; Rosalind Brooke, *Early Franciscan Government: Elias to Bonaventure* (Cambridge: Cambridge University Press, 1959), pp. 270-285.

two biographies of Francis and three extended lecture series, as well as numerous sermons and other works. In 1273 he was named cardinal bishop of Albano by Pope Gregory X and spent the following year assisting him in preparations for the Second Council of Lyons. He played a major role in the council's reform of the Church, reconciling the secular clergy with the mendicant orders; he also was involved in the reconciliation of the Greek Church with Rome. He died at the council on July 15, 1274, and was buried the same day at the Franciscan church in Lyons, in a solemn ceremony in the presence of the pope, the cardinals and the prelates of the council. The scene is described by a chronicler as follows: "Greeks and Latins, clergy and laity followed his bier with bitter tears, grieving over the lamentable loss of so great a person."[16] Two hundred years later Bonaventure was canonized on April 14, 1482, by Pope Sixtus IV; and on March 14, 1588, he was declared a Doctor of the Universal Church by Pope Sixtus V, with the title "Doctor Seraphicus."[17]

BONAVENTURE'S WORKS

Three Periods

Bonaventure's writings are extensive, covering some nine folio volumes in the Quaracchi critical edition, with the individual volumes averaging over seven hundred pages, printed in double columns. This critical text was prepared by a team of Franciscan scholars at Collegio S. Bonaventura at Quaracchi in the vicinity of Florence over a twenty year period from 1882 to 1902.[18] Their work was considered a landmark in medieval

---

16. *Chronica XXIV generalium*, in *Analecta franciscana*, III, 356; cf. the report of Bonaventure's death and funeral in the *ordinatio* of the council, printed in Antonio Franchi, Il Concilio II di Lione (1274) secundo la Ordinatio Councilii Generalis Lugdunensis (Roma: Edizioni francescane, 1965), p. 95.

17. Cf. the bulls of Sixtus IV and Sixtus V, printed in the Quaracchi critical edition (I, xxxix-lii).

18. *Doctoris Seraphici S. Bonaventurae opera omnia*, edita studio et cura pp. Collegii a S. Bonaventura, 10 vols. (Quaracchi: Collegium S. Bonaventurae, 1882-1902).

textual criticism and has stood up well through the succeeding years.[19] Between 1926 and 1946 the *Analecta franciscana* published critical texts of the early biographies of Francis, including an updated critical text of Bonaventure's two biographies of Francis and his treatise on Francis's miracles.[20] Just recently a new edition of Bonaventure's Sunday sermons has appeared, edited by Jacques Guy Bougerol.[21] Our present translations were made from the original Quaracchi critical text for *The Soul's Journey into God* and *The Tree of Life*, with footnotes for the former checked against the new printing in *Opera theologica selecta*.[22] Our translation of the major biography of Francis was made from the critical text in the *Analecta franciscana*.

In addition to his sermons and administrative writings, Bonaventure's works can be classified under three general headings: the scholastic treatises, spiritual writings and lecture series. These three different genres of writing fall into three successive periods of his life. The first period covers his years at the University of Paris, during which he composed his scholastic treatises: his *Commentary on the Sentences;* biblical commentaries on Ecclesiastes, Luke and the Gospel of John; and three sets of disputed questions: *On Evangelical Perfection, On Christ's Knowledge* and *On the Mystery of the Trinity.* During this period he also produced the *Breviloquium*, a summary of his theology, and perhaps also his treatise *On the Reduction of the Arts to Theology*.[23] The

---

19. Cf. Ignatius Brady, "The Edition of the 'Opera Omnia' of Saint Bonaventure (1882-1902)," *Archivum franciscanum historicum* 70 (1977), 352-353; "The *Opera Omnia* of Saint Bonaventure Revisited," in *Proceedings of the American Catholic Philosophical Association* 48 (1974): 295-304.

20. *Analecta franciscana*, X; *Legendae s. Francisci Assisiensis saeculis XIII et XIV conscriptae ad codicum fidem recensitae a patribus Collegii, editae a patribus Collegii S. Bonaventurae adiuvantibus aliis eruditis viris (Quaracchi: Collegium S. Bonaventurae, 1926-1946), pp. 555-678.*

21. *Sancti Bonaventurae sermones dominicales,* ad fidem codicum nunc denuo editi studio et cura Jacques Guy Bougerol (Grottaferrata: Collegio S. Bonaventura, 1977).

22. *Opera theologica selecta,* vol. V (Quaracchi: Collegium S. Bonaventurae, 1966), 179-214.

23. *Commentarius in I, II, III, IV librum Sententiarum* (I-IV); *Commentarius in librum Ecclesiastes* (VI, 3-103); *Commentarius in Evangelium Lucae* (VII, 1-604); *Commentarius in Evangelium Joannis* (VI, 239-532); *Quaestiones disputatae de perfectione evangelica* (V, 117-198); *Quaestiones disputatae de scientia Christi* (V, 3-43); *Quaestiones disputatae de mysterio Trinitatis* (V, 45-115); *Breviloquium* (V, 201-291); *De reductione artium ad theologiam* (V, 319-325).

writings of this period reflect the academic environment of the University of Paris and are replete with the analytic and logical techniques characteristic of 13th-century scholasticism.

The second period, from 1257-1267, begins with his election as minister general of the Franciscan Order and flowers in a host of spiritual writings which have a distinctive Franciscan flavor. The work that ushers in this new phase is *The Soul's Journey into God*, which Bonaventure conceived while at La Verna meditating on Francis's vision of the six-winged Seraph. The work is pivotal because it contains the speculative content of the first period while moving into the spiritual vision of the second period, with Francis as its explicit inspiration and model. After this work, while in the midst of administrative duties, he managed to compose a number of spiritual treatises: *The Tree of Life*, his classic meditation on the life of Christ, and *The Triple Way*, his systematic treatment of the stages of the spiritual life. Also during this period he composed the *Soliloquy on the Four Spiritual Exercises*, *On the Government of the Soul* and *On the Five Feasts of the Child Jesus*. It was during this middle period that he was commissioned by the Chapter of Narbonne in 1260 to write the official biography of Francis, which has come to be known as the *Legenda maior* and which is translated in this volume under the title *The Life of St. Francis*. Bonaventure also composed a shorter life of Francis for liturgical use known as the *Legenda minor*. [24]

The third period of Bonaventure's writing is marked by

---

24. *Itinerarium mentis in Deum* (V, 296-313); *Lignum vitae* (VIII, 68-86); *De triplici via* (VIII, 3-18); *Soliloquium de quatuor mentalibus exercitiis* (VIII, 28-67); *De regimine animae* (VIII, 128-130); *De quinque festivitatibus pueri Jesu* (VIII, 88-95); *Legenda maior sancti Francisci* (VIII, 504-565); *Legenda minor sancti Francisci* (VIII, 565-579). Several other spiritual writings are usually ascribed to Bonaventure and assigned to this period: *De sex alis Seraphim* (VIII, 131-151); *Vitis mystica sive Tractatus de passione Domini* (VIII, 159-189); *Tractatus de praeparatione ad missam* (VIII, 99-106); and *Officium de passione Domini* (VIII, 152-168). There is reason to think that they are not by Bonaventure; cf. Brady, "The Edition of the 'Opera Omnia' of Saint Bonaventure (1882-1902)," 372-374; "The Writings of Saint Bonaventure regarding the Franciscan Order," in *San Bonaventura maestro di vita Francescana de di sapienza cristiana*, ed. Alfonso Pompei, vol. I (Rome: Pontificia Facoltà Teologica "San Bonaventura," 1976), pp. 104-106; and "The Opera Omnia of Saint Bonaventure Revisited," p. 299.

controversy. In 1269 Master Gerard of Abbeville launched a new attack against the mendicants which Bonaventure countered with his *Defense of the Poor*. A new problem arose at the University of Paris, a heterodox form of Aristotelianism taught in the faculty of arts of the university. Influenced by the commentary of Averroes, this Aristotelianism seemed to threaten the integrity of Christian belief, causing a storm of controversy in the intellectual milieu of Paris. In response to the controversy Bonaventure gave three series of university lectures or sermons, called in Latin *collationes: On the Ten Commandments*, *On the Seven Gifts of the Holy Spirit* and on *The Six Days of Creation (Collationes in Hexaemeron)*.[25] This latter series was delivered in Paris the year before his death and contains the full flowering of his thought. In a certain sense it represents the final integration of the two previous periods, for it unites in a complex symbolic structure the speculation of the first period with the Franciscan spirituality of the second. The series was interrupted after twenty-three lectures, never to be completed, when Bonaventure was raised to the cardinalate by Pope Gregory X on May 23, 1273.

Choice of Classics

Out of this rich corpus of writings, it was necessary to make a choice for inclusion in the present volume. In some respects the choice was obvious and in others, problematic. It would be natural to choose writings of the middle period, for these are distinctively spiritual and represent a specifically Franciscan quality. Yet it would not be out of the question to consider publishing the *Lectures on the Six Days of Creation* because these represent the mature flowering of Bonaventure's thought. However, these constitute a volume in themselves and would prevent including other significant material. Furthermore, they

---

25. *Apologia pauperum* (VIII, 233-330); *Collationes de decem praeceptis* (V, 507-532); *Collationes de septem donis Spiritus Sancti* (V, 457-503); *Collationes in Hexaemeron* (V, 329-449).

are permeated more with the mood of speculative controversy than with that of the spiritual journey. Another possibility that suggested itself was a selection from the sermons; but in keeping with the goals of The Classics of Western Spirituality, it seemed more appropriate to select longer complete works where available. I have, then, made my selection from the middle period, and in so doing have chosen according to two criteria: (1) works that clearly qualify as classics both because of their content and because they have been acknowledged as such by their acceptance and influence; (2) works which taken together present an integral picture of the essence of Franciscan spirituality as Bonaventure perceived it.

I believe that the three works chosen meet these criteria. The most obvious choice was *The Soul's Journey into God*, which is considered Bonaventure's masterpiece. It is an extraordinarily dense *summa* of medieval Christian spirituality, which was widely disseminated during the Middle Ages and is the most widely read of Bonaventure's works at the present time. The second selection, *The Tree of Life*, a meditation on the life of Christ, is a gem of Christian devotional literature, imbued with deep feeling and intellectual power without the sentimentality and flights of fancy that characterized much of the later writings in the same genre, for example, the Pseudo-Bonaventurian *Meditations on the Life of Christ*.[26] Unfortunately not as influential as this latter work, Bonaventure's *The Tree of Life* was widely read as the manuscript tradition indicates. It had a significant influence on the 14th century, for example on Ubertino di Casale, who adopted its main theme and even certain details in his version of the Tree of Life which he wrote on Mount La Verna in 1305. In addition, Bonaventure's *The Tree of Life* stimulated a rich tradition in the visual arts.[27] The third selection, Bonaventure's

---

26. *Meditationes vitae Christi* in *Sancti Bonaventurae Opera Omnia*, ed. A. C. Peltier, vol. XII (Paris: Vives, 1868).
27. Cf. P. Gerlach in *S. Bonaventura 1274-1974*, vol. I, pp. 6-9, and Francesco Petrangeli Papini, *ibid.*, 30-48.

longer biography of Francis, is a masterful work of spiritual biography. Because it was adopted as the official biography in the Franciscan Order, its influence was extensive, as we will see later. However, in recent times it has fallen under severe criticism, which I will have to take into account, when I comment on the work, in order to justify my choice.

In making the final selection, I attempted to meet the second criterion: to choose works which taken together present an integral picture of the essence of Franciscan spirituality as Bonaventure perceived it. *The Soul's Journey into God* expresses the Franciscan awareness of the presence of God in creation: the physical universe and the soul are seen as mirrors reflecting God and as rungs in a ladder leading to God. Bonaventure expresses here, in his own way, Francis's joy in the sacrality and sacramentality of creation and, in so doing, captures an essential element in Franciscan spirituality. Basic though this element is, it would not be complete without its flowering in devotion to the humanity of Christ. There is a natural link between the Franciscan attitude toward material creation, as sacramentally manifesting God, and the Franciscan devotion to the incarnation as the fulness of this manifestation.

While *The Soul's Journey* contains significant Christological material, the emphasis is on the mystical Christ, who as the crucified figure in the midst of the Seraph's wings is the gateway and door into mystical consciousness. Christ is also presented as the Bridegroom united to the soul in the embrace of love, and the God-man — the remarkable coincidence of opposites — who draws us into the wonder of contemplation and ultimately into the darkness of unknowing. In *The Soul's Journey* we do not find the human Christ, the historical Jesus as described in the Gospels, who was born humble and poor in a manger, who wandered about preaching and healing, who suffered and died on Calvary, with his body bleeding and broken — not only to redeem mankind, but to give, at every step of the way, an example of virtue to be imitated. This picture, however, is presented in

The Tree of Life, where Bonaventure meditates on Christ in the concrete details of his life as a man. In *The Soul's Journey* Bonaventure evokes the mystical affections of desire, longing, wonder and joy; he sighs for the Bridegroom and loses himself in wonder at the mystery of the God-man. In *The Tree of Life,* on the other hand, he elicits our tender love for the infant in the crib, our admiration at Jesus' humility and obedience, our compassion for his suffering. With delicacy and power he calls forth that complex cluster of human sentiments which the Middle Ages cultivated in compassion for the suffering Savior and which flowered in the great pietàs of Michelangelo. Yet in these two works we do not have two radically different Christologies, but one. In *The Tree of Life* Bonaventure situates his meditation on the humanity of Christ within the context of his speculative theology of the Trinity, thus making the link with the mystical Christ of *The Soul's Journey.* In his different treatises Bonaventure meditates on the mystery of Christ in the book of the soul, the book of creation and the book of Scripture. It is true that he did not produce a single book himself in which these diverse meditations were fully expressed and integrated extensively into an organic whole. In part we hope to supply such a synthesis by publishing the two works together in this present volume and urging the reader to see them as complementary expressions of Bonaventure's Christology.

The picture of Franciscan spirituality would not be complete without Francis himself. Just as one enters into the fulness of the mystery of Christ by meditating on his humanity and by imitating his virtues, so the Franciscan imitates Christ by following the example of Francis. For in the Middle Ages Francis was looked upon as the one who most closely imitated Christ. He had grasped the secret of Gospel simplicity; he had followed Christ in complete poverty; throughout his life he entered more deeply into the mystery of the cross until toward the end God gave a miraculous approbation of his conformity to Christ in the gift of the stigmata. The Franciscan spiritual journey, then, takes its point of departure from Francis, proceeding from Francis to the humanity of Christ and through this into the sacramental cosmos, the mystical marriage and the divine darkness of ecstasy. It was imperative, then, to include the life of Francis in the present volume, especially since Bonaventure's biography is an interpretation of Francis as the model of the spiritual journey in the light of Bonaventure's spiritual and speculative theology. In *The Soul's Journey* Francis is presented as the example of one who has attained the height of the mystical ascent, just as Christ is presented there in his mystical dimension. *The Life of St. Francis*, however, parallels *The Tree of Life* in its focus on the concrete historical details of a human life. *The Life of St. Francis* and *The Tree of Life* are treatises on the life of Christian virtue which leads ultimately to the spiritual ascent of *The Soul's Journey*. In each treatise there is a movement from the lowest to the highest, through a threefold dynamic of purgation, illumination and perfection. Although Bonaventure did not write a single treatise integrating the contents of these three works (perhaps no genre of writings can contain such complexity), nevertheless by seeing these classics in interrelation, the reader can obtain an integral view of the richness of Bonaventure's Franciscan spirituality. Thus by including all three pieces in this volume, we hope to give a comprehensive picture of Franciscan spirituality according to Bonaventure. There were many reasons for placing *The Soul's Journey* first in this volume, chiefly because it is his best known work and because it gives a compact picture of this total theological vision and so can provide an overview for the other two works. However, from the standpoint of the Franciscan spiritual journey, in its total ambit, one could best begin with *The Life of St. Francis*, then proceed to *The Tree of Life* and then to *The Soul's Journey*.

In selecting one of Bonaventure's two biographies of Francis, I have chosen the *Legenda maior*, or longer biography, rather than the *Legenda minor*, since the former contains a fuller exposition of Francis's life and Bonaventure's spiritual theology. However I have omitted Bonaventure's lengthy account of the miracles that occurred after Francis's death, which accompanies the *Legenda maior*.

If there were one addition I would like to make, it would be *The Triple Way*. It certainly qualifies as a classic since it contains one of the most significant studies of the three stages of spiritual development—purgation, illumination and perfection (or union)—which were in the Middle Ages derived from the writings of the Pseudo-Dionysius and which have become accepted in Western spirituality as the classical way of formulating the dynamics of spiritual growth. Limits of space led to the decision not to include it in the present volume. However, the theme is treated explicitly in *The Soul's Journey* and in the biography of Francis, and implicitly in *The Tree of Life*. All three of these pieces exemplify the dynamics spelled out systematically in *The Triple Way*. I suggest, then, that the reader supplement the treatment here by a careful reading of that treatise.[28]

STRUCTURE OF BONAVENTURE'S THOUGHT

Scholastic thought in the Middle Ages has been compared to a Gothic cathedral, especially in the architectonic form it took in the great *summae*. This comparison is particularly apt in the case of Bonaventure's spirituality, for he provides an overarching structure for the elements of the Christian spiritual tradition. If we were to apply the comparison, we could see that his theology and philosophy provide the equivalent of this structure, especially his treatment of the Trinity, creation and Christology. This theological speculation is comparable to the nave, towers and apse of the Gothic cathedral. More specifically, the movement of the stone as it reaches up toward heaven reflects the ascent through creation which Bonaventure describes in *The*

---

28. Cf. the translation by José de Vinck in *The Works of Bonaventure*, vol. I (Paterson, N.J.: St. Anthony Guild Press, 1960), pp. 61-94.

Soul's Journey, and the light streaming through the stained glass windows reflects the downward movement of God expressing himself in the variety of creatures and in his gifts of grace. The crossing of the axes of the design at the center, where the nave and the transepts intersect, suggests the cross of Christ, and together with the focus of the eye on the altar, suggests the convergence of all creation on Christ the center, which is a major theme in Bonaventure's later writing. All of these themes are developed in *The Soul's Journey*, as we will see shortly.

In addition to its superstructure, which reflects a cosmic design, the Gothic cathedral also contains a historical dimension. Depicted in sculpture on the portals, as well as in the stained glass windows, is the history of salvation from the creation of the world, through the drama of sin and redemption, from the kings and prophets of the Old Testament to the saints of the New and the later history of the Church, finally to the last judgment, which was usually depicted on the west portal at the entrance of the cathedral. Bonaventure's meditation on the life of Christ in *The Tree of Life* and his biography of Francis correspond to this historical dimension. By progressing along the various stages of the spiritual journey described in these three treatises, the reader enters ever more deeply into the cathedral, as it were, from its outer portals of salvation history to its inner focus on the altar and then from the altar up to God. In fact, this is the very image used by Bonaventure in the latter part of *The Soul's Journey*, where the reader proceeds through the symbol of the tabernacle or temple ever more deeply into the holy of holies, where he perceives Christ symbolized by the Mercy Seat. In meditating on Christ as the greatest coincidence of opposites, one is drawn up like Francis to the heights of union with God.[29]

Bonaventure's meditation on Christ at the center of the holy of holies reveals the logic of the coincidence of opposites, which, I have argued, permeates all of his thought: his philosophy,

---

29. Cf. III, 1; V, 1, pp. 79-80, 94.

theology and spirituality.[30] Bonaventure sees in Christ, marvelously united, "the first and the last, the highest and the lowest, the circumference and the center, *the Alpha and the Omega*, the caused and the cause, the Creator and the creature."[31] Throughout chapters five to seven of *The Soul's Journey* Bonaventure contemplates the coincidence of opposites in God as Being, in the Trinity as the self-diffusive Good and in Christ as the union of the divine and the human. Then with Christ crucified we move through death to life, from the limits of the finite to the vastness of eternity. Expressed here in a concentrated form, the coincidence of opposites is found, I believe, throughout his thought and can be seen graphically in his interpretation of Francis as the humble, simple poor man who is wondrously exalted by God. As we proceed now in our more detailed analysis of the three treatises, we will see further examples of the coincidence of opposites reflecting the architectonic structure of his thought as a whole.

THE SOUL'S JOURNEY INTO GOD

Circumstances of Composition

The immediate circumstances of the composition of *The Soul's Journey into God* are told by Bonaventure himself in his prologue. He received his inspiration for the treatise while meditating on Francis's vision of the six-winged Seraph on Mount La Verna in Tuscany at the very site where Francis had the vision and received the stigmata some thirty-five years before. The time was late September or early October 1259, as

---

30. Cf. Ewert H. Cousins, "The Coincidence of Opposites in the Christology of Saint Bonaventure," *Franciscan Studies* 28 (1968): 27-45; idem, "La 'Coincidentia Oppositorum' dans la théologie de Bonaventure," *Études franciscaines* 18 (Supplément annuel, 1968): 15-31; idem, "Bonaventure, the Coincidence of Opposites and Nicholas of Cusa," in *Studies Honoring Ignatius Charles Brady, Friar Minor,* (St. Bonaventure, N.Y.: The Franciscan Institute, 1976), pp. 177-197; cf. also idem, *Bonaventure and the Coincidence of Opposites* (Chicago: Franciscan Herald Press, in press).
31. VI, 7, p. 108.

Bonaventure says: "It happened that about the thirty-third anniversary of the Saint's death, under divine impulse, I withdrew to Mount La Verna seeking a place of quiet and desiring to find there peace of spirit."[32] At the time of this visit Bonaventure was forty-two years old and had been for two years minister general of the Franciscan Order. In the prologue he refers both to his office as general and to his desire to seek peace: "Following the example of our most blessed father Francis, I was seeking this peace with panting spirit—I a sinner and utterly unworthy who after our blessed father's death had become the seventh Minister General of the Friars."[33] Through these statements, the reader can detect in Bonaventure a sense of the burden of administration and the tensions within the Order. His very election to the generalate two years before grew out of these tensions since his predecessor John of Parma was bidden to resign because of controversy.

The setting and Bonaventure's own observations indicate that he was also searching out his Franciscan roots, for he went to meditate on the holy mountain of La Verna, which is one of the most venerated Franciscan shrines. It was here in 1224 that Francis had the climactic vision of his life—the apparition of the six-winged Seraph in the form of the Crucified, which left the marks of Christ's passion in his hands, feet and side. He bore these marks in his body during the last two years of his life as a sign of God's final seal on the man who was accounted as the closest imitator of Christ. Here in this setting Bonaventure could search more deeply into Francis's ideal, both for his own life and for guiding the Order in its difficult attempt to embody this ideal.

Plan of the Soul's Journey

While meditating on Francis's vision of the six-winged

---

32. Prol., 2, p. 54.
33. *Ibid.*

Seraph, Bonaventure tells us, there suddenly came to his mind
its symbolic meaning: "While reflecting on this, I saw at once
that this vision represented our father's rapture in contemplation
and the road by which this rapture is reached."[34] The vision,
then, symbolizes both the goal and the journey. This symbolic
interpretation of Francis's vision becomes for Bonaventure the
framework of his treatise, with the first six chapters tracing the
stages of the journey and the seventh describing the goal of
ecstatic rapture. The soul progresses along this journey by
contemplating God's reflection in the material world, sensation,
the natural faculties of the soul and these same faculties reformed by grace. The soul then turns to God himself and
contemplates him as Being and the Good and from there passes
over into the final stage of mystical ecstasy.

Bonaventure's division of the journey into six stages is a
refinement of a larger division of three stages, which represent
three major types of meditation or religious consciousness:
meditation on nature, on the soul and on God. These three types
of religious consciousness are found throughout the world, cultivated in various ways by world religions. Within Christianity
they were given a distinct development and were elaborated by
various spiritual traditions in the Western Middle Ages. In his
treatise Bonaventure shapes these traditions into an integrated
whole, drawing in each case from a major representative of the
tradition: from Francis of Assisi on nature, from Augustine on
the soul and from Dionysius on God. In this way Bonaventure
creates a type of *summa*, comparable in its own sphere to the
Summa theologiae of Thomas Aquinas, for he draws together into
a comprehensive synthesis major strands of Christian spirituality.

In his *summa* Bonaventure unites the various traditions
through the image of the journey. The Latin title of the work is
Itinerarium mentis in Deum, which I have translated as *The Soul's*

---

34. *Ibid.*

Journey into God. The Latin term *itinerarium*, which could be rendered by the English "itinerary," in Bonaventure's day meant what pertains to a journey in general, a plan for a journey or a description of a journey; in ecclesiastical terminology it also meant a prayer for a safe journey or a pilgrimage to, or a description of a pilgrimage to, the Holy Land.[35] In his title, Bonaventure seems to include all of these meanings symbolically since they are all contained in some way in the piece itself. The translation of the term *mentis* presents a problem. Etymologically the Latin *mens (mentis)* is related to our English "mind" and has been translated in the past as such both in the title and the text of Bonaventure's treatise. However, for Bonaventure and medieval spiritual usage in general, as influenced by Augustine, the term *mens* was not limited to the intellectualist connotations of the English term "mind." Among the medieval spiritual writers *mens* encompassed the soul in its three faculties of memory, intelligence and will, which constitute the soul as image of God. Although there is no single English term that captures this precise meaning, I have chosen "soul" in preference to "mind" or "spirit." However "soul" must not be taken here in its Aristotelian sense of the animating principle of the body, but rather as the image of God in the depths of the person, the most profound dimension of man's spiritual being. In the text itself I have translated the term *mens* as "soul" and as "mind" depending on the connotations of the context. In the final phrase of the title there is implied a movement not merely toward or to God but into God, since Bonaventure does not use the phrase *ad Deum* (to God) as might be expected from ordinary usage, but the much bolder *in Deum* (into God). By this choice he is very likely underscoring the mystical nature of the goal of the journey.

True to the spirit of Francis, Bonaventure claims that one can enter on this journey only through Christ Crucified: "There

---

35. Cf. Philotheus Boehner in *Works of Saint Bonaventure*, vol. II: *Saint Bonaventure's Itinerarium Mentis in Deum* (Saint Bonaventure, N.Y.: The Franciscan Institute, 1956), p. 105.

is no other path but through the burning love of the Crucified."[36] This is the symbolic meaning of the crucified Seraph in Francis's vision: Christ crucified is the gateway, the door. Here at the very outset of the journey we encounter Bonaventure's mystical Christology, which will be complemented by his meditation on the humanity of Christ in *The Tree of Life*. In his biography of Francis, Bonaventure emphasizes the meaning of the cross in his spiritual journey, ennumerating seven visions of the cross which are like the seven stages of *The Soul's Journey into God*, the seventh being the climactic vision of the six-winged Seraph and the reception of the marks of the Crucified in his hands, feet and side.[37]

The prologue closes with a forceful rejection of pure intellectualism and an affirmation of affectivity—but affectivity that is not mere emotion or sentimentality. Although the main thrust of the treatise is speculative, with much logic and metaphysics, Bonaventure contends that this speculation should be approached in a prayerful attitude and with characteristic Franciscan affectivity. This is a striking example of Bonaventure's coincidence of opposites. Here in *The Soul's Journey into God* philosophical speculation is joined with mystical affectivity; in *The Tree of Life* the more interpersonal emotions of love and compassion are placed in a speculative-mystical framework. At the outset Bonaventure elicits the affectivity that underlies and motivates the soul's journey. In order to embark on this journey, in order to make this ascent, one must be a man of desires; he must be burning with spiritual passion. To elicit these desires, Bonaventure invites the reader "to the groans of prayer through Christ crucified, through whose blood we are cleansed from the filth of vice." He continues:

> . . . so that he not believe that reading is sufficient without unction, speculation without devotion, investigation without

---

36. Prol., 3, p. 54.
37. XIII, 12, pp. 312-314.

wonder, observation without joy, work without piety, knowledge without love, understanding without humility, endeavor without divine grace, reflection as a mirror without divinely inspired wisdom.[38]

Bonaventure and Francis on Nature

With Christ as the road and the door, Bonaventure begins his ascent through the six stages symbolized by the six wings of the Seraph. He begins his journey in the material world, moves into sensation, then to the spiritual faculties of the soul and then into God. From his other writings, there is considerable evidence that he does not hold that one must move precisely in this direction. For example, one could bypass the journey through nature and begin at once by turning into the soul; or one could bypass nature and the soul and turn at once to contemplate God. In his epistemology, he holds that knowledge of God is innate in the soul and does not have to be derived from sense data by a reasoning process. Although he holds that such a reasoning process is valid, it is not required for us to know God. Consequently in a classical text on his doctrine of knowledge of God, he gives three major ways of approaching God that correspond to the three major stages of *The Soul's Journey*. However, each is presented as an autonomous way, not dependent on the other.[39]

It is not surprising, though, that Bonaventure should begin by contemplating the material world since Francis took such joy in nature as God's creation. Francis felt at one with creatures, especially animals and birds, as many stories in his early biographies attest. In introducing a charming series of animal stories, Bonaventure observes: "When he [Francis] considered the primordial source of all things, he was filled with even more

---

38. Prol., 4, p. 55-56.
39. On Bonaventure's epistemology, cf. *Sc. Chr.*, q. 4 (V, 17-20); *Chr. un. omn. mag.* (V, 567-574); *M. Trin.*, q. 1, a. 1 (V, 45-51); *Itin.*, c. 1-4 (V, 296-308); *Red. art.* (V, 319-325); *Hexaem.*, I, n. 13; XII (V, 331, 384-387); the classical text referred to is *M. Trin.*, q. 1, a. 1 (V, 45-51).

abundant piety, calling creatures, no matter how small, by the name of brother or sister, because he knew they had the same source as himself."[40] Echoing Francis, Bonaventure says: "Let us place our first step in the ascent at the bottom, presenting to ourselves the whole material world as a mirror through which we may pass over to God, the supreme Craftsman."[41] Yet when Bonaventure begins his meditation, he proceeds in a very different fashion from Francis. The immediacy and spontaneity of Francis are transformed into a speculative reflection on creatures as vestiges of the Trinity, reflecting the power, wisdom and goodness of their divine Source. His ascent in the first stage reaches its climax in a panoramic view of material creation seen from seven perspectives—origin, magnitude, multitude, beauty, plenitude, activity and order. For example, he considers "the magnitude of things, in the mass of their length, width and depth, in their great power extending in length, width and depth as appears in the diffusion of light, in the efficiency of their operations which are internal, continuous and diffused, as appears in the operation of fire." Seen in this panoramic sweep, the magnitude of things "clearly manifests the immensity of the power, wisdom and goodness of the triune God, who by his power, presence and essence exists uncircumscribed in all things."[42]

Bonaventure's Theological System

Behind this meditation on the material world, and the entire treatise, stands Bonaventure's theological vision, which is based on the doctrine of the Trinity as the mystery of the self-diffusion of the Good. Drawing from the tradition of the Greek Fathers rather than from Augustine, Bonaventure begins his speculative Trinitarian theology with the Father as the fountain-source of the divine fecundity. For Bonaventure the

---

40. *The Life of St. Francis*, VIII, 6, p. 254-255.
41. I, 9, p. 63.
42. I, 14, p. 65.

Father is the fountain-fulness, *fontalis plenitudo*, in whom the divinity is fecund, dynamic, self-expressive.[43] Out of his boundless fecundity, the Father generates his Son, expressing himself in his perfect Image, his eternal Word. This fecundity issues further in the procession of the Spirit from the Father and the Son as their mutual love and the Gift in whom all good gifts are given. Treated explicitly in chapter six of *The Soul's Journey*, this theme is developed extensively elsewhere in his writings and is the focus of the entire treatise *On the Reduction of the Arts to Theology*, where in contrast to the contemplative ascent of *The Soul's Journey* the reader shares in the dynamism of the self-diffusion of the Father through all of his productive activity.[44] Although this is not underscored in *The Soul's Journey*, it is important to realize that the notion of the fecund Trinity developed in chapter six stands behind even the contemplative ascent of the soul through the world to God.

In *The Soul's Journey* Bonaventure develops the notion of the divine fecundity by applying to the Trinity the principle, derived from the Pseudo-Dionysius, that the Good is self-diffusive. Using the logic of perfection of Anselm, he applies this principle in a general way to God claiming that God must contain the fulness of self-diffusion. But this cannot be realized in God's outpouring of himself in creation since creation is too limited to sustain the full force of the divine fecundity; it is like a mere speck in relation to the immensity of the divine goodness. Therefore this diffusion must be realized in the Trinity, where for all eternity there can be actualized the fullest expression of fecundity in the Trinitarian processions.[45]

Although the divine fecundity is not dependent on the world for its actualization, the world itself is an overflow and an expression of this fecundity. When the Father generates the

---

43. *I Sent.*, d. 27, p. 1, a. un., q. 2 (I, 468-474); cf. *I Sent.*, d. 11, a. un., q. 2 (I, 214-216).

44. Cf. the English translation of *On the Reduction of the Arts to Theology* by José de Vinck in *The Works of Bonaventure*, vol. III (Paterson, N.J.: St. Anthony Guild Press, 1966), pp. 13-32.

45. VI, 2, pp. 102-104; cf. Anselm, *Proslogion*, 2-5, 15.

Son, he produces in the Son the archetypes or *rationes aeternae* of all he can create. When God decrees to create *ad extra* in space and time, this creative energy flows from the Trinitarian fecundity and expresses itself according to the archetypes in the Son. Thus the Son is the link between the divinity and creation; for all of created reality is the expression of him and refers back to him, by way of exemplarism, that is by way of being grounded in him as in its eternal Exemplar.[46] This doctrine of exemplarism makes possible the contemplation of *The Soul's Journey*, for we can look upon any object in creation and trace it back to its archetype in the divine mind; and since it flowed from the divine mind out of the dynamic fecundity of the inner Trinitarian life, we can see it reflecting the power, wisdom and goodness of God as moments in the inner dynamism of God. The movement of creatures out from God and their return to God is the central focus of Bonaventure's entire vision. In a celebrated text he summed up his world view as follows: "This is our whole metaphysics: emanation, exemplarity, consummation; to be illumined by spiritual rays and to be led back to the highest reality."[47] In Franciscan fashion, then, for Bonaventure, creatures are a reflection of God. They are like a stained glass window: "Just as you see that a ray of light entering through a window is colored in different ways according to the different colors of the various parts, so the divine ray shines forth in each and every creature in different ways and in different properties."[48] He says further that "creatures are shadows, echoes and pictures of that first, most powerful, most wise and most perfect Principle . . . . They are vestiges, representations, spectacles proposed to us and signs divinely given so that we can see God." He continues: "These creatures, I say, are exemplars or rather exemplifications presented to souls still untrained and immersed in sensible things so that through sensible things

---

46. *Hexaem.*, I, 12-17 (V, 331-332).
47. *Ibid.*, 17 (V, 332).
48. *Ibid.*, XII, 14 (V, 386).

26

which they see they will be carried over to intelligible things which they do not see as through signs to what is signified."[49]

It is this doctrine of exemplarism that is at the base of Bonaventure's contemplation of creatures as vestiges and images in *The Soul's Journey*. In his *Commentary on the Sentences*, he gives a detailed analysis of how creatures reflect God:[50] All creatures reflect the power, wisdom and goodness of God and are technically called vestiges (literally, footprints) of the Trinity. Rational creatures, however, reflect God in a special way because they have him present within themselves as the object of their knowledge and love. More specifically, since they have him present in themselves in their faculties of memory, understanding and will, they are images of the Trinity. A third form of reflection is found in Bonaventure through the technical term *similitude*, whereby rational creatures transformed by grace reflect the Trinity in a more intimate way. By Bonaventure's contemplation of the material world as a vestige of the Trinity, he is led back to the power, wisdom and goodness of the divinity and ultimately self-diffusing fecundity of the Father, Son and Spirit.

Although Bonaventure's meditation is in the spirit of Francis, it contrasts significantly with Francis's expression in *The Canticle of Brother Sun*, which we print here so that the reader can compare it with Bonaventure's approach to God in *The Soul's Journey*, especially the sevenfold contemplation of creatures in chapter one, number 14:

THE CANTICLE OF BROTHER SUN[51]

Most high omnipotent good Lord,
Yours are the praises, the glory, the honor and all blessing.
To you alone, Most High, do they belong,
And no man is worthy to mention you.

---

49. II, 11, p. 76.
50. *I Sent.*, d. 3, a. un., q. 2, ad 4 (I, 72-74).
51. Cf. the text in Kajetan Esser, ed., *Die Opuscula des Hl. Franziskus von Assisi* (Grottaferrata: Collegium S. Bonaventurae, 1976), pp. 122-133; the English translation is my own.

INTRODUCTION

Praised be you, my Lord, with all your creatures,
Especially Sir Brother Sun,
Who makes the day and through whom you give us light.
And he is beautiful and radiant with great splendor,
And bears the signification of you, Most High One.

Praised be you, my Lord, for Sister Moon and the stars,
You have formed them in heaven clear and precious and beautiful.

Praised be you, my Lord, for Brother Wind,
And for the air—cloudy and serene—and every kind of weather,
By which you give sustenance to your creatures.

Praised be you, my Lord, for Sister Water,
Which is very useful and humble and precious and chaste.

Praised be you, my Lord, for Brother Fire,
By whom you light the night,
And he is beautiful and jocund and robust and strong.

Praised be you, my Lord, for our sister Mother Earth,
Who sustains and governs us,
And produces various fruits with colored flowers and herbs.

Praised be you, my Lord, for those who give pardon for your love
And bear infirmity and tribulation,
Blessed are those who endure in peace,
For by you, Most High, they will be crowned.

Praised be you, Lord, for our Sister Bodily Death,
From whom no living man can escape.
Woe to those who die in mortal sin.
Blessed are those whom death will find in your most holy will,
For the second death shall do them no harm.

Praise and bless my Lord and give him thanks
And serve him with great humility.

The lines concerning pardon and death (23-31) were added by Francis later to the original verses which sing of the material universe. Francis's *Canticle* is a hymn of praise to God in the Biblical tradition of Psalm 148 and the "Canticle of the Three Young Men" in the Book of Daniel (3:52-90), but it adds to this tradition a medieval flavor and Francis's own charm and spontaneity.

Instead of singing a direct hymn of praise like Francis, Bonaventure contemplates the vast sweep of creation and sees in it a reflection of the power, wisdom and goodness of God as a vestige of the Trinity. In contrast to Francis's simple directness, Bonaventure's approach presupposes the speculative tradition of Christian theology derived from the Pseudo-Dionysius, Augustine and Anselm. Imbedded in the text of his meditation are theological and philosophical elements which had been elaborated and refined for centuries in both the Greek East and the Latin West. Although this complex theoretical structure stands behind Bonaventure's meditation on creation, it contains a point of convergence with Francis's *Canticle* in the simple experience of religious awe awakened in us by the wonders of creation. Francis's hymn evokes a sense of the majesty of creation reflecting the grandeur of God, his power and beauty, especially in Brother Sun, who "is beautiful and radiant with great splendor, and bears the signification of you, Most High One." This correlates with Bonaventure's meditation on creation as reflecting the power of the Father and the wisdom of the Son. More than Francis, Bonaventure was captivated by the intelligible structure of creation and meditates extensively on this aspect as reflecting the wisdom of the Son. In its scientific speculation it echoes the sense of nature expressed in the lyrical simplicity of Francis's praise to God "for Sister Moon and the stars," which he has "formed in heaven clear and precious and beautiful." Throughout his hymn Francis responds to the goodness of creation, praising God for Sister Water, "which is very useful," and "for our sister Mother Earth, who sustains and governs us,

and produces various fruits with colored flowers and herbs."
This correlates with Bonaventure's meditation on the goodness
of creation as reflecting the Holy Spirit.

Although Bonaventure's meditation on creation is more
abstract than Francis's hymn, it is not for that reason without
strong feeling. The force of this feeling is captured in the rich
imagery Bonaventure employs to describe creation. Seen with
the eye of contemplation, creatures are vestiges, that is, the very
footprints of God; they are roads leading to God, ladders on
which we can climb to God; they are signs divinely given so that
we can see God—shadows, echoes, pictures, statues, representations of God; creation is a book in which we can read God, a
mirror in which the divine light shines in various colors.[52] In
view of this strong feeling, it is not surprising that he should
close his meditation on the material world with one of his most
rhetorical passages:

> Whoever, therefore, is not enlightened by such splendor of
> created things is blind; whoever is not awakened by such outcries
> is deaf; whoever does not praise God because of all these effects is
> dumb; whoever does not discover the First Principle from such
> clear signs is a fool. Therefore, open your eyes, alert the ears of
> your spirit, open your lips and apply your heart so that in all
> creatures you may see, hear, praise, love and worship, glorify and
> honor your God lest the whole world rise against you.[53]

Meditation on the Soul

Having painted such a picture of the universe, Bonaventure
proceeds on his journey by turning within, to the experience of
sensation where once again he discovers a reflection of the
Trinity. From there he moves further into subjectivity into the
spiritual faculties where in the depths of memory we see the
reflection of the eternity of the Father, in the intellect the

---

52. II, 11, p. 76.
53. I, 15, pp. 67-68.

reflection of the Son as truth and in the will the reflection of the goodness of the Holy Spirit. Bonaventure's meditation on the faculties of the soul, which is begun in chapter three and completed in chapter four, is a classic example of inner way or introspective meditation. Derived chiefly from Augustine, this tradition is not found as such in Francis, but is quite compatible with his general perception of God's presence throughout creation.

Bonaventure's starting point here is more concrete than in the previous meditation on nature. He begins with specific objects of our knowledge: for example, the first principle that the whole is greater than any of its parts. We grasp such a principle as if we always knew it, as eternally true. In a similar way, he illustrates that when our intellect knows truth, it does so in the light of eternal Truth, and when our will desires or judges something as good, it does so in the light of the absolute Good. Behind this *reductio* stands Augustine's speculative analysis that the objects of our perception and our minds themselves are changeable; yet the truth we grasp is eternal and unchangeable. This means that we grasp truth in God himself, who shines as the light of truth and goodness in our souls. "See, therefore," Bonaventure says, "how close the soul is to God, and how, in their operations, the memory leads to eternity, the understanding to truth and the power of choice to the highest good."[54]

This introspective meditation is completed in the next or fourth stage, in which Bonaventure contemplates God present in the soul as image reformed by grace. Here he describes the plight of the fallen soul. It is strange, he observes, that given the fact that God is so close to the soul, so few are concerned with perceiving God within themselves. Distracted by cares, clouded by sense images, drawn away by concupiscence, the soul cannot reenter into itself as image of God. It lies fallen, immersed in the things of sense, in need of someone to lift it up so that it can see

---

54. III, 4, p. 84.

its true self as image of God, with the eternal Truth shining within itself. Christ has come and lifted up the soul, restoring the fallen image. Eternal Truth itself took on human form in Christ and became "a ladder, restoring the first ladder that had been broken in Adam."[55] Through Christ the spiritual senses are restored in the soul so that like the bride in the Canticle of Canticles, the soul can respond to her beloved.

Meditation on God

In the fifth and sixth stages, Bonaventure turns to God himself and meditates upon him first as Being and then as the Good. This type of meditation is more directly metaphysical and speculative than the preceding types. Beginning with a dialectical speculation on being and nonbeing, Bonaventure observes that Being itself cannot be rightly thought not to be, for the most pure being does not enter our minds except in full flight from nonbeing. Our intellect is strangely blind, for it does not consider that in the light of which it knows everything else. Our mind is like the eye of the bat that is so attuned to darkness that it is blinded by the light. "Thus our mind, accustomed to the darkness of beings and images of the things of sense, when it glimpses the light of the Supreme Being, seems to itself to see nothing. It does not realize that this very darkness is the supreme illumination of our mind, just as when the eye sees pure light, it seems to itself to see nothing."[56] Bonaventure closes his meditation on God as Being with a focus on the coincidence of opposites. God is the beginning and the end, the first and the last, the Alpha and the Omega; he "is an intelligible sphere whose center is everywhere and whose circumference is nowhere."[57] Because God as Being is most perfect and beyond all measurement, he

---

55. IV, 2, p. 88.
56. V, 4, pp. 96-97.
57. V, 8, p. 100; the statement on the intelligible sphere is quoted from Alan of Lille, *Regulae theologicae*, reg. 7.

"is, therefore, within all things, but not enclosed, outside all things, but not excluded, above all things, but not aloof, below all things, but not debased."[58]

From the contemplation of God as Being, Bonaventure turns to the contemplation of the Trinity as self-diffusive Good. This stage consists of a speculative meditation on emanation, not in the Neoplatonic sense of descending hypostases, but in the consubstantial sense of the Christian Trinity. There must be an eternal emanation on the level of the divinity itself, within the inner life of God; for, as Bonaventure says, "the good is said to be self-diffusive, therefore the highest Good must be most self-diffusive."[59] This dynamic self-diffusiveness of the Good can be realized only in the Trinitarian processions of the Son and Spirit from the Father. Creation can not bear the impact of this divine diffusion, for "the diffusion in time in creation is no more than a center or point in relation to the immensity of the divine goodness."[60] The self-diffusion of the Good leads Bonaventure to a contemplation of the coincidence of opposites within the Trinity: of unity and difference, of communication and intimacy, of equality and distinction.

At this point Bonaventure turns to Christ and contemplates him as an even greater coincidence of opposites, for "in him is joined the First Principle with the last, God with man, who was formed on the sixth day; the eternal is joined with temporal man . . . , the most simple with the most composite, the most actual with the one who suffered supremely and died, the most perfect and immense with the lowly, the supreme and all-inclusive one with a composite individual distinct from others, that is, the man Jesus Christ."[61] Gazing thus on Christ, one is filled with wonder and is drawn to the seventh stage of the journey, to the heights of mystical ecstasy, like Francis with his vision of the

---

58. V, 8, pp. 100-101.
59. VI, 2, p. 103.
60. *Ibid.*
61. VI, 5, p. 107.

Seraph, where "all intellectual activities must be left behind and the height of our affection must be totally transferred and transformed into God."[62] Bonaventure quotes the *Mystical Theology* of the Pseudo-Dionysius and draws his treatise to a close with the image of God as fire. He tells us to ask for "the fire that totally inflames and carries us into God by ecstatic unctions and burning affections."[63] This fire, he tells us, is God himself. We must die to ourselves and enter into darkness and silence and with Christ pass out of this world to the Father, so that when the Father is shown to us, we will say with the disciple Philip: "*It is enough for us*" (John 14:8).[64]

THE TREE OF LIFE

If we were to limit our study to the paths mapped out in *The Soul's Journey*, we would omit a major strand of the Christian tradition. The most characteristic form of Christian spirituality in the West focuses on the mystery of Christ, who is seen as the Mediator between God and man and the Savior freeing man from the burden of sin and leading him to salvation. In the Middle Ages this spirituality took the form of devotion to the humanity and passion of Christ, with concentration on vivid details, an awakening of human emotions, especially compassion, and the imitation of Christ in his moral virtues. This devotion is rooted in the fundamental orientation of Western culture toward the concrete, the particular, the human and the moral. Gounded in classical Roman culture, this orientation developed in the spirituality of the Middle Ages and blossomed in the 13th century into a complex form of religious sensibility, with Francis of Assisi as its chief expression. Francis attempted to imitate Christ literally, especially in poverty and in his suffering. His devotion to Christ covered a wide spectrum: from

62. VII, 4, p. 113.
63. VII, 6, p. 115.
64. *Ibid*, p. 116.

tender love of the infant Jesus, expressed in his producing the crib at Greccio, to his identification with the suffering Savior, expressed in his austere asceticism, and finally in his receiving the stigmata.

There are elements of this Franciscan devotion to the humanity and passion of Christ in *The Soul's Journey*. In the prologue Bonaventure states that no one can make this journey except by passing through Christ crucified. As the six wings of the Seraph symbolize the six stages of the journey, so the passage into God is symbolized by the form of the Crucified. In chapter four Bonaventure meditaties on Christ as the Bridegroom of the soul, and in chapter six he contemplates Christ as the greatest coincidence of opposites evoking wonder that leads to the mystical rapture of chapter seven. Thus Bonaventure meditates on Christ as the beginning, the middle and the end of the journey; but in each case he focuses not on the historical Jesus in the concrete details of his earthly life as an example of moral virtue, but on the mystical Christ who opens the deeper dimensions of the soul and leads to union with God.

In *The Tree of Life*, however, Bonaventure provides a meditation that touches the very heart of Franciscan devotion to the humanity and passion of Christ. He presents Christ as the tree of life upon which blossom such virtues as humility, piety, patience, constancy. The central object of the meditation is the historical Jesus as he is depicted in the New Testament: in his birth, public life, death and resurrection. In each specific meditation, Bonaventure summarizes the narrative details of an event in Christ's life, with references to his foreshadowing in Old Testament texts. There is a vivid application of the senses, an imaginative re-creation of the Gospel scene, a drawing of the reader into the drama of the event as a witness and a participator. Most of the meditations contain a prayer or direct address to the reader, evoking strong emotions through graphic, dramatic imagery. For example, after describing the scene of Jesus' birth in Bethlehem, he draws the reader into the midst of the event:

Now, then, my soul, embrace that divine manger; press your lips upon and kiss the boy's feet. Then in your mind keep the shepherds' watch, marvel at the assembling host of angels, join in the heavenly melody, singing with your voice and heart: *"Glory to God in the highest and on earth peace to men of good will."*[65]

One third of the treatise is devoted to Christ's suffering and death, with meditations in vivid detail on the bloody sweat in the garden, the scourging, the crowning with thorns, the piercing of the hands and feet with nails, the bitterness of the gall offered to drink and the final agony of death. For example, one of the meditations is entitled "Jesus Dripping with Blood."[66] Bonaventure concludes his meditation on Christ's death with the following address to the human heart:

O human heart, you are harder than any hardness of rocks, if at the recollection of such great expiation you are not struck with terror, nor moved with compassion, nor shattered with compunction, nor softened with devoted love.[67]

In this type of meditation, one applies the senses to a vividly imagined scene and evokes human emotions ranging from tender love to anguish. In the history of Christian piety, this form of meditation has been problematic, especially in its focus on the passion of Christ. Since it evokes human emotions, it can fall into a superficial sentimentalism. If it avoids this, it might remain exclusively on the moral level, proposing Christ's virtues for imitation in everyday life. It can, however, be a gateway into deeper mystical states of consciousness. Bonaventure indicates how this can be done when in *The Soul's Journey* he speaks of Christ as the doorway into the Franciscan contemplative vision, then later as the Bridegroom of the soul and finally as the passage to mystical ecstasy. If one were, for example, to link Bonaventure's meditations on the life of Christ in *The Tree of Life* to these

---

65. 4, p. 129.
66. 31, p. 156.
67. 29, p. 154.

36

three points, he could integrate these two forms of meditation in an organic fashion.

In this context Bonaventure can be seen in relation to the *Spiritual Exercises* of Ignatius of Loyola. Bonaventure's *The Tree of Life* is in many respects a forerunner of Ignatian meditation, in both its subject matter and its techniques. Ignatian meditation also runs the risk of the problems indicated above. From one point of view, the Ignatian *Exercises* can be seen as an initiation into the contemplative vision that Bonaventure proposes in *The Soul's Journey*; and from another point of view, one could follow Bonaventure's suggestions as how to open the meditation on the humanity of Christ in the *Exercises* to a more mystical contemplation of Christ.

THE LIFE OF ST. FRANCIS

Circumstances of Composition

At the General Chapter of Narbonne in 1260, Bonaventure was commissioned to write a biography of Francis. The chapter decreed as follows: "Likewise, we order that one good legend of blessed Francis be compiled from all those already in existence."[68] The Latin term *legenda*, used by the Chapter and retained in the title of Bonaventure's work, presents a problem in English translation. It would be inaccurate to translate it by the English term *legend*, meaning an account that is imaginative and historically untrue. The Latin term *legenda* is derived from the verb *legere* meaning to read and for the entire Middle Ages meant an account intended to be read publicly. It also indicated that the account followed the laws of literary composition in contradistinction to the *florilegia*, like the *Fioretti*, which were simply collections of anecdotes.[69] The biography which Bona-

---

68. *Archivum franciscanum historicum* 3 (1910): 76, no. 74.
69. Cf. Damien Vorreux in *Saint François d'Assise: Documents, écrits et premières biographies*, ed. Théophile Desbonnets and Damien Vorreux (Paris: Éditions franciscaines, 1968), pp. 565-566, n. 1.

venture wrote in response to this commission has been known as the *Legenda maior* to distinguish it from the shorter *Legenda minor* which he composed later for liturgical usage. The biography which we have translated here under the title *The Life of St. Francis* is Bonaventure's *Legenda maior*.

Precisely why this new biography was commissioned is not known with certainty and remains a matter of conjecture and even dispute among historians. As the Chapter indicated, earlier biographies existed: chiefly the two lives of Francis by Thomas of Celano along with his treatise on Francis's miracles, and the life by Julian of Speyer. Yet from a structural point of view there was need for a unified and complete biography. Thomas of Celano wrote two distinct lives over a twenty-four-year period. By itself each was incomplete, and together they contained many repetitions. The life of Julian was brief, omitting and compressing important material. Furthermore, there was need for a life of Francis that would be interpreted within the context of a profound and consistent spiritual theology. Bonaventure was eminently qualified; yet historians have maintained that his motivation was chiefly political, since the early biographies contained too much of the primitive spirit of Francis to be acceptable to Bonaventure's policies in shaping the Order along institutional lines. This is a complex question which we shall address ourselves to shortly.

Bonaventure took up the task of writing the biography with a sense of personal inadequacy balanced by his deep devotion to Francis. In his prologue he writes: "I feel that I am unworthy and unequal to the task of writing the life of a man so venerable and worthy of imitation. I would never have attempted it if the fervent desire of the friars had not aroused me, the unanimous urging of the General Chapter had not induced me and the devotion which I am obliged to have toward our holy father had not compelled me."[70] He then goes on to describe how as a boy

---

70. Prol., 3, p. 182.

he was cured through Francis, as we cited above. According to his own testimony, he did extensive research in the sources: "In order to have a clearer and more certain grasp of the authentic facts of his life, which I was to transmit to posterity, I visited the sites of the birth, life and death of this holy man."[71] At that time some of Francis's early companions were still alive, for example, Brothers Giles, Illuminato, Leo, Masseo and Rufino. Although he does not mention them by name, Bonaventure writes: "I had careful interviews with his companions who were still alive, especially those who had intimate knowledge of his holiness and were its principal followers."[72]

His chief purpose, he tells us, was to "*gather together* the accounts of his [Francis's] virtues, his actions and his words—like so many *fragments*, partly forgotten and partly scattered—although I cannot accomplish this fully, *so that they may not be lost* (John 6:12) when those who lived with this servant of God die."[73] In this passage Bonaventure is evoking the Scriptural image of the gathering of the fragments into baskets after the miraculous multiplication of the loaves and fish. As a matter of fact, however, Bonaventure does not add substantially to the material in the earlier biographies.[74] Rather his work is primar-

---

71. *Ibid*, 4, p. 183.
72. *Ibid*.
73. *Ibid*., 3, pp. 182-183.
74. The new material which Bonaventure adds to Celano and Julian is as follows: The simple man spreads his mantle before Francis I, 1; Francis has a vision of Christ crucified before his conversion I, 5; the crucifix speaks three times II, 1; Francis marks the mantle with a cross II, 4; kisses and cures II, 6; Brother Giles in ecstasy III, 4; Sylvester sees a dragon over Assisi III, 5; the defense of Cardinal John of St. Paul III, 9; the small tonsure which is conferred III, 10; Francis preaches in San Rufino IV, 4; friars among the infidels IV, 7; Fra Morico IV, 8; Chapter of the Protinucula IV, 10; the *Regula Bullata* IV, 11; details on practice of austerity V, 1; words on use of few clothes V, 2; gift of tears V, 8; the light at night V, 12; manner of his preaching in Assisi VI, 2; why called Minors VI, 5; poverty as foundation of Order VII, 2; details on vision of three ladies VII, 6; begs his meal from friars VII, 9; miracle of doctor's house VII, 11; reliance on providence VII, 13; details on compassion VIII, 5; on lambs at Portiuncula, and Rome VIII, 7; birds near Venice VI, 9; birds at LaVerna VIII, 10; Epiphany fast IX, 2; devotion to apostles IX, 3; intrepid in Holy Land IX, 7; goes to camp of Saracens IX, 8; return and desire for martyrdom IX, 9; ecstasy in prayer X, 4; some new details on crib at Christmas X, 7; more explicit regarding studies XI, 1; knowledge of Scriptures from God XI, 2; Siena and a prophecy, ability to read hearts XI, 7; doubts regarding preaching and a life of prayer XII, 1; consultation of Sylvester and Clare XII, 2;

ily a compilation of Celano and Julian of Speyer, largely verbatim. How much is verbatim from Celano and Julian can be seen at a glance in the remarkable printing of the critical text in the *Analecta franciscana* in which the phrases from the earlier biographies are printed in small type and Bonaventure's words in larger type. Although it was impossible to reproduce this effect in our translation, we have indicated in the footnotes the sources of each section in Celano and Julian. What is unique to Bonaventure, however, is his organization of the material and his interpretation of it within the context of his highly developed spiritual theology.

In 1263 at the General Chapter of Pisa Bonaventure presented a copy of his biography to each of the thirty-four provincials present. At the General Chapter of Paris in 1266, his biography was officially approved and the controversial decree was passed directing the friars to dispose of the earlier biographies:

> The General Chapter likewise orders under obedience that all the Legends of the Blessed Francis which have been made should be deleted, and where these may be found outside the Order, the friars should strive to remove them, since this Legend made by the minister general has been compiled as he received it from the mouth of those who were always with the blessed Francis and had certain knowledge of everything, and proven facts have been diligently placed in it.[75]

This decree, which strikes the modern reader as strange, is not clear in its intent. Whatever its purpose, it did lead to the

---

preaching at Gaeta XII, 6; testimonies that Francis was Herald of Christ XII, 12; details of experience of LaVerna XIII, 3; consults friars about concealing XIII, 4; hides stigmata— details XIII, 5; touches and warms peasant XIII, 7; Alexander IV's sermon: sees stigmata XIII, 8; jubilation of Bonaventure on stigmata XIII, 9; seven signs listed XIII, 10; reaction of a simple brother to Francis's sufferings XIV, 2; gratitude for suffering XIV, 2; Francis's desire for total conformity XIV, 4; the saint's example of Gospel perfection XV, 1; the witnesses to his stigmatized body after his death XV, 4; the stigmata as the signs of approval of the Most High King XV, 8.

75. *Miscellanea francescana* 72 (1972): 247.

widespread influence of Bonaventure's biography in the 13th and later centuries. There are more than four hundred surviving manuscripts of Bonaventure's work, but only twenty of the first life of Celano and only two complete manuscripts of his second life and only one of his treatise on the miracles. The Chapter of Paris in 1266 decreed that each friary in the Order should be supplied with its own copy of Bonaventure's biography. In the second half of the 14th century the number of friaries had reached 1,530, and there were about 400 houses of the Poor Clares. These statistics indicate that Bonaventure's biography was one of the most widely disseminated texts of the later Middle Ages. Its influence was enormous in popularizing the story of Francis in poetry, painting and religious devotion. Apart from its content, which we will examine shortly, it would qualify to be included in this series of classics of Western spirituality on its influence alone.

Since the time of Sabatier there has been a revival in interest among historians in early Franciscan material and in the primitive spirit which was seen in opposition to Bonaventure and his policies.[76] A number of these historians have been critical of Bonaventure's biography, viewing it as a purely political tool to achieve peace in the Order or to soften the message of Francis. They maintain that the earlier biographies contain too much of the primitive spirit for Bonaventure and his adherents who wanted to institutionalize the simple ideal of Francis. For example, A. G. Little writes that Bonaventure's biography "was compiled mainly with a view of pacifying the discords in the Order. It adds little that is new, and its chief historical value lies in its omissions and in its subsequent influence."[77] Bishop John H. R. Moorman claims that Bonaventure "never really understood the Franciscan ideal," and Rosalind Brooke judges Bonaventure's biography "disappointing" when compared to

---

76. Cf. Paul Sabatier, *Vie de Saint François d'Assise* (Paris: Fischbacker, 1894).
77. A.G. Little, "Guide to Franciscan Studies," *Études franciscaines* 41 (1929): 64-78.

Celano and the *Scripta Leonis*.[78] However this historical question will be resolved, which we cannot do here, this much is clear: Modern scholarship has been distracted by this historical question from taking adequate account of the distinct spiritual dimensions of Bonaventure's biography. My inclusion of the biography here is justified not only in terms of its influence but in terms of its spiritual content. In fact, the present series of classics in Western spirituality may well provide the appropriate context for evaluating the work. Once it is examined within the context of spirituality, its depth, power and wisdom become clear. An analysis of the biography reveals that it is a remarkable spritual work which penetrates deeply into the spirituality of Francis and interprets it in the light of Bonaventure's theology as a whole. Without this biography, the picture of Bonaventure's spirituality would be incomplete, and one of the most important and influential traditions of interpreting Francis's spirituality would be left ignored. It is hoped that the inclusion of the biography in this series may lead to a reexamination of the question of the relation of Francis and Bonaventure within the large context of Western spirituality and not merely within the framework of the history of the Franciscan Order in the 13th century.

Spirituality of The Life of St. Francis

The spirituality of Bonaventure's biography can best be seen through its structure. In his prologue he claims that he is not following a strict chronological order, but organizing the material according to themes.[79] As a matter of fact, there are two patterns of order: (1) There is a general chronological framework in the beginning and end. The initial section from chapter one

---

78. John Moorman, *The Sources for the Life of St. Francis of Assisi* (Manchester: University Press, 1940), p. 141; Rosalind B. Brooke, "St. Bonaventure as Minister General," in *S. Bonaventura Francescano: Convegni del Centro di Studi sulla Spiritualità Medievale XIV* (Todi: Presso L'Accademia Tudertina, 1974), pp. 75-105.

79. Prol., 4, p. 183.

through chapter four deals with his early life, his conversion, the foundation and spread of the Order; the final section from chapter thirteen through chapter fifteen deals with his receiving the stigmata, his death and canonization. (2) Within this general chronological framework is the core of the treatise, nine chapters on the virtues which are organized according to themes. Here Bonaventure draws together incidents from various periods in Francis's life as illustrations of the practice of virtues, for example, poverty, obedience, piety.[80]

The section on the virtues has an inner order according to the three stages of the spiritual life: purgation, illumination and perfection. For example, the first three virtues treated are purgative virtues and correspond to the three vows of the religious life: mortification (including here chastity), obedience and poverty. This pattern can be seen in the following outline of the chapters:

PURGATION
CHAPTER V: On the austerity of his life and how creatures provided him comfort
CHAPTER VI: On his humility and obedience and God's condescension to his slightest wish
CHAPTER VII: On his love of poverty and the miraculous fulfillment of his needs

ILLUMINATION
CHAPTER VIII: On his affectionate piety and how irrational creatures were affectionate toward him
CHAPTER IX: On the fervor of his charity and his desire for martyrdom
CHAPTER X: On his zeal for prayer and the power of his prayer

---

80. For the main points of this interpretation, I am indebted to Regis J. Armstrong, "The Spiritual Theology of the *Legenda Major* of Saint Bonaventure" (Ph.D. dissertation, Fordham University, 1978).

PERFECTION
CHAPTER XI: On his understanding of Scripture and his
spirit of prophecy
CHAPTER XII: On the efficacy of his preaching and his grace
of healing
CHAPTER XIII: On his sacred stigmata

There is a further pattern within the three stages. In the purgative virtues we find a remarkable coincidence of opposites. In chapter five Francis practices radical physical austerity; yet creatures provide him with bodily comfort, under God's miraculous providence. For example all of his senses are so comforted: taste and smell by a miracle which changed water into wine; his sight by a miraculous light that illumined his path in the darkness of night; his hearing by an angelic melody; his touch by the fire that did not cause pain when he was being cauterized. The same paradoxical pattern is followed in chapter six, where his humble obedience is balanced by God's obedience to him in working miracles. Again in chapter seven, his extreme poverty is balanced by God's miraculously supplying his needs in providing him with food, drink and lodging.

When we move into the illuminative virtues, this pattern of the coincidence of opposites is not so strikingly present, although there are instances of it. In the case of piety in chapter seven, Francis has deep affection for all of God's creatures and the animals respond affectionately to him. In chapter nine his charity is so intense that it leads him to seek martyrdom by going to the land of the Muslims, even to the Soldan's court. Paradoxically he is not granted his desire but is saved for a symbolic martyrdom in the stigmata. Finally, in chapter ten God responds to his prayer by working miracles.

In the third class, the virtues of perfection, the paradoxical pattern is present, but not so vividly as in the purgative virtues. For example, in chapter twelve, although he is a poor, simple unlettered man, his preaching has an enormous impact on his hearers. The treatment of the virtues reaches its climax in chapter thirteen when Francis receives the stigmata, which is God's seal on his virtuous life. At this point the thematic order intersects with the chronological order, for with the reception of the stigmata Bonaventure draws us into the final events of his story, Francis's last years, his death and canonization. At this point of intersection we begin to see that the outer chronological framework also follows the pattern of purgation, illumination and perfection. For there has been a direct development from the purgation involved in his conversion through the illumination of the virtues to the perfection achieved in the stigmata, and in the transformation in his death, or passing (in Latin *transitus*), as it is traditionally called. One of the most beautiful scenes in the entire biography is Francis's death, when his body seems already to be a resurrected, glorified body; for his flesh seems full of light, the wounds of the stigmata seem like jewels and the wound in his side like a rose. Finally his state of perfection reaches its fulness in his canonization and the extraordinary miracles that flow from him.

What is the image of Francis in the biography? Bonaventure is proposing him to the friars and to Christians in general as a model of the Gospel way of life. In him one can see the dynamics of spiritual growth and the ideal realization of all the virtues. In the prologue Bonaventure associates him with an abundance of Scriptural images, linking him to John the Baptist as the herald of the Gospel, with the fiery chariot of Elijah, with the Angel of the sixth seal of the Apocalypse. Although he is a new prophet and an angelic spirit, he is first and foremost an imitator of Christ. As the work progresses, we see that Francis is being assimilated to Christ by his growth in the very virtues which are presented as Christ's in *The Tree of Life*. Finally he is lifted up on Mount La Verna as Christ was in his transfiguration on Mount Tabor. There Francis is assimilated to Christ to such an extent that he bears the marks of Christ's passion in his body. At this point Bonaventure bursts into some of his most poetic passages as he praises this knight of Christ, who carries the standard of the Most High King, and recounts the seven visions of the cross that have led Francis, like the stages of *The Soul's Journey*, to the heights of sanctity.

This image of Francis, then, leads the reader to the image of Christ in *The Tree of Life* and into the various stages of *The Soul's Journey*, thus completing the picture of Bonaventure's spirituality. It represents a major contribution to the history of Western spirituality within the Franciscan Order, the medieval period and Christianity as a whole. What relevance does this spirituality have for the present? It remains a vital resource for grounding one's self in the tradition of Christian spirituality and for meeting the challenges of the present and future. In an age when the environment is being threatened by pollution, modern man can learn much from Francis's respect and love for creation. At a time when our natural resources are being depleted and when the Third World is demanding in justice its equal share of available goods, Franciscan poverty may have a new prophetic message for our age. Bonaventure's Franciscan joy in the fecundity of God and creation may be extended into the sphere of religious experience and provide a theoretical context for opening to ecumenism and the convergence of world spiritualities. If the decisive event of the last quarter of the 20th century is the movement of the human race toward a global community, then it would be of crucial importance to develop from our cultural resources images of global wholeness, such as are found in the structure of the Gothic cathedral and Bonaventure's spiritual vision.

TRANSLATION IN SENSE LINES

In the present translation I have taken the liberty to break Bonaventure's text into sense lines where it seemed appropriate because of the rhetorical and poetic quality of a passage. This may seem a bold and even unwarranted innovation since there is no precedent for it in the manuscript tradition. Yet there are stong internal reasons for doing so and a trend in similar literature, as is evidenced in *The Jerusalem Bible* and on a limited scale in the French translation of Bonaventure's biography of Francis by Damien Vorreux.[81]

Bonaventure's Latin presents special problems to the translator. His style is highly complex, composed of long stately sentences, with rhythmically balanced phrases and clusters of symbols whose meaning is enhanced by the subtle relations suggested by their position in the rhetorical structure. Contemporary English cannot convey this complexity. So the translator is faced with a dilemma: He can retain the long sentence structure and run the risk of losing the reader in the middle of a passage; or he can break the structure into shorter English sentences and lose much of the flavor of Bonaventure's style and often much of his meaning. After working on translating Bonaventure for more than ten years, I saw no solution to this dilemma.

In the course of my preparation of the present volume, however, Richard Payne, the editor-in-chief of The Classics of Western Spirituality, suggested that I experiment with breaking the text into sense lines in order to make it more available for meditative reading. I followed his suggestion, but with some reluctance because of the lack of precedent. To my surprise, I discovered that the sense lines not only aided meditative reading, but resolved the dilemma. The visual pattern supplied what noninflected English grammar could not do. It allowed the translator to retain the original sentence structure, with its rhetorical and poetic qualities, and to produce an English version that was readable at the same time. Sustained by the visual pattern, the reader's attention did not break down in the middle of a paragraph but was carried along by the rhythm and balance of the structure. Bonaventure's symbols could now speak for

---

81. Cf. Desbonnets and Vorreux (eds.), *Saint François d'Assise: Documents, écrits et premières biographies*, pp. 579-581, 709-711.

themselves, mounted in their original rhetorical framework; and his speculative mysticism could carry the reader to its heights on the strength of this linguistic structure.

Granted the advantages of the sense lines, they are not without problems. For a number of reasons some readers may prefer the unbroken, solid text. Even if others are sympathetic to the sense lines, they may judge my choice arbitrary. Since there is no absolute formula, I have followed my own criteria and practical judgment on precisely which passages to treat this way and specifically how to arrange them in sense lines. Many readers, I am sure, would prefer a different pattern. Yet, if the sense lines have opened a new approach to understanding and appreciating Bonaventure, individuals can divide passages in sense lines according to their own judgment and taste.

With the freedom that the sense lines give, I have striven for a translation that reflects, as much as possible, Bonaventure's Latin style without being awkward or archaic in English. I have inclined more to a literal translation than a paraphrase, striving for precision of technical meaning, attempting to retain some of the medieval flavor of passages, not only in sentence structure, but in the use of technical terms and in the turn of phrase. This is not intended, then, to be a translation of a medieval Latin text into 20th century dress, but rather a rendition that attempts to touch the reader in his own time and to draw him into the life-world of the Middle Ages, without seeming foreign, and from there into the universal issues that are at the perennial center of spirituality. This is the ideal, but I realize that the performance will fail to measure up to its demand.

One final point—in keeping with a current tradition, I have italicized quotations from Scripture and cited their sources. Like his medieval contemporaries, Bonaventure was steeped in the Bible and interwove texts from Scripture throughout the fabric of his writing. It is hoped that this visual device will show the reader at a glance how profoundly Bonaventure's spirituality was grounded in the biblical tradition.

Bonaventure

THE SOUL'S JOURNEY INTO GOD ·
THE TREE OF LIFE · THE LIFE OF ST. FRANCIS

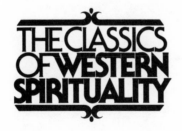

THE CLASSICS OF WESTERN SPIRITUALITY

PROLOGUE

1. In the beginning
I call upon the First Beginning,[1]
from whom
all illuminations descend
as from the *Father of Lights*,
from whom
comes *every good and every perfect gift*.[2]

I call upon the Eternal Father
through his Son, our Lord Jesus Christ,
that through the intercession of the most holy Virgin Mary,
the mother of the same God and Lord Jesus Christ,
and through the intercession of blessed Francis,
our leader and father,
he *may enlighten the eyes* of our soul
to guide our feet
in the way of that *peace*
which surpasses all understanding.[3]

This is the peace
proclaimed and given to us
by our Lord Jesus Christ
and preached again and again
by our father Francis.

At the beginning and end of every sermon he announced peace;
in every greeting he wished for peace;
in every contemplation he sighed for ecstatic peace—

---

1. The Latin for "beginning" is *principium*, which also means principle; the *First Beginning*, then, is God as First Principle. The initial phrase *in the beginning* alludes to the opening words of Genesis (1:1) and of the Gospel of John (1:1).
2. James 1:17.
3. Cf. Eph. 1:18; Luke 1:79; Phil. 4:7.

> like a citizen of that Jerusalem of which
> that Man of Peace says,
> who *was peaceable with those who hated peace:*
> *Pray for the peace of Jerusalem.*[4]

For he knew that the throne of Solomon would not stand
except in peace,
since it is written:
In peace is his place and his abode in Sion.[5]

2. Following the example of our most blessed father Francis, I was seeking this peace with panting spirit—I a sinner and utterly unworthy who after our blessed father's death had become the seventh Minister General of the Friars. It happened that about the time of the thirty-third anniversary of the Saint's death,[6] under divine impulse, I withdrew to Mount La Verna, seeking a place of quiet and desiring to find there peace of spirit. While I was there reflecting on various ways by which the soul ascends into God, there came to mind, among other things, the miracle which had occurred to blessed Francis in this very place: the vision of a winged Seraph in the form of the Crucified.[7] While reflecting on this, I saw at once that this vision represented our father's rapture in contemplation and the road by which this rapture is reached.

3. The six wings of the Seraph can rightly be taken to symbolize the six levels of illumination by which, as if by steps or stages, the soul can pass over to peace through ecstatic elevations of Christian wisdom. There is no other path but through the burning love of the Crucified, a love which so transformed Paul into Christ when he *was carried up to the third heaven* (2 Cor. 12:2) that he could say: *With Christ I am nailed to the cross. I live,*

---

4. Ps. 119:7, 121:6.

5. Ps. 75:3.

6. Since Francis died on October 4, 1226, Bonaventure is referring here to September or October 1259, some two and one-half years after he had been elected Minister General.

7. Cf. Bonaventure's description of Francis's vision in his biography of the saint, XIII, 3, pp. 305-306. On the winged Seraph, cf. Isa. 6:2.

now not I, but Christ lives in me (Gal. 2:20). This love also so absorbed the soul of Francis that his spirit shone through his flesh when for two years before his death he carried in his body the sacred stigmata of the passion. The six wings of the Seraph, therefore, symbolize the six steps of illumination that begin from creatures and lead up to God, whom no one rightly enters except through the Crucified. For *he who enters not through the door, but climbs up another way is a thief and a robber.* But *if anyone enter* through this door, *he will go in and out and will find pastures* (John 10:1, 9). Therefore John says in the Apocalypse: *Blessed are they who wash their robes in the blood of the Lamb that they may have a right to the tree of life and may enter the city through the gates* (Apoc. 22:14). It is as if John were saying that no one can enter the heavenly Jerusalem by contemplation unless he enter through the blood of the Lamb as through a door. For no one is in any way disposed for divine contemplation that leads to mystical ecstasy unless like Daniel he is a *man of desires* (Dan. 9:23). Such desires are enkindled in us in two ways: by an outcry of prayer that makes us *call aloud in the groaning of our heart* (Ps. 37:9) and by the flash of insight by which the mind turns most directly and intently toward the rays of light.

4. First, therefore, I invite the reader
to the groans of prayer
through Christ crucified,
through whose blood
we are cleansed from the filth of vice—
so that he not believe
that reading is sufficient without unction,
speculation without devotion,
investigation without wonder,
observation without joy,
work without piety,
knowledge without love,
understanding without humility,

endeavor without divine grace,
reflection as a mirror[8] without divinely inspired wisdom.
To those, therefore, predisposed by divine grace,
the humble and the pious,
the contrite and the devout,
those anointed with *the oil of gladness*,[9]
the lovers of divine wisdom, and
those inflamed with a desire for it,
to those wishing to give themselves
to glorifying, wondering at and even savoring God,
I propose the following considerations,
suggesting that the mirror presented by the external world
is of little or no value
unless the mirror of our soul
has been cleaned and polished.

Therefore, man of God,
first exercise yourself in remorse of conscience
before you raise your eyes
to the rays of Wisdom reflected in its mirrors,
lest perhaps from gazing upon these rays
you fall into a deeper pit of darkness.

5. It seemed good to divide this work into seven chapters,
giving each a title for a better understanding of the contents.

I ask you, then,
to weigh the writer's intention rather than his work,
the meaning of his words rather than his uncultivated style,
truth rather than beauty,
the exercise of affection rather than erudition of the intellect.
To do this,

---

8. The mirror referred to here is the soul, whose powers of reflection must be illumined by divine wisdom.
9. Ps. 44:8.

you should not run rapidly
over the development of these considerations,
but should mull them over slowly
with the greatest care.

HERE ENDS THE PROLOGUE

CHAPTER HEADINGS

CHAPTER ONE
On the Stages of the Ascent into God and on Contemplating Him through His Vestiges in the Universe

CHAPTER TWO
On Contemplating God in His Vestiges in the Sense World

CHAPTER THREE
On Contemplating God through His Image Stamped upon our Natural Powers

CHAPTER FOUR
On Contemplating God in His Image Reformed by the Gifts of Grace

CHAPTER FIVE
On Contemplating the Divine Unity through Its Primary Name Which Is Being

CHAPTER SIX
On Contemplating the Most Blessed Trinity in Its Name Which Is Good

CHAPTER SEVEN
On Spiritual and Mystical Ecstasy in Which Rest Is Given to Our Intellect When through Ecstasy Our Affection Passes Over Entirely into God

CHAPTER ONE

ON
THE STAGES OF THE ASCENT
INTO GOD AND ON CONTEMPLATING HIM
THROUGH HIS VESTIGES
IN THE UNIVERSE[1]

1. *Blessed is the man*
whose help is from you;
in his heart
he has prepared to ascend by steps
in the valley of tears,
in the place which he has set.[2]

Since happiness is nothing other than
the enjoyment of the highest good
and since the highest good is above,
no one can be made happy unless he rise above himself,
not by an ascent of the body,
but of the heart.
But we cannot rise above ourselves
unless a higher power lift us up.
No matter how much our interior progress is ordered,
nothing will come of it
unless accompanied by divine aid.
Divine aid is available
to those who seek it from their hearts,

---

1. The Latin term for "contemplating" in this and the other chapter headings is *speculatio*, which has as its root *speculum*, meaning "mirror." Bonaventure uses the word to mean "reflection," "speculation," "contemplation," "consideration." As is customary in his use of certain key words, he often intends all of these meanings in a given instance. The Latin term for "vestige" is *vestigium*, which primarily means "footprint." Since this seemed too graphic for the context, we have chosen the less concrete term "vestige."

2. Ps. 83:6-7.

59

humbly and devoutly;
and this means to sigh for it
in this *valley of tears*, through fervent prayer.
Prayer, then, is the mother and source
of the ascent.
Dionysius, therefore, in his book *Mystical Theology*,
wishing to instruct us in mystical ecstasy,
places a prayer at the outset.[3]
Let us pray, therefore, and say to the Lord our God:
Lead me, Lord, in your path,
and I will enter in your truth.
Let my heart rejoice
that it may fear your name.[4]

2. By praying in this way, we receive light to discern the steps of the ascent into God. In relation to our position in creation, the universe itself is a ladder by which we can ascend into God. Some created things are vestiges, others images; some are material, others spiritual; some are temporal, others everlasting; some are outside us, others within us. In order to contemplate the First Principle, who is most spiritual, eternal and above us, we must pass through his vestiges, which are material, temporal and outside us. This means *to be led in the path of God.* We must also enter into our soul, which is God's image, everlasting, spiritual and within us. This means *to enter in the truth of God.* We must go beyond to what is eternal, most spiritual and above us, by gazing upon the First Principle. This means to *rejoice in the knowledge of God and in reverent fear of his majesty* (cf. Ps. 85:11).[5]

---

3. Dionysius, *De mystica theologia*, I, 1; Bonaventure has incorporated the prayer into the present work; VII, 5, p. 114-115.

4. Ps. 85:11.

5. Bonaventure develops the beginning of his treatise like a medieval sermon, giving first the text Psalm 83:6-7: *Blessed is the man.* . . . This *prothema*, as it is called, exhorts to prayer and leads to the *thema*, or main theme, expressed in the text Psalm 85:11: *Lead me, Lord.* . . . From this latter verse he derives the threefold division of his treatise developed in 2: the reflection of God in his vestige, his image and in himself. Note the correlation of this division with the text, as indicated in the italicized phrases in 2.

3. This threefold division, then, corresponds to the three days' journey into the wilderness (Exod. 3:18), and to the threefold intensity of light during a single day: The first is like evening, the second like morning, the third like noon. This division reflects the threefold existence of things: in matter, in the mind and in the Eternal Art,[6] according to which it was said: *Let it be made; he made it*; and *it was made* (Gen. 1:3ff.). It reflects also the threefold substance in Christ, who is our Ladder: bodily, spiritual and divine.

4. Corresponding to this threefold movement, our mind has three principal perceptual orientations. The first is toward exterior material objects and is the basis for its being designated as animal or sensual. The second orientation is within itself and into itself and is the basis for its being designated as spirit. The third is above itself and is the basis for its being designated as mind.[7] By all of these we should dispose ourselves to ascend into God so as to love him *with our whole mind, with our whole heart and with our whole soul* (Mark 12:30; Matt. 22:37; Luke 10:27). In this consists both perfect observance of the Law and Christian wisdom.

5. Any one of these ways can be doubled, according to whether we consider God as *the Alpha and the Omega* (Apoc. 1:8). Or in each of these ways we can see him through a mirror or in a mirror. Or we can consider each way independently or as joined to another. Therefore it is necessary that these three principal stages be multiplied to a total of six. Just as God completed the whole world in six days and rested on the seventh, so the smaller world of man is led in a most orderly fashion by six successive stages of illumination to the quiet of contemplation. This is symbolized by the following: Six steps led up to the throne of Solomon (3 Kings 10:19); the Seraphim which Isaiah saw had six

---

6. For Bonaventure the Eternal Art means the Son in the Trinity as the expression of the Father, in whom the Father expresses all that he can make. Thus the Son contains the ideas of all things, which have an eternal existence in him.

7. The Latin is *mens*, which we translate here as "mind" although in the title as "soul," for here the context focuses on cognition; cf. our introduction, pp. 20-21.

wings (Isa. 6:2); after six days the Lord called Moses *from the midst of the cloud* (Exod. 24:16); and *after six days*, as is said in Matthew, Christ *led his disciples up a mountain and was transfigured before them* (Matt. 17:1-2).

6. Just as there are six stages in the ascent into God, there are six stages in the powers of the soul, through which we ascend from the lowest to the highest, from the exterior to the interior, from the temporal to the eternal. These are the senses, imagination, reason, understanding, intelligence, and the summit of the mind or the spark of conscience.[8] We have these stages implanted in us by nature, deformed by sin and reformed by grace. They must be cleansed by justice, exercised by knowledge and perfected by wisdom.

7. In the initial state of creation, man was made fit for the quiet of contemplation, and therefore *God placed him in a paradise of delights* (Gen. 2:15). But turning from the true light to changeable good, man was bent over by his own fault, and the entire human race by original sin, which infected human nature in two ways: the mind with ignorance and the flesh with concupiscence. As a result, man, blinded and bent over, sits in darkness and does not see the light of heaven unless grace with justice come to his aid against concupiscence and unless knowledge with wisdom come to his aid against ignorance. All this is done through Jesus Christ, *whom God made for us wisdom, justice, sanctification and redemption* (1 Cor. 1:30). Since he is *the power of God and the wisdom of God* (1 Cor. 1:24), the incarnate Word *full of grace and truth* (John 1:14), he made *grace* and *truth*. That is, he pours out the grace of charity, which, since it flows *from a pure heart and a good conscience and faith unfeigned* (1 Tim. 1:5), rectifies the entire soul in the threefold orientation mentioned above. He has taught the knowledge of truth according to the threefold mode of theology: symbolic, literal and mystical, so that

---

8. The Latin is *apex mentis seu synderesis scintilla*, the highest point of the soul, from which mystical union proceeds. For Bonaventure it is conscience as the natural tendency of the soul toward goodness.

through the symbolic we may rightly use sensible things, through the literal we may rightly use intelligible things and through the mystical we may be lifted above to ecstasy.

8. Whoever wishes to ascend to God must first avoid sin, which deforms our nature, then exercise his natural powers mentioned above: by praying, to receive restoring grace; by a good life, to receive purifying justice; by meditating, to receive illuminating knowledge; and by contemplating, to receive perfecting wisdom. Just as no one comes to wisdom except through grace, justice and knowledge, so no one comes to contemplation except by penetrating meditation, a holy life and devout prayer. Since grace is the foundation of the rectitude of the will and of the penetrating light of reason, we must first pray, then live holy lives and thirdly concentrate our attention upon the reflections of truth. By concentrating there, we must ascend step by step until we reach the height of the mountain *where the God of gods is seen in Sion* (Ps. 83:8).

9. Since we must ascend Jacob's ladder before we descend it, let us place our first step in the ascent at the bottom, presenting to ourselves the whole material world as a mirror through which we may pass over to God, the supreme Craftsman.[9] Thus we shall be true Hebrews passing over from Egypt to the land promised to their fathers (Exod. 13:3ff.); we shall also be Christians passing over with Christ *from this world to the Father* (John 13:1); we shall be lovers of wisdom, which calls to us and says: *Pass over to me all who long for me and be filled with my fruits* (Ecclus. 24:26). *For from the greatness and beauty of created things, their Creator can be seen and known* (Wisd. 13:5).

10. The Creator's supreme power, wisdom and benevolence shine forth in created things, as the bodily senses convey this to the interior senses in three ways. For the bodily senses assist the intellect when it investigates rationally, believes faith-

---

9. Cf. Gen. 28:12; although Bonaventure begins here with the material world, it is clear from many other texts that he does not believe we must begin from sense perception in order to come to knowledge of God.

fully or contemplates intellectually. In contemplating, it considers the actual existence of things; in believing, the habitual course of things; and in reasoning, the potential excellence of things.

11. In the first way, that of contemplation, we consider things in themselves and see in them weight, number and measure: weight, by which they tend to their position; number, by which they are distinguished; and measure, by which they are limited. Thus we see in them mode, species and order as well as substance, power and operation. From these, as from a vestige, we can rise to knowledge of the immense power, wisdom and goodness of the Creator.

12. In the second way, that of faith, we consider this world, in its origin, process and end. For *by faith* we believe that *the world was fashioned by the Word of life* (Heb. 11:3). By faith we believe that the periods of the three laws—of nature, Scripture and grace—succeeded each other and progressed in a most orderly way. By faith we believe that the world must come to an end with the final judgment. In the first, we consider the power of the supreme Principle; in the second, his providence; and in the third, his justice.

13. In the third way, that of investigating by reason, one sees that some things merely exist, others exist and live, and others exist, live and discern. He sees that the first are less perfect; the second, intermediate; and the third, more perfect. Likewise he sees that some things are material, others partly material and partly spiritual. From this he realizes that others are purely spiritual and are better and more noble than the two previous classes. He sees, finally, that some things are changeable and corruptible, as are earthly bodies; others are changeable and incorruptible, as are heavenly bodies. From this he realizes that other things are unchangeable and incorruptible, as are supercelestial realities.

From these visible things, therefore, one rises to consider the power, wisdom and goodness of God as existing, living, intelligent, purely spiritual, incorruptible and unchangeable.

14. This reflection can be extended according to the seven-fold properties of creatures—which is a sevenfold testimony to the divine power, wisdom and goodness—if we consider the origin, magnitude, multitude, beauty, fulness, activity and order of all things.

The *origin* of things,
according to their
creation, distinction and embellishment,
as the work of the six days,
proclaims
the divine power that produces all things from nothing,
the divine wisdom that clearly distinguishes all things,
and the divine goodness that lavishly adorns all things.

The *magnitude* of things,
in the mass of their
length, width and depth;
in their great power extending
in length, width and depth
as appears in the diffusion of light;
in the efficiency of their operations which are
internal, continuous and diffused
as appears in the operation of fire—
all this clearly manifests the immensity
of the power, wisdom and goodness
of the triune God,
who by his
power, presence and essence
exists uncircumscribed in all things.

The *multitude* of things
in their generic, specific and individual
diversity
in substance, form or figure, and efficiency—

beyond all human calculation—
clearly suggests and shows
the immensity
of the three previously mentioned attributes
in God.

The *beauty* of things,
in the variety
of light, shape and color
in simple, mixed and even organic bodies—
such as heavenly bodies,
and minerals (like stones and metals),
and plants and animals—
clearly proclaims
the three previously mentioned attributes.

The *fulness* of things
by which
matter is full of forms because of seminal principles,[10]
form is full of power because of its active potency,
power is full of effects because of its efficiency,
clearly declares
the same attributes.

The *activity*,
multiple inasmuch as it is
natural, artificial and moral,
by its manifold variety
shows the immensity
of that power, art and goodness
which is
"the cause of being, the basis of understanding
and the order of living"[11]

---

10. The Latin term here is *rationes seminales*, the potencies in matter out of which forms emerge in the future.
11. Augustine, *De civitate Dei*, VIII, 4.

The *order*
in duration, position and influence,
that is, before and after, higher and lower, nobler and less noble,
in the book of creation
clearly indicates
the primacy, sublimity and dignity
of the First Principle
and thus the infinity of his power.
The order
of the divine law, precepts and judgments
in the book of Scripture
shows
the immensity of his wisdom.
And the order
of the divine sacraments, benefits and recompense
in the body of the Church
shows
the immensity of his goodness.
In this way
order itself
leads us most clearly into
the first and highest, the most powerful, the wisest and the best.

15. Whoever, therefore, is not enlightened
by such splendor of created things
is blind;
whoever is not awakened by such outcries
is deaf;
whoever does not praise God because of all these effects
is dumb;
whoever does not discover the First Principle
from such clear signs
is a fool.
Therefore, open your eyes,
alert the ears of your spirit, open your lips

and *apply your heart*[12]
so that in all creatures you may
see, hear, praise, love and worship, glorify and honor
your God
lest the whole world rise against you.
For because of this
the whole world will fight against the foolish.[13]
On the contrary,
it will be a matter of glory for the wise,
who can say with the Prophet:
You have gladdened me, Lord, by your deeds
and in the works of your hands I will rejoice.
How great are your works, Lord!
You have made all things in wisdom;
the earth is filled with your creatures.[14]

---

12. Prov. 22:17.
13. Wisd. 5:20.
14. Ps. 91:5-6, 103:24.

CHAPTER TWO

ON
CONTEMPLATING GOD
IN HIS VESTIGES IN
THE SENSE WORLD

1. Concerning the mirror of things
perceived through sensation,
we can see God
not only through them as through his vestiges,
but also in them
as he is in them
by his essence, power and presence.
This type of consideration is higher than the previous one;
therefore it holds second place
as the second level of contemplation
by which we are led to contemplate God
in all creatures
which enter our minds through our bodily senses.

2. It should be noted that this world, which is called the macrocosm, enters our soul, which is called the smaller world, through the doors of the five senses as we perceive, enjoy and judge sensible things. This is clear from the following: In the world, some things generate, some are generated and some govern the former and the latter. Those that generate are simple bodies, such as heavenly bodies and the four elements. Whatever is generated and produced by the operation of natural power is generated and produced from these elements by the power of the light which unites contrary elements in composite things. Generated things are composite bodies made from the elements, such as minerals, plants, animals and the human

body. Those which rule over these groups are spiritual substances, either completely united to matter, as the souls of brute animals; or united to but separable from matter, as rational spirits; or completely separated from matter, as heavenly spirits, which the philosophers call intelligences and we, angels. According to the philosophers, these latter move the heavenly bodies. Because of this, the governance of the universe is attributed to them, by their receiving from the First Cause, God, an influx of power which, in turn, they distribute in their task of governing, which has to do with the natural consistency of things. According to the theologians, the ruling of the universe is attributed to the angels in relation to the work of restoration, under the dominion of the most high God. Hence they are called *ministering spirits, sent for the sake of those who inherit salvation* (Heb. 1:14).

3. So man, who is called the smaller world, has five senses like five doors through which knowledge of all things which are in the sense world enters his soul. For through sight enter the sublime and luminous heavenly bodies and other colored objects; through touch, solid and terrestrial bodies; through the three intermediate senses, intermediate objects; through taste, liquid; through hearing, sounds; and through smell, vapors which have something of humid nature, something of air, and something fiery or hot, as is evidenced in the smoke from incense.

Through these doors, then, enter both simple bodies and composite bodies made of mixtures of these. We perceive with our senses not only these particular sense objects, which are light, sound, odor, taste and the four primary qualities which touch apprehends; but also the common sense objects, which are number, size, shape, rest and motion. "Everything that is moved is moved by something else";[1] and certain things move and come to rest by themselves, such as animals. When through these five senses we perceive the motion of bodies, we are led to

---

1. Aristotle, *Physic.*, VII, t. 1, c.1 (241b 24).

the knowledge of spiritual movers, as from effect to cause.

4. The entire sense world, therefore, in its three classes of objects, enters the human soul through apprehension. The exterior sense objects are the first which enter into the soul through the gates of the five senses. They enter, I say, not through their substance, but through their likenesses, which are first produced in the medium; and from the medium they enter into the organ and from the exterior organ into the interior organ and from this into the apprehensive faculty. And thus the production of the image in the medium and from the medium in the organ and the turning of the apprehensive faculty upon it bring about the apprehension of all objects that the soul grasps from outside.

5. From this apprehension, if it is of a suitable object, there follows pleasure. The senses take delight in an object perceived through an abstracted likeness either because of its beauty, as in sight, or because of its sweetness, as in smell and hearing, or because of its wholesomeness, as in taste or touch, if we speak by way of appropriation. Now, all enjoyment is based on proportion. But the species has the notion of form, power or operation according to whether it is viewed in relation to the principle from which it flows; or to the medium through which it passes; or to the term on which it acts. Therefore proportion can be viewed in the likeness, insofar as it involves species or form, and then it is called beauty since "beauty is nothing other than harmonious symmetry" or "a certain arrangement of parts with pleasing color."[2] Or proportion can be viewed as involving potency or power, and then it is called agreeableness since the acting power does not disproportionally exceed the recipient; for the senses are pained by extremes and delighted in the mean. Or proportion can be viewed as productive and impressive; it is proportioned when the agent by its impression fills a need of the recipient, that is, strengthening and nourishing the recipient, which is most apparent in taste and touch. And thus through

2. Augustine, *De musica*, VI, c.13, no. 38; *De civitate Dei*, XXII, c. 19, no. 2.

pleasure, exterior agreeable objects enter into the soul by their likenesses according to a threefold form of delight.

6. After this apprehension and pleasure comes judgment, by which we determine not only whether something is white or black, because this pertains to a particular sense, not only whether it is wholesome or harmful, because this pertains to an interior sense, but we judge also and give a reason why it is pleasurable. In this judgment we inquire into the reason of the pleasure which is experienced in the senses from the object. Now this occurs when we ask the reason why a thing is beautiful or pleasant or wholesome, and we find that the reason lies in the proportion of harmony. The basis of harmony is the same in large and small objects; neither is it increased by size nor does it change or pass away as things pass away, nor is it altered by motion. It abstracts, therefore, from place, time and motion, and consequently is unchangeable, unlimited, endless and is completely spiritual. Judgment, therefore, is an action which causes the sensible species, received in a sensible way through the senses, to enter the intellective faculty by a process of purification and abstraction. And thus the whole world can enter into the human soul through the doors of the senses by the three operations mentioned above.

7. All these are vestiges in which we can see our God. For the species which is apprehended is a likeness generated in a medium and then impressed on the organ itself. Through this impression, it leads to its source, namely the object to be known. This clearly suggests that the Eternal Light generates from itself a coequal Likeness or Splendor, which is consubstantial and coeternal. It further suggests that he who is *the image of the invisible God* (Col. 1:15) and *the brightness of his glory and the image of his substance* (Heb. 1:3), who is everywhere through his initial generation, as the object generates its likeness in the entire medium, is united by the grace of union to an individual of rational nature, as the species is united to the bodily organ. Through this union he leads us back to the Father as to the

fountain-source and object. If, therefore, all things that can be known generate a likeness of themselves, they manifestly proclaim that in them as in mirrors we can see the eternal generation of the Word, the Image and Son, eternally emanating from God the Father.

8. In this way the species which delights as beautiful, pleasant and wholesome suggests that there is primordial beauty, pleasure and wholesomeness in that first Species, in which there is supreme proportion and equality with the generating Source, in which there is power flowing not from images of the imagination but from the truth of apprehension, in which there is an impression which preserves and satisfies and dispels all need in the one who apprehends. If, therefore, "pleasure is the union of the harmonious with the harmonious,"[3] and if the Likeness of God alone contains in the highest degree the notion of beauty, delight and wholesomeness and if it is united in truth and intimacy and in a fulness that fulfills every capacity, it is obvious that in God alone there is primordial and true delight and that in all of our delights we are led to seek this delight.

9. In a more excellent and immediate way, judgment leads us to see eternal truths more surely. Judgment takes place through our reason abstracting from place, time and mutability, and thus from dimension, succession and change, through reason which is unchangeable, unlimited and endless. But nothing is absolutely unchangeable, unlimited and endless unless it is eternal. Everything that is eternal is either God or in God. If, therefore, everything which we judge with certainty we judge by such a reason, then it is clear that he himself is the reason of all things and the infallible rule and light of truth, in which all things shine forth infallibly, indelibly, indubitably, irrefutably, indisputably, unchangeably, boundlessly, endlessly, indivisibly and intellectually. Therefore those laws by which we judge with certainty about all sensible things that come under our

---

3. William of Auxerre, *Summa aurea*, II, tr. 20, c.1.

consideration—since they are infallible and cannot be doubted by the intellect of the one who apprehends them, since they are as if ever present and cannot be erased from the memory of the one who recalls them, since they cannot be refuted or judged by the intellect of the one who judges because, as Augustine says, "no one passes judgment on them, but by them"[4]—these laws must be unchangeable and incorruptible since they are necessary; boundless since they are without limits; and endless since they are eternal—and for this reason they must be indivisible since they are intellectual and incorporeal, not made, but uncreated, existing eternally in the Eternal Art, by which, through which and according to which all beautiful things are formed.[5] Therefore we cannot judge with certainty except in view of the Eternal Art which is the form that not only produces all things but also conserves and distinguishes all things, as the being which sustains the form in all things and the rule which directs all things. Through it our mind judges all things that enter it through the senses.

10. We can extend this reflection by considering the seven different kinds of numbers by which, as by seven steps, we ascend to God.[6] Augustine shows this in his book *On True Religion* and in the sixth book *On Music*,[7] where he indicates the differences of numbers which ascend step by step from sensible things to the Maker of all so that God may be seen in all things.

For he says that there are numbers in bodies, especially in sounds and voices, and these he calls *sounding numbers*. There are numbers which we abstract from the above and receive in our senses; these he calls *encountered numbers*. There are numbers which proceed from the soul into the body, as seen in gestures and dance; these he calls *expressive numbers*. There are numbers in

---

4. Augustine, *De libero arbitrio*, II, c.12, no. 34; *De vera religione*, XXXI, 58.

5. Cf. note 6 to Chapter One, p. 61.

6. Although the Latin term *numerus* could be translated here in a general way by "harmony," we have chosen to retain the literal meaning "number" for technical reasons. As Bonaventure states, he is following Augustine, whose notion of number includes not only natural numbers, but also ratios, harmonies, proportions and rhythms.

7. Augustine, *De vera religione*, XL, 74-76; *De musica*, VI, *passim*.

the pleasures of the senses from turning attention to the species received; these he calls *sensual numbers*. There are numbers retained in the memory, and these he calls *remembered numbers*. There are also numbers by which we judge all the others, and these he calls *judicial numbers*. As has been said, these are necessarily above the mind since they are infallible and beyond judgment. From these there are impressed on our minds *artistic numbers*, which, however, Augustine does not enumerate among these classes because they are connected with the judicial numbers. From these latter flow the expressive numbers, from which are created the numerous forms of artifacts. Thus an orderly descent is made from the highest numbers, through the intermediate, to the lowest. To these highest numbers we ascend step by step from the sounding numbers, by means of the encountered, the sensual and the remembered numbers.

Since, therefore, all things are beautiful and in some way pleasurable, and since beauty and pleasure do not exist without proportion, and since proportion exists primarily in numbers, all things must necessarily involve numbers. Thus "number is the foremost exemplar in the mind of the Creator,"[8] and in things, the foremost vestige leading to Wisdom. Since this is most evident to all and very close to God, it leads us most closely to God by means of these seven divisions; and it makes him known in all bodily and sensible things when we apprehend the numerical, delight in numerical proportions and judge irrefutably according to the laws of numerical proportion.

11. From the first two stages
in which we are led to behold God
in vestiges,
like the two wings covering the Seraph's feet,[9]
we can gather that all the creatures of the sense world
lead the mind

---

8. Boethius, *De institutione arithmetica*, I, 2.
9. Cf. Isa. 6:2.

of the contemplative and wise man
to the eternal God.
For these creatures are
shadows, echoes and pictures
of that first, most powerful, most wise and most perfect
Principle,
of that eternal Source, Light and Fulness,
of that efficient, exemplary and ordering Art.
They are
vestiges, representations, spectacles
proposed to us
and signs divinely given
so that we can see God.
These creatures, I say, are
exemplars
or rather exemplifications
presented to souls still untrained
and immersed in sensible things
so that through sensible things
which they see
they will be carried over to intelligible things
which they do not see
as through signs to what is signified.

12. The creatures of the sense world
signify
the invisible attributes of God,[10]
partly because God is
the origin, exemplar and end
of every creature,
and every effect is
the sign of its cause, the exemplification of its exemplar
and the path to the end, to which it leads:

---

10. Rom. 1:20.

partly by their own proper representation,
partly from prophetic prefiguration,
partly from angelic operation,
partly from additional institution.
For every creature is by its nature
a kind of effigy and likeness of the eternal Wisdom,
but especially one
which in the book of Scripture
has been elevated through the spirit of prophecy
to prefigure spiritual things;
and more especially, those creatures
in whose likeness God wished to appear
through the ministry of angels;
and most especially, a creature
which God willed to institute
as a symbol
and which has the character
not only of a sign in the general sense
but also of a sacrament.

13. From all this, one can gather that
*from the creation of the world
the invisible attributes of God are clearly seen,
being understood
through the things that are made.*[11]
And so those who do not wish to heed these things,
and to know, bless and love
God
in all of them
are without excuse;[11]
for they are unwilling to be transported
*out of darkness
into the marvelous light* of God.

---

11. Rom. 1:20.

But thanks be to God
through our Lord Jesus Christ,
who *has transported* us
out of darkness
into his marvelous light[12]
when through these lights exteriorly given
we are disposed to reenter
the mirror of our mind
in which divine realities shine forth.

---

12. 1 Cor. 15:57; 1 Pet. 2:9.

CHAPTER THREE

ON
CONTEMPLATING GOD
THROUGH HIS IMAGE
STAMPED UPON OUR NATURAL POWERS

1. The two previous stages, by leading us
into God
through his vestiges,
through which he shines forth
in all creatures,
have led us to the point
of reentering into ourselves, that is,
into our mind,
where the divine image shines forth.
Here it is that, now in the third stage,
we enter into our very selves;
and, as it were, leaving the outer court,
we should strive to see God
through a mirror
in the sanctuary, that is, in the forward area of the tabernacle.[1]
Here the light of truth,
as from a candelabrum,
glows upon the face of our mind,
in which the image of the most blessed Trinity
shines in splendor.[2]
Enter into yourself, then, and see
that your soul loves itself most fervently;
that it could not love itself

---

1. On the description of the tabernacle in Scripture, cf. Exod. 26:33-35, 27:9-18, 37:17-24, 38:9-20.
2. Cf. Ps. 4:7.

unless it knew itself,
nor know itself
unless it remembered itself,
because our intellects grasp only what is present to our memory.
From this you can observe,
not with the bodily eye, but with the eye of reason,
that your soul has a threefold power.
Consider, therefore,
the operations and relationships of these three powers,
and you will be able to see God
through yourself as through an image,
which is to see *through a mirror in an obscure manner.*[3]

2. The function of memory is to retain and represent not only present, corporeal and temporal things but also successive, simple and eternal things. For the memory retains the past by remembrance, the present by reception and the future by foresight. It retains also simple things, such as the principles of continuous and discrete quantities like the point, the instant and the unit. Without these it is impossible to remember or to think of things which originate from them. The memory also retains the principles and axioms of the sciences, as everlasting truths held everlastingly. For while using reason, one can never so completely forget these principles that he would fail to approve and assent to them once they are heard, not as if he perceives them anew, but rather as if he recognizes them as innate and familiar. This is clearly shown when we propose to someone the following: "On any matter, one must either affirm or deny," or "Every whole is greater than its part," or any other axiom which cannot be contradicted "by our inner reason."[4]

In its first activity, therefore—the actual retention of all temporal things, past, present and future—the memory is an

___
3. 1 Cor. 13:12.
4. Aristotle, *Anal. Post.*, I, t. 77, c.10 (76b 24-27); the first quote is a formulation of the principle of contradiction and is derived from Aristotle, *Metaph.*, IV, t. 15, c. 4. (1006a 1-29); the second is derived also from Aristotle, *ibid*, V, t. 30f., c. 25f. (1023b 12-36).

image of eternity, whose indivisible presence extends to all times. From its second activity, it is evident that memory is informed not only from outside by sensible images, but also from above by receiving and holding within itself simple forms which cannot enter through the doors of the senses by means of sensible images. From the third activity, we hold that the memory has an unchangeable light present to itself in which it remembers immutable truths. And so from the activities of the memory, we see that the soul itself is an image of God and a likeness so present to itself and having God so present that the soul actually grasps him and potentially "is capable of possessing him and of being a partaker in him."[5]

3. The function of the intellective faculty consists in understanding the meaning of terms, propositions and inferences. Now, the intellect grasps the meaning of terms when it comprehends in a definition what a thing is. But definitions are constructed by using more universal terms; and these are defined by more universal terms until we come to the highest and most universal. Consequently, unless these latter are known, the less universal cannot be grasped in a definition. Unless we know what being per se is, we cannot fully know the definition of any particular substance. We cannot know being per se unless we also know its properties, which are: one, true, good. Now, being can be considered as incomplete or complete, as imperfect or perfect, as being in potency or being in act, qualified being or unqualified being, partial being or total being, transient being or permanent being, being through another or being through itself, being mixed with nonbeing or pure being, dependent being or absolute being, posterior being or prior being, changeable being or unchangeable being, simple being or composite being. Since privations and defects can in no way be known except through something positive, our intellect does not come to the point of

---

5. Augustine, *De Trinitate*, XIV, c. 8, no. 11.

understanding any created being by a full analysis[6] unless it is aided by a knowledge of the Being which is most pure, most actual, most complete and absolute, which is unqualified and Eternal Being, in which are the principles of all things in their purity. How could the intellect know that a particular being is defective and incomplete if it had no knowledge of the Being which is free from all defect? The same holds true for the other properties previously mentioned.

The intellect can be said truly to comprehend the meaning of propositions when it knows with certitude that they are true. To know this is really to know because the intellect cannot be deceived in this kind of comprehension. For it knows that this truth cannot be otherwise; therefore, it knows that this truth is unchangeable. But since our mind itself is changeable, it can see such a truth shining forth unchangingly only by means of some light which shines in an absolutely unchangeable way; and it is impossible for this light to be a changeable creature. Therefore our intellect knows in that Light *which enlightens every man coming into this world*, which is *the true Light* and the *Word* who *was in the beginning with God* (John 1:9, 1).

Our intellect truly grasps the meaning of an inference when it sees that the conclusion follows necessarily from the premises. It sees this not only in necessary but also in contingent terms such as the following: If a man is running, the man is moving. Our intellect perceives this necessary relationship not only in existing things, but also in nonexisting things. For if a man actually exists, it follows that if he is running, he is moving; the same conclusion follows even if he does not exist. The necessity, therefore, of this inference does not come from the existence of the thing in matter since it is contingent; nor from the existence of the thing in the soul because that would be a fiction if the thing did not exist in reality. Therefore the necessity of such an

---

6. We translate by "full analysis" Bonaventure's technical term *plene resolvens*, which means a movement of the mind back to the absolute Being, whereby what is understood is known in relation to the absolute Being.

inference comes from its exemplarity in the Eternal Art, according to which things are mutually oriented and related to one another because they are represented in the Eternal Art. As Augustine says in *On the True Religion:* The light of everyone who reasons truly is enkindled by that Truth which he also strives to reach.[7] From this it is obvious that our intellect is joined to Eternal Truth itself since it can grasp no truth with certitude if it is not taught by this Truth. You can see, therefore, through yourself the Truth which teaches you, if your desires and sensory images do not hinder you and interpose themselves like clouds between you and the rays of Truth.

4. The function of the power of choice is found in deliberation, judgment and desire. Deliberation consists in inquiring which is better, this or that. But *better* has meaning only in terms of its proximity to *best*; and this proximity is in terms of greater resemblance. No one, therefore, knows whether this is better than that unless he knows that it bears a greater resemblance to the best. No one knows that something bears a greater resemblance to another unless he knows the other. For I do not know that a certain man resembles Peter unless I know Peter or have some acquaintance with him. Therefore, the notion of the highest good is necessarily imprinted in everyone who deliberates.

A judgment of certitude on matters of deliberation is made according to some law. But no one judges with certitude according to law unless he is certain that the law is right and that he should not judge the law itself. But our mind judges about itself. Since, then, it cannot judge about the law through which it judges, that law is higher than our mind; and our mind judges by means of that law insofar as it is imprinted on our mind. But nothing is higher than the human mind except him alone who made it. Therefore in judging, our deliberative power touches the divine laws if it reaches a solution by a full analysis.[8]

---

7. Augustine, *De vera religione*, XXXIX, 72; this is a paraphrase, not a direct quotation.
8. The Latin is *plena resolutione*; cf. note 6, p. 82.

Now desire tends principally toward what moves it most; but what moves it most is what is loved most, and what is loved most is happiness. But happiness is had only in terms of the best and ultimate end. Therefore human desire seeks nothing except the highest good or what leads to or has some likeness to it. So great is the power of the highest good that nothing can be loved by a creature except out of a desire for it. Creatures, when they take the image and copy for the Truth, are deceived and in error.

See, therefore, how close the soul is to God, and how, in their operations, the memory leads to eternity, the understanding to truth and the power of choice to the highest good.

5. These powers lead us to the most blessed Trinity itself in view of their order, origin and interrelatedness. From memory, intelligence comes forth as its offspring, since we understand when a likeness which is in the memory leaps into the eye of the intellect in the form of a word. From memory and intelligence love is breathed forth as their mutual bond. These three—the generating mind, the word and love—are in the soul as memory, understanding and will, which are consubstantial, coequal and coeval, and interpenetrate each other. If, then, God is a perfect spirit, he has memory, understanding and will; and he has the Word generated and Love breathed forth, which are necessarily distinct since one is produced by the other—not in the order of essence, not in the order of accident, therefore in the order of persons.

When, therefore, the soul considers itself, it rises through itself as through a mirror to behold the blessed Trinity of the Father, the Word and Love: three persons, coeternal, coequal and consubstantial. Thus each one dwells in each of the others; nevertheless one is not the other but the three are one God.

6. When the soul considers its Triune Principle through the trinity of its powers, by which it is an image of God, it is aided by the lights of the sciences which perfect and inform it and represent the most blessed Trinity in a threefold way. For all philosophy is either natural or rational or moral. The first

deals with the cause of being and therefore leads to the power of the Father; the second deals with the basis of understanding and therefore leads to the wisdom of the Word; the third deals with the order of living and therefore leads to the goodness of the Holy Spirit.

Again, the first, natural philosophy, is divided into metaphysics, mathematics and physics. The first deals with the essences of things; the second with numbers and figures; and the third with natures, powers and diffusive operations. Therefore the first leads to the First Principle, the Father; the second to his Image, the Son; and the third to the gift of the Holy Spirit.

The second, rational philosophy, is divided into grammar, which makes men able to express themselves; logic, which makes them skillful in arguing; and rhetoric, which makes them capable of persuading and moving others. This likewise suggests the mystery of the most blessed Trinity.

The third, moral philosophy, is divided into individual, domestic and political. The first suggests the unbegottenness of the First Principle; the second, the relatedness of the Son; and the third, the liberality of the Holy Spirit.

7. All these sciences have certain and infallible rules,
     like rays of light shining down upon our mind
               from the eternal law.
     And thus our mind, illumined and flooded
               by such brilliance,
               unless it is blind,
          can be led through itself
     to contemplate that Eternal Light.
     The radiation and contemplation
               of this Light
     lifts up the wise in wonder;
          and on the contrary
     it leads to confusion the fools
who do not believe so that they may understand.

Thus this prophecy is fulfilled:
You enlighten wonderfully
from the eternal hills;
all the foolish of heart
were troubled.[9]

---

9. Ps. 75:5-6.

CHAPTER FOUR

ON
CONTEMPLATING GOD
IN HIS IMAGE
REFORMED BY THE GIFTS OF GRACE

1. Since we can contemplate the First Principle
not only by passing through ourselves
but also in ourselves,
and since the latter contemplation is superior to the former,
this mode of consideration
occupies the fourth stage of contemplation.
It seems amazing
when it has been shown
that God is so close to our souls
that so few should be aware
of the First Principle within themselves.
Yet the reason is close at hand:
for the human mind, distracted by cares,
does not enter into itself through memory;
clouded by sense images,
it does not turn back to itself through intelligence;
allured away by concupiscence,
it does not turn back to itself through desire
for inner sweetness and spiritual joy.

Thus lying totally in these things of sense,
it cannot reenter into itself
as into the image of God.

2. When one has fallen down,
he must lie there

---

1. Cf. Ps. 40:9; Is. 24:20.

unless someone lend a helping hand for him to rise.[1]
So our soul could not rise completely
from these things of sense
to see itself
and the Eternal Truth in itself
unless Truth, assuming human nature in Christ,
had become a ladder, restoring the first ladder
that had been broken in Adam.

Therefore, no matter how enlightened one may be
by the light of natural and acquired knowledge,
he cannot enter into himself
to delight within himself *in the Lord*[2]
unless Christ be his mediator, who says:
I am the door.
If anyone enters through me,
he will be saved;
and he will go in and out and will find pastures.[3]
But we do not draw near
to this door
unless we believe in him, hope in him and love him.
Therefore, if we wish to enter again
into the enjoyment of Truth as into paradise,
we must enter
through faith in, hope in and love of Jesus Christ,
the mediator between God and men,[4]
who is like
the tree of life
in the middle of paradise.[5]

---

2. Ps. 36:4.
3. John 10:9.
4. 1 Tim. 2:5.
5. Gen. 2:9; Apoc. 22:2; cf. Bonaventure's *The Tree of Life*, prol., 1-5, pp. 119-122.

3. The image of our soul, therefore, should be clothed with the three theological virtues, by which the soul is purified, illumined and perfected.[6] And so the image is reformed and made like the heavenly Jerusalem and a part of the Church militant which, according to the Apostle, is the offspring of the heavenly Jerusalem. For he says: *That Jerusalem which is above is free, which is our mother* (Gal. 4:26). The soul, therefore, believes and hopes in Jesus Christ and loves him, who is the incarnate, uncreated and inspired Word—*the way, the truth and the life* (John 14:6). When by faith the soul believes in Christ as the uncreated Word and Splendor of the Father,[7] it recovers its spiritual hearing and sight: its hearing to receive the words of Christ and its sight to view the splendors of that Light. When it longs in hope to receive the inspired Word, it recovers through desire and affection the spiritual sense of smell. When it embraces in love the Word incarnate, receiving delight from him and passing over into him through ecstatic love, it recovers its senses of taste and touch. Having recovered these senses, when it sees its Spouse and hears, smells, tastes and embraces him, the soul can sing like the bride the Canticle of Canticles, which was composed for the exercise of contemplation in this fourth stage. *No one* grasps this *except him who receives* (Apoc. 2:17), since it is more a matter of affective experience than rational consideration. For in this stage, when the inner senses are restored to see the highest beauty, to hear the highest harmony, to smell the highest fragrance, to taste the highest sweetness, to apprehend the highest delight, the soul is prepared for spiritual ecstasy through devotion, admiration and exultation according to the three exclamations in the Canticle of Canticles. The first of these flows from the fulness of devotion, by which the soul becomes *like a column of smoke from aromatic spices of myrrh and frankincense* (Cant. 3:6). The second arises from intense admiration, by

---

6. These are the classical three stages of the spiritual life or the threefold dynamics of spiritual growth; cf. Bonaventure's treatment of them in *De triplici via*.

7. Cf. John 1:1; Heb. 1:3.

which the soul becomes *like the dawn, the moon and the sun* (Cant. 6:10), according to the progressive stages of enlightenment that lift up the soul to gaze in admiration upon its Spouse. The third arises from the superabundance of exultation, by which the soul, *overflowing with delights* of the sweetest pleasure, *leans wholly upon her beloved* (Cant. 8:5).

4. When this is achieved, our spirit is made hierarchical[8] in order to mount upward, according to its conformity to the heavenly Jerusalem which no man enters unless it first descend into his heart through grace, as John saw in the Apocalypse.[9] It descends into our heart when our spirit has been made hierarchical—that is, purified, illumined and perfected— through the reformation of the image, through the theological virtues, through the delights of the spiritual senses and through mystical ecstasies. Our soul is also marked with nine levels when within it the following are arranged in orderly fashion: announcing, declaring, leading, ordering, strengthening, commanding, receiving, revealing and anointing. These correspond level by level to the nine choirs of angels. In the human soul the first three of these levels pertain to human nature; the next three, to effort and the last three, to grace. Having attained these, the soul, by entering into itself, enters the heavenly Jerusalem, where beholding the choirs of angels, it sees in them God, who dwells in them and performs all their operations. Hence Bernard says to Eugene that "God loves in the Seraphim as charity, knows in the Cherubim as truth, is seated in the Thrones as equity, reigns in the Dominations as majesty, rules in the Principalities as principle, guards in the Powers as salvation, acts in the Virtues as strength, reveals in the Archangels as light, assists in the Angels as piety."[10] From all this, God is seen as *all in all* (1

---

8. Influenced by the Pseudo-Dionysius, Bonaventure sees the soul ordered in a hierarchical pattern. As developed in the present chapter, the soul is hierarchical in its threefold act of purgation, illumination and perfection. In a larger context, the hierarchical soul reflects the hierarchical patterns in the Trinity, the angelic choirs and the Church.

9. Cf. Apoc. 21:2.

10. Bernard of Clairvaux, *De consideratione*, V, c. 5, no. 12. This is addressed to Pope Eugene III; Bernard does not explicitly name the choirs of angels in this text, but in the previous passage.

Cor. 15:28) when we contemplate him in our minds, where he dwells through the gifts of the most abundant charity.

5. For this stage of contemplation the study of the divinely imparted Scripture is especially helpful just as philosophy is for the preceding stage. For Sacred Scripture deals principally with the works of reparation. Hence it treats mainly of faith, hope and charity by which the soul is reformed, and most especially of charity. Of charity the Apostle says: *The aim of the command-ment is charity* insofar as it comes *from a pure heart and a good conscience, and a faith that is not feigned* (1 Tim. 1:5). Charity *is the fulfillment of the Law* (Rom. 13:10), as the same Apostle says. And our Savior asserts that the whole Law and the prophets depend on these two commandments: love of God and of our neighbor (cf. Matt. 22:40). These two are signified in the one Spouse of the Church, Jesus Christ, who is at the same time our neighbor and God, brother and lord, king and friend, the Word uncreated and incarnate, our maker and remaker, the *Alpha and Omega* (Apoc. 1:8; 21:6; 22:13), who is also the supreme Hierarch, who purifies, illumines and perfects his spouse, that is, the entire Church and every holy soul.

6. All Sacred Scripture, therefore, deals with this Hierarch and the ecclesiastical hierarchy. By Scripture we are taught that we should be purged, illumined and perfected ac-cording to the threefold law handed down in it: the law of nature, of Scripture and of grace; or rather, according to its three principal parts: the law of Moses which purifies, prophetic revelation which illumines, and the gospel teaching which per-fects; or especially, according to its threefold spiritual meaning: the tropological, which purifies one for an upright life; the allegorical, which illumines one for clarity of understanding; and the anagogical, which perfects through spiritual ecstasies and sweet perceptions of wisdom. This takes place through the three previously mentioned theological virtues and the spiritual senses which have been reformed and the three above-mentioned ecstatic stages and hierarchical acts of the soul, by

which our soul enters back into its interior, there to behold God *in the splendor of the saints* (Ps. 109:3). There, as in a chamber, the soul *sleeps and rests* (Ps. 4:9), while the Bridegroom entreats that she be not awakened until she pleases to come forth (cf. Cant. 2:7).

7. These two middle stages,
through which we enter into the contemplation of God
within us
as in mirrors of created images,
are like the two middle wings
of the Seraph spread out for flight.[11]
Through them we can understand
that we are led to divine things
through the rational soul's naturally implanted faculties
in their operations, relationships
and habitual scientific knowledge,
as is apparent in the third stage.

Likewise, we are led
through the reformed faculties of the soul, that is,
through the infused virtues, spiritual senses
and mystical ecstasies,
as is apparent in the fourth stage.

Moreover, we are led
by the hierarchical operations, that is,
the purifying, illumining and perfecting
of human souls;
and by the hierarchical revelations
of Sacred Scripture
given to us by the angels, as the Apostle says,
that the Law was given *by angels in the hand of a mediator*.[12]
And, finally, we are led

---

11. Cf. Isa. 6:2.
12. Gal. 3:19.

through the hierarchies and hierarchical orders
which are to be arranged
in our soul
as in the heavenly Jerusalem.

8. Filled with all these intellectual illuminations,
our mind like the house of God
is inhabited by divine Wisdom;
it is made
a daughter of God, his spouse and friend;
it is made
a member of Christ the Head, his sister and coheir;
it is made
a temple of the Holy Spirit,
grounded on faith, built up by hope
and dedicated to God
by holiness of mind and body.
All of this is accomplished
by a most sincere love of Christ
which *is poured forth in our hearts
by the Holy Spirit
who has been given to us*,[13]
without whom
we cannot know the secret things of God.
No one can know *the things of man
except the spirit of man which is in him;
so no one knows the things of God
except the spirit of God.*[14]

Let us, therefore, be rooted and grounded
in charity
so that *with all the saints
we may be able to comprehend* what is
the length of eternity, *the breadth* of liberality, *the height* of majesty
and *the depth* of discerning wisdom.[15]

13. Rom. 5:5.
14. 1 Cor. 2:11.
15. Eph. 3:17-18.

CHAPTER FIVE

ON
CONTEMPLATING THE DIVINE UNITY
THROUGH ITS PRIMARY NAME
WHICH IS BEING

1. We can contemplate God
not only outside us and within us
but also above us:
outside through his vestiges, within through his image
and above through the light
which shines upon our minds,[1]
which is the light of Eternal Truth,
since "our mind itself is formed immediately
by Truth itself."[2]
Those who have become practiced in the first way
have already entered the court before the tabernacle;
those practiced in the second way
have entered the sanctuary;
and those practiced in the third way
enter with the high priest
into the Holy of Holies
where the Cherubim of glory stand over the ark
overshadowing the Mercy Seat.[3]
By these Cherubim we understand
the two modes or stages
of contemplating the invisible and eternal things of God:
one is concerned with the essential attributes of God
and the other with those proper to the Persons.

2. The first method

---

1. Cf. Ps. 4:7.
2. Augustine, *De diversis quaestionibus* 83, q. 51, no. 2, 4.
3. Cf. Exod. 25:10-22; 26:33-35; Heb. 9:2-5.

fixes the gaze primarily and principally
on Being itself,
saying that God's primary name is
He who is.[4]
The second method
fixes the gaze
on the Good itself,
saying that this is God's primary name.
The first looks chiefly to the Old Testament,
which proclaims most of all
the unity of the divine essence.
Hence Moses was told:
I am who am.[5]
The second method looks to the New Testament
which determines
the plurality of Persons
by baptizing
in the name of the Father and of the Son and of the Holy Spirit.[6]
Therefore, Christ our Teacher,
wishing to raise to evangelical perfection
the youth who had observed the Law,
attributed to God principally and exclusively
the name of goodness.
For he says:
No one is good but God alone.[7]
Damascene, therefore, following Moses, says that
He who is
is God's primary name;
Dionysius, following Christ, says that
the Good
is God's primary name.[8]

---

4. Exod. 3:14.
5. *Ibid.*
6. Matt. 28:19.
7. Mark 10:18; Luke 18:19.
8. John Damascene, *De fide orthodoxa*, I, 9; Dionysius, *De divinis nominibus*, III, 1; IV, 1.

3. Let him who wishes to contemplate the invisible things of God in the unity of his essence fix his attention first on being itself, and let him see that being itself is so certain in itself that it cannot be thought not to be. For pure being occurs only in full flight from nonbeing just as nothing is in full flight from being. Therefore, just as absolute nothing has nothing of being or its attributes, so contrariwise being itself has nothing of nonbeing either in act or potency, either in objective truth or in our estimation. Since nonbeing is the privation of being, it does not come into our understanding except through being; but being does not come to us through something else because everything which is understood is understood as nonbeing or being in potency or being in act. If, therefore, nonbeing can be understood only through being and being in potency only through being in act, and if being signifies the pure act of being, then being is what first comes into the intellect and this being is pure act. But this is not particular being, which is limited because mixed with potency; nor is it analogous being because that has only a minimum of actuality because it has only a minimum of being. It remains that the being in question must be divine Being.

4. Strange, then, is the blindness of the intellect, which does not consider that which it sees first and without which it can know nothing. The eye, concentrating on various differences of color, does not see the very light by which it sees other things; and if it does see this light, it does not advert to it. In the same way, the mind's eye, concentrating on particular and universal being, does not advert to being itself, which is beyond every genus, even though it comes to our minds first and through it we know other things. Hence it is most truly apparent that "as the eye of the bat is in regard to light so is the eye of our mind in regard to the most evident things of nature."[9] Thus our mind, accustomed to the darkness of beings and the images of

9. Aristotle, *Metaph.* I minor (II), t. 1, c. 1 (993b 9-11).

the things of sense, when it glimpses the light of the supreme Being, seems to itself to see nothing. It does not realize that this very darkness is the supreme illumination of our mind (cf. Ps. 138:11), just as when the eye sees pure light, it seems to itself to see nothing.

5. Behold, then, if you can, purest being itself and you will realize that it cannot be thought of as received from another. From this, it must necessarily be thought of as absolutely first since it cannot come from nothing or from something. For what exists of itself, if being itself does not exist of itself and by itself? It will also appear to you as completely lacking nonbeing and therefore as never beginning nor ceasing, but rather eternal. It will also appear to you as having in itself nothing but being itself and hence as not composite but utterly simple. It will appear to you as having no potentiality since every potential being has in some way something of nonbeing; and hence it will appear as supremely actual. It will appear as having no possibility for defect and hence as most perfect. Finally, it will appear as having no diversity and hence as supremely one.

Therefore that being which is pure being and simple being and absolute being is Primary Being, eternal, utterly simple, most actual, most perfect and supremely one.

6. These things are so certain that their opposites cannot be conceived by a man who understands being itself, and one of these necessarily implies the other. For since being exists without qualification, it is without qualification first. Since it is without qualification first, it is not made by another, nor could it be made by itself; therefore it is eternal. Likewise, since it is first and eternal, it is not made from other things; therefore it is utterly simple. Also, since it is first, eternal and utterly simple, there is in it no potency mixed with its actuality; therefore it is most actual. Also, since it is first, eternal, utterly simple and most actual, it is most perfect; it lacks absolutely nothing, nor can any addition be made to it. Since it is first, eternal, utterly simple, most actual and most perfect, it is su-

ST. BONAVENTURE

premely one. What is said with all-embracing superabundance
is said of all things. But "what is said through superabundance
unqualifiedly can be applied to only one thing."[10] Hence, if God
is called primary being, eternal, utterly simple, most actual, and
most perfect, it is impossible that he be thought not to be or to be
other than unique. *Hear, therefore, Israel, your God is one God.*[11] If
you see this in the pure simplicity of your mind, you will
somehow be bathed in the brilliance of eternal light.

7. But you have something here to lift you up
in wonder.
for Being itself
is first and last;
it is eternal and most present;
it is utterly simple and the greatest;
it is most actual and most unchangeable;
it is most perfect and most immense;
it is supremely one and yet all-inclusive.
If you wonder at this with a pure mind,
you will be flooded with a greater light
when you see further
that it is last because it is first.
For because it is first,
it does all things
for itself;
and therefore it must necessarily be the ultimate end,
the beginning and the consummation,
the Alpha and the Omega.[12]
It is most present
precisely because it is eternal.
For because it is eternal,
it does not flow from another,

---

10. Aristotle, *Topica*, V, c. 5 (134b 23-24).
11. Deut. 6:4; the text in Deuteronomy reads: "Hear, Israel, the Lord our God is one
Lord."
12. Apoc. 1:8, 21:6, 22:13.

nor of itself cease to be,
nor pass from one state into another;
therefore it has neither past nor future,
but only present being.
It is greatest
precisely because it is utterly simple.
For because it is utterly simple in essence,
it is greatest in power,
because the more power is unified,
the more it is infinite.
It is unchangeable
precisely because it is most actual.
For because it is most actual,
it is pure act;
and what is pure act
can acquire nothing new,
can lose nothing it already has;
hence it cannot be changed.
It is immense
precisely because it is most perfect.
For because it is most perfect,
nothing can be thought beyond it
better, nobler or more worthy,
hence nothing greater;
and such a being is immense.
It is all-inclusive
precisely because it is supremely one.
For what is supremely one
is the universal principle of all multiplicity;
hence it is the universal
efficient, exemplary and final cause
of all things
as "the cause of being, the basis of understanding
and the order of living"[13]

---

13. Augustine, *De civitate Dei*, VIII, 4.

It is, therefore, all-inclusive
not as the essence of all things,
but as the supremely excellent and most universal
and most sufficient
cause of all essences,
whose power is
supremely infinite and multiple in its efficacy
because it is supremely unified in its essence.

8. Once again reflecting upon these things,
let us say that
because the most pure and absolute Being,
which is being without qualification,
is the first and the last,
it is, therefore,
the origin and consummating end of all things.
Because it is eternal and most present,
it therefore encompasses and enters all duration
as if it were at one and the same time
its center and circumference.
Because it is utterly simple and the greatest,
it is, therefore,
totally within all things and totally outside them
and thus "is an intelligible sphere
whose center is everywhere
and whose circumference is nowhere."[14]
Because it is most actual and unchangeable,
therefore "while remaining stable,
it gives motion to all things."[15]
Because it is most perfect and immense,
it is, therefore,
within all things, but not enclosed;
outside all things, but not excluded;

14. Alan of Lille, *Regulae theologicae*, reg. 7.
15. Boethius, *De consolatione philosophiae*, III, metr. 9.

above all things, but not aloof;
below all things, but not debased.
Finally, because it is supremely one and all-inclusive,
it is, therefore,
all in all,[16]
although all things are many and it is itself only one,
and this is so because,
through its most simple unity,
most serene truth and most sincere goodness,
there is in it
all power, all exemplarity and all communicability.
Consequently,
from him, through him and in him
are all things;[17]
for he is
all-powerful, all-knowing and all-good,
and to see him perfectly is to be blessed,
as was said to Moses:
I will show you all good.[18]

---

16. 1 Cor. 15:28.
17. Rom. 11:36.
18. Exod. 33:19.

CHAPTER SIX

ON
CONTEMPLATING THE MOST BLESSED
TRINITY
IN ITS NAME
WHICH IS GOOD

1. After considering the essential attributes of God,
the eye of our intelligence
should be raised to look upon
the most blessed Trinity,
so that the second Cherub
may be placed alongside the first.
Now just as being itself is
the root principle
of viewing the essential attributes,
and the name
through which the others become known,
so the good itself is
the principal foundation
for contemplating the emanations.

2. See, then, and observe
that the highest good is without qualification
that than which no greater can be thought.
And it is such
that it cannot rightly be thought
not to be,
since to be is in all ways better than not to be;[1]
it is such

---

1. Cf. Anselm, *Proslogion*, c. 2-5, 15.

that it cannot rightly be thought of unless it be thought of
as three and one.
For good is said to be
self-diffusive;[2]
therefore the highest good must be
most self-diffusive.
But the greatest self-diffusion cannot exist unless it is
actual and intrinsic,
substantial and hypostatic,
natural and voluntary,
free and necessary,
lacking nothing and perfect.
Therefore, unless there were eternally in the highest good
a production which is actual and consubstantial,
and a hypostasis as noble as the producer,
as in the case in a producing by way of generation and spiration,
so that it is from an eternal principle eternally coproducing
so that there would be a beloved
and a cobeloved,
the one generated and the other spirated,
and this is
the Father and the Son and the Holy Spirit—
unless these were present,
it would by no means be the highest good
because it would not diffuse itself in the highest degree.
For the diffusion in time in creation
is no more than a center
or point
in relation to the immensity of the divine goodness.
Hence another diffusion can be conceived
greater than this,
namely, one in which
the one diffusing communicates to the other
his entire substance and nature.

2. Cf. Dionysius, *De caelesti hierarchia*, IV, 1 *De divinis nominibus*, IV, 1, 20.

Therefore it would not be the highest good
if it could lack this,
either in reality or in thought.
If, therefore, you can behold with your mind's eye
the purity of goodness,
which is the pure act
of a principle loving in charity
with a love
that is both free and due and a mixture of both,
which is the fullest diffusion
by way of nature and will,
which is a diffusion by way of the Word,
in which all things are said,
and by way of the Gift, in which other gifts are given,
then you can see
that through the highest communicability of the good,
there must be
a Trinity of the Father and the Son and the Holy Spirit.
From supreme goodness,
it is necessary that there be in the Persons
supreme communicability;
from supreme communicability, supreme consubstantiality;
from supreme consubstantiality, supreme configurability;
and from these supreme coequality
and hence supreme coeternity;
finally, from all of the above, supreme mutual intimacy,
by which one is necessarily in the other
by supreme interpenetration
and one acts with the other
in absolute lack of division
of the substance, power and operation
of the most blessed Trinity itself.

3. But when you contemplate these things,
do not think

that you comprehend the incomprehensible.
For you still have something else to consider
in these six properties
which strongly leads our mind's eye
to amazement and admiration.
For here is
supreme communicability with individuality of persons,
supreme consubstantiality with plurality of hypostases,
supreme configurability with distinct personality,
supreme coequality with degree
supreme coeternity with emanation,
supreme mutual intimacy with mission.
Who would not be lifted up in admiration
at the sight of such marvels?
But we understand with complete certitude
that all these things are in the most blessed Trinity
if we lift up our eyes
to the superexcellent goodness.
For if there is here
supreme communication and true diffusion,
there is also here
true origin and true distinction;
and because the whole is communicated and not merely part,
whatever is possessed is given,
and given completely.
Therefore, the one emanating and the one producing
are distinguished by their properties
and are one in essence.
Since, then, they are distinguished by their properties,
they have
personal properties and plurality of hypostases
and emanation of origin
and order, not of posteriority but of origin,
and a sending forth,
not involving a change of place but free inspiration

by reason of the producer's authority
which the sender has in relation to the one sent.
Moreover, because they are one in substance,
there must be unity
in essence, form, dignity, eternity, existence and unlimitedness.
Therefore, when you consider these in themselves one by one,
you have matter for contemplating the truth;
when you compare them with one another,
you have reason to be lifted up to the highest wonder.
Therefore, that your mind may ascend
through wonder to wondering contemplation,
these should be considered together.

4. For the Cherubim who faced each other
also signify this.
The fact that they faced each other,
with their faces turned toward the Mercy Seat,[3]
is not without a mystical meaning,
so that what Our Lord said in John
might be verified:
This is eternal life,
that they may know you, the only true God,
and Jesus Christ, whom you have sent.[4]
For we should wonder
not only at the essential and personal properties of God
in themselves
but also in comparison with
the superwonderful union of God and man
in the unity of the Person of Christ.

5. For if you are the Cherub
contemplating God's essential attributes,
and if you are amazed

---

3. Exod. 25:20.
4. John 17:3.

because the divine Being is both
first and last,
eternal and most present,
utterly simple and the greatest or boundless,
totally present everywhere and nowhere contained,
most actual and never moved,
most perfect and having nothing superfluous or lacking,
and yet immense and infinite without bounds,
supremely one and yet all-inclusive,
containing all things in himself,
being all power, all truth, all goodness—
if you are this Cherub,
look at the Mercy Seat and wonder
that in him there is joined
the First Principle with the last,
God with man, who was formed on the sixth day;[5]
the eternal is joined with temporal man,
born of the Virgin in the fulness of time,
the most simple with the most composite,
the most actual with the one who suffered supremely and died,
the most perfect and immense with the lowly,
the supreme and all-inclusive one
with a composite individual distinct from others,
that is, the man Jesus Christ.

6. But if you are the other Cherub
contemplating the properties of the Persons,
and you are amazed
that communicability exists with individuality,
consubstantiality with plurality,
configurability with personality,
coequality with order,
coeternity with production,
mutual intimacy with sending forth,

---

5. Cf. Gen. 1:26.

because the Son is sent by the Father
and the Holy Spirit by both,
who nevertheless is with them and never departs from them—
if you are this Cherub,
look at the Mercy Seat and wonder
that in Christ
personal union exists
with a trinity of substances and a duality of natures;
that complete agreement exists
with a plurality of wills;
that mutual predication of God and man exists
with a plurality of properties;
that coadoration exists
with a plurality of excellence,
that coexaltation above all things exists
with a plurality of dignity;
that codomination exists
with a plurality of powers.

7. In this consideration is
the perfection of the mind's illumination
when, as if on the sixth day of creation,
it sees man made to the image of God.[6]
For if an image is an expressed likeness,
when our mind contemplates
in Christ the Son of God,
who is the image of the invisible God by nature,
our humanity
so wonderfully exalted, so ineffably united,
when at the same time it sees united
the first and the last,
the highest and the lowest,
the circumference and the center,

---

6. Ibid.

the Alpha and the Omega,[7]
the caused and the cause,
the Creator and the creature,
that is, *the book written within and without*,[8]
it now reaches something perfect.
It reaches the perfection of its illuminations
on the sixth stage,
as if with God on the sixth day of creation;
nor does anything more remain
except the day of rest on which
through mystical ecstasy
the mind's discernment comes to rest
from all the work which it *has done*.[9]

---

7. Apoc. 1:8, 21:6, 22:13.
8. Apoc. 5:1; Ezech. 2:9.
9. Gen. 2:2.

CHAPTER SEVEN

ON
SPIRITUAL AND MYSTICAL ECSTASY
IN WHICH REST IS GIVEN TO OUR
INTELLECT
WHEN THROUGH ECSTASY OUR
AFFECTION
PASSES OVER ENTIRELY INTO GOD

1. We have, therefore, passed through
these six considerations.
They are like
the six steps of the true Solomon's throne,
by which we arrive
at peace,
where the true man of peace
rests in a peaceful mind
as in the interior Jerusalem.

They are also like
the six wings of the Seraph[1]
by which the mind of the true contemplative
can be borne aloft,
filled with the illumination of heavenly wisdom.

They are also like the first six days,
in which the mind has been trained so that it may reach
the sabbath of rest.

After our mind has beheld God
outside itself

---

1. Although the critical text has "Cherub," we have read "Seraph," since Bonaventure is clearly referring to the six-winged Seraph of Francis's vision (cf. prologue, 2-3, p. 54), which serves as the symbolic matrix of the entire treatise.

through his vestiges and in his vestiges,
within itself
through his image and in his image,
and above itself
through the similitude of the divine Light shining above us
and in the Light itself,
insofar as this is possible in our state as wayfarers
and through the exercise of our mind,
when finally in the sixth stage
our mind reaches that point
where it contemplates
in the First and Supreme Principle
and in the *mediator of God and men*,[2]
Jesus Christ,
those things whose likenesses can in no way be found
in creatures
and which surpass all penetration
by the human intellect,
it now remains for our mind,
by contemplating these things,
to transcend and pass over not only this sense world
but even itself.
In this passing over,
Christ is the *way and the door*;[3]
Christ is the ladder and the vehicle,
like the Mercy Seat placed above the ark of God[4]
and the *mystery hidden from eternity*.[5]

2. Whoever turns his face fully to the Mercy Seat
and with faith, hope and love,
devotion, admiration, exultation,
appreciation, praise and joy

---

2. 1 Tim. 2:5.
3. Cf. John 14:6, 10:7.
4. Cf. Exod. 25:21.
5. Eph. 3:9

beholds him hanging upon the cross,
such a one makes the Pasch, that is, the passover,
with Christ.
By the staff of the cross
he passes over the Red Sea,[6]
going from Egypt into the desert,
where he will taste the *hidden manna*;[7]
and with Christ
he rests in the tomb,
as if dead to the outer world,
but experiencing,
as far as is possible in this wayfarer's state,
what was said on the cross
to the thief who adhered to Christ;
Today you shall be with me in paradise.[8]

3. This was shown also
to blessed Francis,
when in ecstatic contemplation
on the height of the mountain —
where I thought out these things I have written —
there appeared to him
a six-winged Seraph fastened to a cross,
as I and several others heard
in that very place
from his companion who was with him then.[9]
There he passed over into God in ecstatic contemplation
and became an example of perfect contemplation
as he had previously been of action,
like another Jacob and Israel,[10]
so that through him,
more by example than by word,

---

6. Cf. Exod. 12:11.
7. Apoc. 2:17.
8. Luke 23:43.
9. Cf. Bonaventure's *Life of St. Francis*, XIII, 3., pp. 305-306.
10. Cf. Gen. 35:10.

God might invite all truly spiritual men
to this kind of passing over
and spiritual ecstasy.

4. In this passing over,
if it is to be perfect,
all intellectual activities must be left behind
and the height of our affection
must be totally transferred and transformed
into God.
This, however, is mystical and most secret,
which *no one knows*
except him who receives it,[11]
no one receives
except him who desires it,
and no one desires except him
who is inflamed in his very marrow by the fire of the Holy Spirit
whom Christ sent into the world.[12]
And therefore the Apostle says that
this mystical wisdom is revealed
by the Holy Spirit.[13]

5. Since, therefore, in this regard
nature can do nothing
and effort can do but little,
little importance should be given to inquiry,
but much to unction;
little importance should be given to the tongue,
but much to inner joy;
little importance should be given to words and to writing,
but all to the gift of God,
that is, the Holy Spirit;

11. Apoc. 2:17.
12. Cf. Luke 12:49.
13. Cf. 1 Cor. 2:10ff.

little or no importance should be given to creation,
but all to the creative essence,
the Father, Son and Holy Spirit,
saying with Dionysius
to God the Trinity:
"Trinity,
superessential, superdivine and supereminent
overseer of the divine wisdom of Christians,
direct us into
the super-unknown, superluminous and most sublime
summit
of mystical communication.
There
new, absolute and unchangeable mysteries of theology
are hidden
in the superluminous darkness
of a silence
teaching secretly in the utmost obscurity
which is supermanifest—
a darkness which is super-resplendent
and in which everything shines forth
and which fills to overflowing
invisible intellects
with the splendors of invisible goods
that surpass all good."[14]
This is said to God.
But to the friend to whom these words were written,
let us say with Dionysius:
"But you, my friend,
concerning mystical visions,
with your journey more firmly determined,
leave behind
your senses and intellectual activities,

14. Dionysius, *De mystica theologia*, I, 1.

sensible and invisible things,
all nonbeing and being;
and in this state of unknowing
be restored,
insofar as is possible,
to unity with him
who is above all essence and knowledge.
For transcending yourself and all things,
by the immeasurable and absolute ecstasy of a pure mind,
leaving behind all things
and freed from all things,
you will ascend
to the superessential ray
of the divine darkness."[15]

6. But if you wish to know how these things come about,
ask grace not instruction,
desire not understanding,
the groaning of prayer not diligent reading,
the Spouse not the teacher,
God not man,
darkness not clarity,
not light but the fire
that totally inflames and carries us into God
by ecstatic unctions and burning affections.
This fire is God,
and *his furnace is in Jerusalem*;[16]
and Christ enkindles it
in the heat of his burning passion,
which only he truly perceives who says:
My soul chooses hanging and my bones death.[17]

15. *Ibid.*
16. Isa. 31:9.
17. Job 7:15.

Whoever loves this death
can see God
because it is true beyond doubt that
man will not see me and live.[18]
Let us, then, die
and enter into the darkness;
let us impose silence
upon our cares, our desires and our imaginings.
With Christ crucified
let us pass *out of this world to the Father*[19]
so that when the Father is shown to us,
we may say with Philip:
It is enough for us.[20]
Let us hear with Paul:
My grace is sufficient for you.[21]
Let us rejoice with David saying:
My flesh and my heart have grown faint;
You are the God of my heart,
and the God that is my portion forever.
Blessed be the Lord forever
and all the people will say:
Let it be; let it be.
Amen.[22]

HERE ENDS THE SOUL'S JOURNEY INTO GOD.

---

18. Exod. 33:20.
19. John 13:1.
20. John 14:8.
21. 2 Cor. 12:9.
22. Ps. 72:26, 105:48.

THE TREE OF LIFE

PROLOGUE

1. *With Christ I am nailed to the cross,*[1]
from Galatians, chapter two.

The true worshiper of God and disciple of Christ,
who desires to conform perfectly
to the Savior of all men
crucified for him,
should, above all, strive
with an earnest endeavor of soul
to carry about continuously,
both in his soul and in his flesh,
the cross of Christ
until he can truly feel in himself
what the Apostle said above.
Moreover an affection and feeling of this kind
is merited to be experienced in a vital way only by one
who, not unmindful of the Lord's passion nor ungrateful,
contemplates
the labor, suffering and love
of Jesus crucified,
with such vividness of memory, such sharpness of intellect
and such charity of will
that he can truly say with the bride:
A bundle of myrrh is my beloved to me;
he will linger
between my breasts.[2]

2. To enkindle in us this affection, to shape this understanding and to imprint this memory, I have endeavored to
gather this bundle of myrrh from the forest of the holy Gospel,

---

1. Gal. 2:19.
2. Cant. 1:12.

which treats at length the life, passion and glorification of Jesus Christ. I have bound it together with a few ordered and parallel words to aid the memory. I have used simple, familiar and unsophisticated terms to avoid idle curiosity, to cultivate devotion and to foster the piety of faith. Since imagination aids understanding, I have arranged in the form of an imaginary tree the few items I have collected from among many, and have ordered and disposed them in such a way that in the first or lower branches the Savior's origin and life are described; in the middle, his passion; and in the top, his glorification. In the first group of branches there are four stanzas placed opposite each other in alphabetical order.[3] So also in the second and third group of branches. From each of these branches hangs a single fruit. So there are, as it were, twelve branches bearing twelve fruits according to the mystery of the tree of life.[4]

3. Picture in your mind a tree whose roots are watered by an ever-flowing fountain that becomes a great and living river with four channels to water the garden of the entire Church. From the trunk of this tree, imagine that there are growing twelve branches that are adorned with leaves, flowers and fruit. Imagine that the leaves are a most effective medicine to prevent and cure every kind of sickness, because the word of the cross *is the power of God for salvation to everyone who believes* (Rom. 1:16). Let the flowers be beautiful with the radiance of every color and perfumed with the sweetness of every fragrance, awakening and attracting the anxious hearts of men of desire. Imagine that there are twelve fruits, *having every delight and the sweetness of every taste* (Wisd. 16:20). This fruit is offered to God's servants to be tasted so that when they eat it, they may always be satisfied, yet never

---

3. Bonaventure implies that the original manuscript contained a picture of a tree. On this was inscribed a poem, which is discussed in note 5, p. 121; cf. the Quaracchi critical edition, *S. Bonaventurae opera omnia*, VIII, xxxix.

4. This and the following passage are based on Apocalypse 22:1-2: *And he showed me a river of the water of life, clear as a crystal, coming forth from the throne of God and of the Lamb. In the midst of the city street, on both sides of the river, was the tree of life, bearing twelve fruits, yielding its fruit according to each month, and the leaves for the healing of nations.* Cf. Esther 10:6; Gen. 2:9-10.

grow weary of its taste. This is the fruit that took its origin from the Virgin's womb and reached its savory maturity on the tree of the cross under the midday heat of the Eternal Sun, that is, the love of Christ. In the garden of the heavenly paradise—God's table—this fruit is served to those who desire it. This is suggested by the first stanza, which says:

> O cross, salvation-bearing tree,
> Watered by a living fountain,
> Your flower is spice-scented,
> Your fruit an object of desire.[5]

4. Although this fruit is one and undivided, it nourishes devout souls with varied consolations in view of its varied states, excellence, powers and works. These can be reduced to twelve. This fruit of the tree of life, therefore, is pictured and is offered to our taste under twelve flavors on twelve branches. On the first branch the soul devoted to Christ perceives the flavor of sweetness, by recalling the distinguished origin and sweet birth of her Savior; on the second branch, the humble mode of life which he condescended to adopt; on the third, the loftiness of his perfect power; on the fourth, the plenitude of his most abundant piety; on the fifth, the confidence which he had in the trial of his passion; on the sixth, the patience which he exhibited in bearing great insults and injuries; on the seventh, the constancy which he maintained in the torture and suffering of his rough and bitter cross; on the eighth, the victory which he achieved in the conflict and passage of death; on the ninth, the novelty of his resurrection embellished with remarkable gifts; on the tenth, the sublimity of his ascension, pouring forth spiritual charisms; on the eleventh, the equity of the future judgment; on the twelfth, the eternity of the divine kingdom.

---

5. This and the two stanzas below, in no. 6, are part of a longer poem which Bonaventure mentions in no. 2; cf. note 3, p. 120. This longer poem, which probably had fifteen stanzas, was changed and added to by later copyists. The editors of the critical edition print within the text only the three stanzas here, but add a number of others in a supplement: cf. the critical edition, *S. Bonaventurae opera omnia*, VIII, 86-87.

5. I call these fruits because they delight with their rich sweetness and strengthen with their nourishment the soul who meditates on them and diligently considers each one, abhoring the example of unfaithful Adam who preferred *the tree of the knowledge of good and evil* (Gen. 2:17) to the tree of life. No one can avoid this error unless he prefers faith to reason, devotion to investigation, simplicity to curiosity and finally the sacred cross of Christ to all carnal feeling or wisdom of the flesh. Through the cross the charity of the Holy Spirit is nourished in devout hearts and the sevenfold grace is poured forth, as is requested in the two first and last verses.

6. Let us, then, say with devotion and tears:

Feed us with these fruits,
Shed light upon our thoughts,
Lead us along straight paths,
Crush the attacks of the enemy.
Fill us with your sacred light,
Breathe holy inspiration,
Be a peaceful way of life
For those who fear Christ. Amen.[6]

---

6. Cf. note 5, p. 121.

CHAPTER HEADINGS

ON THE MYSTERY OF HIS ORIGIN

FIRST FRUIT: HIS DISTINGUISHED ORIGIN
Jesus Begotten of God
Jesus Prefigured
Jesus Sent from Heaven
Jesus Born of Mary

SECOND FRUIT: THE HUMILITY OF HIS MODE OF LIFE
Jesus Conformed to His Forefathers
Jesus Shown to the Magi
Jesus Submissive to the Law
Jesus Exiled from His Kingdom

THIRD FRUIT: THE LOFTINESS OF HIS POWER
Jesus, Heavenly Baptist
Jesus Tempted by the Enemy
Jesus Wonderful in His Miracles
Jesus Transfigured

FOURTH FRUIT: THE PLENITUDE OF HIS PIETY
Jesus, the Solicitous Shepherd
Jesus Bathed with Tears
Jesus Acclaimed King of the World
Jesus, Consecrated Bread

ON THE MYSTERY OF HIS PASSION

FIFTH FRUIT: HIS CONFIDENCE IN TRIALS

Jesus Sold through Guile

Jesus Prostrate in Prayer

Jesus Surrounded by the Mob

Jesus Bound with Chains

SIXTH FRUIT: HIS PATIENCE IN MALTREATMENT

Jesus Denied by His Own

Jesus Blindfolded

Jesus Handed Over to Pilate

Jesus Condemned to Death

SEVENTH FRUIT: HIS CONSTANCY UNDER TORTURE

Jesus Scorned by All

Jesus Nailed to the Cross

Jesus Linked with Thieves

Jesus Given Gall to Drink

EIGHTH FRUIT: VICTORY IN THE CONFLICT OF DEATH

Jesus, Sun Dimmed in Death

Jesus Pierced with a Lance

Jesus Dripping with Blood

Jesus Laid in the Tomb

ON THE MYSTERY OF HIS GLORIFICATION

NINTH FRUIT: THE NOVELTY OF HIS RESURRECTION

Jesus Triumphant in Death

Jesus Rising in Blessedness

Jesus, Extraordinary Beauty

Jesus Given Dominion over the Earth

TENTH FRUIT: THE SUBLIMITY OF HIS ASCENSION

Jesus, Leader of His Army

Jesus Lifted Up to Heaven

Jesus, Giver of the Spirit

Jesus Freeing from Guilt

ELEVENTH FRUIT: THE EQUITY OF HIS JUDGMENT

Jesus, Truthful Witness

Jesus, Wrathful Judge

Jesus, Glorious Conqueror

Jesus, Adorned Spouse

TWELFTH FRUIT: THE ETERNITY OF HIS KINGDOM

Jesus, King, Son of the King

Jesus, Inscribed Book

Jesus, Fountain-Ray of Light

Jesus, Desired End

Arise, then, O soul devoted to Christ, and examine diligently, consider attentively and mull over carefully each of the things that are said about Jesus.

ON
THE MYSTERY
OF HIS ORIGIN

FIRST FRUIT:
HIS DISTINGUISHED ORIGIN

Jesus Begotten of God

1. When you hear that Jesus is begotten of God, beware lest some inadequate thought of the flesh appear before your mind's eye. Rather, with the vision of the dove and the eagle, believe simply and contemplate with penetrating gaze the following: From that Eternal Light which is at the same time measureless and most simple, most brilliant and most hidden, there emerges a coeternal, coequal and consubstantial splendor, who is the power and wisdom of the Father. In him the Father ordered all things from eternity; through him *he made the world* (Heb. 1:2) and governs and directs it to his own glory, partly by nature, partly by grace, partly by justice and partly by mercy, so that he leaves nothing in this world without order.

Jesus Prefigured

2. At the beginning of the creation of nature, our first parents were placed in paradise; but they were driven out by the severity of God's decree because they ate of the forbidden tree. From that time his heavenly mercy has not ceased calling straying man back to the way of penance by giving hope of forgiveness and by promising that a Savior would come. Lest such condescension on God's part should fail to effect our salvation because of ignorance and ingratitude, he never ceased announcing, promising and prefiguring the coming of his Son in the five

ages of history, through the patriarchs, judges, priests, kings and prophets, from Abel the Just to John the Baptist. Through many thousands of years, by many marvelous prophecies he stirred men's minds to faith and inflamed their hearts with living desires.

Jesus Sent from Heaven[1]

3. Finally, the *fulness of time* (Gal. 4:4) had come. Just as man was formed from the earth on the sixth day by the power and wisdom of the divine hand, so at the beginning of the sixth age, the Archangel Gabriel was sent to the Virgin. When she gave her consent to him, the Holy Spirit came upon her like a divine fire inflaming her soul and sanctifying her flesh in perfect purity. But the *power of the Most High overshadowed* her (Luke 1:35) so that she could endure such fire. By the action of that power, instantly his body was formed, his soul created, and at once both were united to the divinity in the Person of the Son, so that the same Person was God and man, with the properties of each nature maintained.

Oh, if you could feel in some way
the quality and intensity of that fire sent from heaven,
the refreshing coolness that accompanied it,
the consolation it imparted;
if you could realize the great exhaltation of the Virgin Mother,
the ennobling of the human race,
the condescension of the divine majesty;
if you could hear the Virgin singing with joy;
if you could go with your Lady
into the mountainous region;
if you could see the sweet embrace
of the Virgin and the woman who had been sterile
and hear the greeting

---

1. Cf. Matt. 1:18-23; Luke 1:26-38.

in which the tiny servant recognized his Lord,
the herald his Judge
and the voice his Word,
then I am sure
you would sing in sweet tones
with the Blessed Virgin
that sacred hymn:
My soul magnifies the Lord . . .;[2]
and with the tiny prophet
you would exalt, rejoice and adore
the marvelous virginal conception!

Jesus Born of Mary[3]

4. Under the reign of Caesar Augustus, the *quiet silence*
(Wisd. 18:14) of universal peace had brought such calm to an age
which had previously been sorely distressed that through his
decree a census of the whole world could be taken. Under the
guidance of divine providence, it happened that Joseph, the
Virgin's husband, took to the town of Bethlehem the young girl
of royal descent who was pregnant. When nine months had
passed since his conception, the King of Peace *like a bridegroom
from his bridal chamber* (cf. 1 Par. 22:9; Ps. 18:6), came forth from
the virginal womb. He was brought forth into the light without
any corruption just as he was conceived without any stain of
lust. Although he was great and rich, he became small and poor
for us. He chose to be born away from a home in a stable, to be
wrapped in swaddling clothes, to be nourished by virginal milk
and to lie in a manger between an ox and an ass. Then "there
shone upon us a day of new redemption, restoration of the past
and eternal happiness. Then throughout the whole world the
heavens became honey-sweet."[4]

---

2. Luke 1:46.
3. Cf. Luke 2:1-18.
4. *Breviarium Romanum*, Officium nativitatis Domini, noc. 1, resp. 2.

Now, then, my soul,
embrace that divine manger;
press your lips upon and kiss the boy's feet.
Then in your mind
keep the shepherds' watch,
marvel at the assembling host of angels,
join in the heavenly melody,
singing with your voice and heart:
Glory to God in the highest
and on earth peace
to men of good will.[5]

SECOND FRUIT:
THE HUMILITY OF HIS MODE OF LIFE

Jesus Conformed to His Forefathers

5. On the eighth day the boy was circumcised and named Jesus (Luke 2:21). Thus not delaying to pour out for you the price of his blood, he showed that he was your true Savior, promised to his forefathers by word and sign, and like them in everything except ignorance and sin. For this reason he received the mark of circumcision so that coming and appearing *in the likeness of sinful flesh*, he might *condemn sin by sin* (Rom. 8:3) and become our salvation and eternal justice, taking his beginning from humility, which is the root and guardian of all virtues.

Why are you proud,
dust and ashes?[6]
The innocent Lamb
who takes away the sins of the world[7]
does not shrink from the wound of circumcision.

5. Luke 2:14.
6. Ecclus. 10:9.
7. John 1:29.

But you,
who are a sinner,
while you pretend to be just,
are fleeing
from the remedy of eternal salvation,
which you can never reach
unless you are willing to follow
the humble Savior.

Jesus Shown to the Magi[8]

6. When the Lord was born in Bethlehem of Judah, a star appeared to the Magi in the east and with its brightness showed them the way to the home of the humble King.

Do not now turn away
from the brilliance of that star in the east
which guides you.
Become a companion of the holy kings;
accept the testimony of the Jewish Scriptures
about Christ
and avert the evil
of the treacherous king.
With gold, frankincense and myrrh,
venerate Christ the King
as true God and man.
Together with the first fruits of the Gentiles to be called to faith,
adore, confess and praise
this humble God
lying in a manger.
And thus, warned in a dream
not to follow Herod's pride,

8. Cf. Matt. 2:1-12.

you will return to your country
in the footsteps
of the humble Christ.

Jesus Submissive to the Law[9]

7. It was not enough for the teacher of perfect humility, who was equal to the Father in all things, to submit himself to the humble Virgin. He must submit himself also to the Law, *that he might redeem those who were under the Law and free them from the slavery of corruption to the freedom of the glory of the sons of God* (Gal. 4:5; Rom. 8:21). He wished that his mother, although she was most pure, should observe the law of purification. And he wished that he himself, the redeemer of all men, should be redeemed as a firstborn son and should be presented to God in the temple and that an offering should be given for him in the presence of the just who were rejoicing.

Rejoice, then,
with that blessed old man and the aged Anna;
walk forth
to meet the mother and Child.
Let love overcome your bashfulness;
let affection dispel your fear.
Receive the Infant
in your arms
and say with the bride:
*I took hold of him
and would not let him go.*[10]
Dance with the holy old man
and sing with him:
*Now dismiss your servant, Lord,
according to your word in peace.*[11]

---

9. Cf. Luke 2:27.
10. Cant. 3:4.
11. Luke 2:29.

131

Jesus Exiled from His Kingdom[12]

8. It is fitting that perfect humility should be adorned and accompanied by three other virtues: poverty in fleeing from riches which are spurs to pride; patience in bearing insults with composure; obedience in following the bidding of others. So in God's design a higher providence allowed that, when the evil Herod sought to kill the tiny King, he was taken into Egypt as a pilgrim and pauper, directed by a warning from heaven. In the children his own age who were killed because of him, he was killed and, as it were, slaughtered in each. Finally, after Herod's death, he was brought back by divine command into the land of Judah; and growing in age and grace, he lived there with his parents and was subject to them. He never left them for a moment except when, at twelve years of age, he remained in Jerusalem, causing his mother much sorrow while she sought him and bringing her much joy when he was found.

Do not, then, leave the mother and Child
as they flee into Egypt
without accompanying them.
With the beloved mother looking for her beloved Son,
do not cease searching
until you have found him.
O, how you would weep
if with devotion
you could look upon so venerable a lady,
so charming a girl,
in a foreign country
with so tender and handsome a little boy;
or if you could hear the sweet complaint
of the loving mother of God:
Son, why have you done this to us?[13]
as if she would say:

---

12. Cf. Matt. 2:13-23.
13. Luke 2:48.

THE TREE OF LIFE

Most beloved Son,
how could you give such sorrow
to your Mother,
whom you love
and who loves you
so much?

THIRD FRUIT:
THE LOFTINESS OF HIS POWER

Jesus, Heavenly Baptist[14]

9. When the Savior reached the age of thirty, wishing to work out our salvation, he began first to act before he taught (cf. Acts 1:1). And beginning with baptism as the doorway of the sacraments and the foundation of virtues, he wished to be baptized by John, in order to show us an example of perfect justice and to "confer regenerative power on water by contact with his most pure flesh."[15]

You also, accompany him faithfully;
and once regenerated in him,
explore his secrets so that
"on the banks of the Jordan
you may discern
the Father in the voice,
the Son in the flesh
and the Holy Spirit in the dove,
and when the heaven of the Trinity
is opened to you,"[16]
you will be taken up
into God.

---

14. Cf. Matt. 3:13-17; Mark 1:9-11; Luke 3:21-22.
15. Bede, *In Lucam*, I, 3:21.
16. Pseudo-Anselm, *Meditationes*, 15.

Jesus Tempted by the Enemy[17]

10. *Then Jesus was led by the Spirit into the desert to be tempted by the devil* (Matt. 4:1). By humbly enduring the enemy's attacks, he would make us humble; and by winning a victory, he would make us courageous. He firmly took up a life that was hard and solitary so that he might arouse the souls of the faithful to strive toward perfection and strengthen them to endure hardships.

Come now, disciple of Christ,
search into the secrets of solitude
with your loving teacher,
so that having become a companion of wild beasts,
you may become an imitator and sharer of
the hidden silence, the devout prayer, the daylong fasting
and the three encounters with the clever enemy.
And so you will learn
to have recourse to him
in every crisis of temptation
because *we do not have a high priest
who cannot have compassion on our infirmities,
but one tried
in all things as we are,
except sin.*[18]

Jesus Wonderful in His Miracles

11. *He is the one who alone does marvelous things* (Ps. 71:18). He transforms the elements, multiples the loaves of bread, walks upon the sea and calms the waves; he curbs the demons and puts them to flight; he cures the sick, cleanses the lepers and raises the dead; he restores sight to the blind, hearing to the deaf, speech to the mute, the power to walk to the crippled, sensation and movement to the paralytics and those with withered limbs.

17. Cf. Matt. 4:1-11; Mark 1:12-13; Luke 4:1-13.
18. Heb. 4:15.

To him our sinning conscience calls out
like the faithful leper:
Lord, if you wish,
you can make me clean.[19]
Now like the centurion:
Lord, my servant boy is lying at home
paralyzed and is suffering intensely.[20]
Now like the woman of Canaan:
Have mercy on me,
Son of David.[21]
Now like the woman with the issue of blood:
If I touch the hem of his garment,
I will be cured.[22]
Now with Mary and Martha:
See, Lord,
the one you love is ill.[23]

Jesus Transfigured[24]

12. To strengthen the human spirit with hope of eternal
reward, *Jesus took Peter, James and John up a high mountain* by
themselves (Matt. 17:1). He revealed to them the mystery of the
Trinity and foretold that he would be rejected in his passion. He
showed the glory of his future resurrection in his transfiguration. The Law and the prophets gave testimony to him in the
apparition of Moses and Elijah, the Father and the Holy Spirit in
the voice and the cloud.

So the soul devoted to Christ,
strengthened in truth and borne to the summit of virtue,

---

19. Luke 5:12; Matt. 8:2.
20. Matt. 8:6.
21. Matt. 15:22.
22. Matt. 9:21.
23. John 11:3.
24. Cf. Matt. 17:1-8; Mark 9:1-13; Luke 9:28-36.

can faithfully say with Peter:
Lord, it is good for us to be here,[25]
in the serene enjoyment of contemplating you.
When heavenly repose and ecstasy are given to the soul,
it will hear *the secret words*
which man is not permitted to speak.[26]

FOURTH FRUIT:
THE PLENITUDE OF HIS PIETY

Jesus, the Solicitous Shepherd[27]

13. How great was this devoted shepherd's solicitous care for the lost sheep and how great his mercy, the Good Shepherd himself indicates with an affectionate metaphor in the parable of the shepherd and the hundredth sheep that was lost, sought with much care, and finally found and joyfully brought back on his shoulders. He openly declares the same thing in an express statement when he says: *"The good shepherd gives his life for his sheep"* (John 10:11). In him is truly fulfilled the prophecy: *Like a shepherd he will feed his flock* (Isa. 40:11). In order to do this, he endured toil, anxiety and lack of food; he traveled through towns and villages preaching the kingdom of God in the midst of many dangers and the plotting of the Pharisees; and he passed the nights in watchful prayer. Fearless of the murmuring and scandal of the Pharisees, he was affable to the publicans, saying that he had come into the world for the sake of those who are sick (Matt. 9:12). He also extended fatherly affection to the repentant, showing them the open bosom of divine mercy. As witnesses to this I call upon and summon Matthew, Zacchaeus, the sinful woman who prostrated herself at his feet and the woman taken in adultery.[28]

---

25. Matt. 17:4.
26. 2 Cor. 12:4.
27. Cf. Luke 15:4-10; Matt. 18:12-14.
28. Matt. 9:9-13, 10:3; Luke 19:1-10, 7:36-50; John 8:3-11.

Like Matthew, therefore
follow this most devoted shepherd;
like Zacchaeus
receive him with hospitality;
like the sinful woman
anoint him with ointment
and wash his feet with your tears,
wipe them with your hair
and caress them with your kisses,
so that finally,
with the woman presented to him for judgment,
you may deserve to hear
the sentence of forgiveness:
Has no one condemned you? Neither will I condemn you.
Go, and sin no more.[29]

Jesus Bathed with Tears[30]

14. To manifest the sweetness of supreme devotedness, the Fountain of all mercy, the good Jesus, wept for us in our misery not only once but many times. First over Lazarus, then over the city and finally on the cross, a flood of tears streamed forth from those loving eyes for the expiation of all sins. The Savior wept abundantly, now deploring the misery of human weakness, now the darkness of a blind heart, now the depravity of obdurate malice.

O hard heart,
insane and impious,
to be pitied as if bereft of true life,
why do you rejoice and laugh
like a madman
in the midst of such misery
while the Wisdom of the Father

---

29. John 8:10-11.
30. Cf. John 11:35; Luke 19:41; Heb. 5:7.

weeps over you?
Consider your weeping physician and
make mourning as for an only son,
a bitter lamentation;
let tears stream down
like a torrent
day and night.
Give yourself no rest,
nor let the pupil of your eye be still.[31]

Jesus Acclaimed King of the World[32]

15. After the raising of Lazarus and the pouring of the jar of ointment on Jesus' head, as the fragrance of his fame had already spread among the people, foreseeing that a crowd would meet him, he mounted an ass in order to give a remarkable example of humility in the midst of the applause of the people who came to him, cut down branches and strewed their garments in his way. Not forgetting compassion, when the crowd was singing a hymn of praise, he lamented over the destruction of the city.

Rise now,
handmaid of the Savior, so that
like one of the daughters of Jerusalem
you may behold
King Solomon in the honor
which his mother the synagogue reverently offered him[33]
as a symbol
of the birth of the Church, so that
with works of piety and triumphs of virtue—
as if with olive branches and palms—
you may follow
the Lord of heaven and earth,
sitting on the back of an ass.

---

31. Jer. 6:26; Lam. 2:18.
32. Cf. Matt. 21:1-11; Mark 11:1-11; Luke 19:29-38; John 12:12-16.
33. Cf. Cant. 3:11.

Jesus, Consecrated Bread[34]

16. Among all the memorable events of Christ's life, the most worthy of remembrance is that last banquet, the most sacred supper. Here not only the paschal lamb was presented to be eaten but also the immaculate Lamb, *who takes away the sins of the world* (John 1:29). Under the appearance of bread *having all delight and the pleasantness of every taste* (Wisd. 16:20), he was given as food. In this banquet the marvelous sweetness of Christ's goodness shone forth when he dined at the same table and on the same plates with those poor disciples and the traitor Judas. The marvelous example of his humility shone forth when, girt with a towel, the King of Glory diligently washed the feet of the fishermen and even of his betrayer. The marvelous richness of his generosity was manifest when he gave to those first priests, and as a consequence to the whole Church and the world, his most sacred body and his true blood as food and drink so that what was soon to be a sacrifice pleasing to God and the priceless price of our redemption would be our viaticum and sustenance. Finally the marvelous outpouring of his love shone forth when, *loving his own to the end* (John 13:1), he strengthened them in goodness with a gentle exhortation, especially forewarning Peter to be firm in faith and offering to John his breast as a pleasant and sacred place of rest.

O how marvelous are all these things,
how full of sweetness,
but only for that soul
who, having been called to so distinguished a banquet,
runs
with all the ardor of his spirit
so that he may cry out
with the Prophet:
As the stag longs for the springs of water
so my soul longs for you,
O God! [35]

---

34. Cf. Matt. 26:17-29; Mark 14:12-25; Luke 22:7-38; John 13-17.
35. Ps. 41:2.

ON
THE MYSTERY
OF HIS PASSION

FIFTH FRUIT:
HIS CONFIDENCE IN TRIALS

Jesus Sold through Guile[1]

17. The first thing that occurs to one who wishes to contemplate devoutly the passion of Jesus Christ is the perfidy of the traitor. So filled was he with the poison of deceit that he betrayed his Teacher and Lord; so on fire with the flame of greed that he sold the all-good God for money and weighed the most precious blood of Christ against the price of a cheap reward. So ungrateful was he that he pursued to death the one who had entrusted everything to him and had elevated him to the height of apostolic dignity. So hardened was he that he could not be called back from the evil he had conceived by the intimacy of the banquet, the humility of Christ's deference or the sweetness of his words.

O marvelous kindness
of the Master
toward this hardened disciple,
toward this wicked servant
of the loving Lord!
Certainly *it were better for that man
if he had not been born.*[2]
But although the traitor's impiety was inexplicable,
the most sweet meekness of the Lamb of God
surpassed it beyond measure.

---

1. Cf. Matt. 26:14-16; Mark 14:10-11; Luke 22:3-6.
2. Matt. 26:24.

This meekness was given
as an example to mortal men, so that
when exasperated by a friend,
our human weakness would no longer say:
If my enemy had reviled me,
I could have borne it,[3]
because here was *a man, another self,*
who seemed to be a companion and friend,
who *ate the bread* of Christ
and at that sacred supper
partook sweet food with him—
he it was
who *raised his heel against him!*[4]
And nevertheless in the very hour of his betrayal
this most mild Lamb did not refuse to apply
with a sweet kiss
his mouth *in which no guile was found*[5]
to the mouth which abounded in iniquity
in order to give the traitor every opportunity
to soften the obstinacy
of his perverse heart.

Jesus Prostrate in Prayer[6]

18. *Jesus, knowing all that was to come upon him* (John 18:4), in accord with the secret disposition of the Most High, *after reciting a hymn went forth to the Mount of Olives* (Matt. 26:30) to pray to his Father, as was his custom. And especially at that moment, when the combat of death was close at hand and the sheep which the devoted Shepherd had embraced with tender affection were about to be dispersed and left abandoned, the imagination of death was so horrible to Christ's sensible nature that he said:

---

3. Ps. 54:13.
4. Ps. 54:14-15; 40:10.
5. 1 Pet. 2:22.
6. Cf. Matt. 26:36-46; Mark 14:32-42; Luke 22:40-46; John 18:1.

Father if it be possible, let this chalice pass from me (Matt. 26:39). The intensity of the anxiety in the Redeemer's spirit, springing from diverse causes, is testified to by the drops of bloody sweat that ran down to the ground from his entire body.

"Ruler, Lord Jesus,
whence comes to your soul
such vehement anxiety and such anxious supplication?
Have you not offered to the Father
an entirely willing sacrifice?"[7]
To shape us in faith
by believing that you have truly shared our mortal nature,
to lift us up in hope
when we must endure similar hardships,
to give us greater incentives to love you—
for these reasons you exhibited
the natural weakness of the flesh
by evident signs which teach us
that you have truly *borne our sorrows*[8]
and that it was not without experiencing pain
that you tasted the bitterness
of your passion.

Jesus Surrounded by the Mob[9]

19. How ready Jesus' spirit was to face his passion was clearly evidenced by the fact that when *men of blood* (Ps. 54:24) together with the betrayer came by night with torches, lanterns and weapons to seek his life, he spontaneously hurried to meet them, showed himself plainly and offered himself to them. That human presumption might know that it can do nothing against him unless he permit it, he cast these evil guards upon the ground with a word of his omnipotent power. But not even then

7. Pseudo-Anselm, *Meditationes*, 9.
8. Isa. 53:4.
9. Cf. Matt. 26:47-56; Mark 14:43-52; Luke 22:47-53; John 18:2-11.

did he *withhold his compassion in anger* (Ps. 76:10) nor did his honeycomb cease to drip the sweetness of kindness.[10] For he healed with the touch of his hand the ear of the impudent servant which had been cut off by his disciple, and he restrained the zeal of his defender who wanted to injure the attackers.

> *Cursed be their fury*
> *because it is violent,*[11]
> for it could be curbed
> neither by a miracle of his majesty
> nor by a favor of his kindness.

Jesus Bound with Chains

20. Finally, who could hear without grief how the cruel executioners laid murderous hands upon the King of Glory and bound with chains the innocent hands of the gentle Jesus, as if he were a robber, and insultingly dragged as a victim to sacrifice that most meek Lamb who offered no objection? What a sting of grief then penetrated the hearts of his disciples when they saw their beloved Master and Lord betrayed by their fellow disciple and led to death, hands bound behind his back like an evildoer, and when that impious Judas, driven by remorse, afterwards was filled with such bitterness because of this that he preferred to die rather than live! (cf. Matt. 27:3-5).

> Yet woe to that man
> who did not return
> to the fountain of mercy
> out of hope of forgiveness
> but, terrified
> by the enormity of his crime,
> despaired!

---

10. Cf. Cant. 4:11.
11. Gen. 49:7.

SIXTH FRUIT:
HIS PATIENCE IN MALTREATMENT

Jesus Denied by His Own[12]

21. When the shepherd is seized, *the sheep are scattered* (Matt. 26:31). When the Master was captured, the disciples fled. Yet Peter, more faithful, *followed at a distance even to the courtyard of the high priest* (Matt. 26:58). There in response to a maidservant he denied with an oath that he knew Christ and repeated it a third time. Then after the cock crowed, his kind Master looked upon his beloved disciple with mercy and grace. Reminded by this of the earlier warning, Peter *went out and wept bitterly* (Matt. 26:75).

O whoever you are,
who at the word of an insistent servant,
that is your flesh,
by will or act
have shamelessly denied Christ,
who suffered for you,
remember the passion of your beloved Master
and go out with Peter
to weep most bitterly over yourself.
When the one
who looked upon the weeping Peter
looks upon you,
you will be inebriated with *the wormwood*[13]
of a twofold bitterness:
remorse for yourself
and compassion for Christ,
so that having atoned with Peter
for the guilt of your crime,
with Peter

12. Cf. Matt. 26:69-75; Mark 14:66-72; Luke 22:56-62; John 18:12-27.
13. Lam. 3:15.

you will be filled
with the spirit of holiness.

Jesus Blindfolded[14]

22. Presented to the council of the malicious high priests, our High Priest Jesus Christ professed the truth that he was the Son of God. He was condemned to death, as if for blasphemy, and endured innumerable insults. For that face, venerable to the elders and desirable to the angels, which fills all the heavens with joy, was defiled by the spittle of polluted lips, struck by impious and sacrilegious hands, and covered in derision with a veil. The Lord of all creation was struck on the ears like a contemptible slave, while he with placid respect and submissive speech gently reprimanded one of the servants of the high priest who had given him a blow: *If I have spoken ill*, he said, *bear witness to the evil; but if well, why do you strike me?* (John 18:23).

O truthful and kind Jesus,
what soul who is devoted to you,
when it sees and hears this,
can restrain itself from tears
and hide the sorrow
of its inner compassion?

Jesus Handed Over to Pilate[15]

23. O horrible impiety of the Jews,[16] which could not be satiated by such insults but went further and, raging with the madness of wild beasts, exposed the life of the Just One to an impious judge as if to be devoured by a mad dog! For the high priests led Jesus bound before the face of Pilate, demanding death by the torture of the cross for him who knew *nothing of sin* (2 Cor. 5:21). But he, like *a lamb before his shearer* (Isa. 53:7), stood

14. Cf. Matt. 26:57-68; Mark 14:53-65; Luke 22:66-71; John 18:13, 19-24.
15. Cf. Matt. 27:11-26; Mark 15:1-15; Luke 23:2-5; John 18:28-19:16.
16. An example of strong language against the Jews that was widespread in the Middle Ages. Such expressions would be contrary to contemporary norms as expressed, for example,

before his judge meek and silent, while deceitful and impious men, accusing him of a mass of false crimes, with tumultuous shouts sought to bring to death the Author of Life; and they saved the life of a man who was a murderer and seditious thief. With as much folly as impiety they preferred the wolf to the lamb, death to life, darkness to light.

Sweet Jesus,
who will be so hardened
as not to groan and cry out in spirit
when he hears with his bodily ear
or considers with his mind
those horrible shouts:
Away with him! Away with him!
Crucify him! [17]

Jesus Condemned to Death [18]

24. Pilate was not ignorant of the fact that the Jewish people were aroused against Jesus not out of zeal for justice but out of envy. Although he clearly asserted that he found in him no cause at all for death, nevertheless, vanquished by human fear, he *filled* his soul *with bitterness* (Lam. 3:15) and handed over the most dutiful King to the judgment of a cruel tyrant, Herod. After Herod mocked Jesus and sent him back to Pilate, the latter issued an even crueler order that Jesus should stand stripped in the sight of men who mocked him so that savage scourgers could lash that virginal and pure-white flesh with fierce blows, cruelly inflicting bruise upon bruise, wound upon wound. The precious blood flowed down the sacred sides of that innocent and loving youth in whom there was found absolutely no basis for accusation.

And you, lost man,
the cause of all this confusion and sorrow,
how is it

_____

in the statement of Vatican II on the Jews in its *Declaration on the Relation of the Church to Non-Christian Religions.*

17. Cf. John 19:15.
18. Cf. Luke 23:8-25; Matt. 27:26-31; Mark 15:16-20; John 19:1-16.

that you do not break down and weep?
Behold, the most innocent Lamb
has chosen on your account
to be condemned by an unjust sentence
in order to rescue you
from a sentence of just damnation.
Behold, he *pays back* for you
what he *did not steal.*[19]
And you, my wicked and impious soul,
you do not repay him
with gratitude and devotion
nor do you recompense him
with compassion.

SEVENTH FRUIT: HIS CONSTANCY UNDER TORTURE

Jesus Scorned by All[20]

25. After Pilate had passed judgment to satisfy the desires of the wicked, those sacrilegious soldiers were not satisfied to crucify the Savior until they had heaped his soul full of mockery. The entire cohort assembled in the praetorium, stripped him of his clothes, dressed him in a scarlet tunic and placed a purple cloak around him, a crown of thorns on his head and a reed in his right hand. They genuflected in mockery, gave him blows, spat upon him and struck that sacred head with the reed.

Attend now,
O pride of the human heart
that flees from reproach and aspires after honors!
Who is it who comes
in the likeness of the King
and yet is filled with the confusion

---

19. Ps. 68:5.
20. Cf. references in note 17, p. 146.

of a despicable slave?
He is your King and your God,
who is accounted *as a leper and the last of men*[21]
in order to snatch you from eternal confusion
and to heal you from the disease of pride.
Woe, therefore, and woe again
to those who, after seeing this outstanding reflection
of humility,
are lifted on high
in pride
placing on display again the Son of God,[22]
who is all the more worthy of all honor from men
because of how much humiliation
he has endured for their sake.

Jesus Nailed to the Cross[23]

26. When the wicked men were sated with insulting the meekest King, our King was again clothed in his own garments, which would be stripped off a second time; and *bearing his cross for himself*, he was led forth *to the place of Calvary* (John 19:17). There he was stripped completely and covered only with a cheap loincloth. Thrown roughly upon the wood of the cross, spread out, pulled forward and stretched back and forth like a hide, he was pierced by pointed nails, fixed to the cross by his sacred hands and feet and most roughly torn with wounds. His garments were given away as spoils and were divided into parts, except his seamless tunic which was not divided but went by lot to one man.

See, now, my soul,
how he who is *God blessed above all things*,

---

21. Isa. 53:4, 3.
22. Heb. 6:6.
23. Cf. Matt. 27:33-37; Mark 15:22-26; Luke 23:33-34; John 19:17-24.

is totally submerged
in the waters of suffering
from *the sole of the foot to the top of the head.*[24]
In order that he might draw you out totally
from these sufferings,
the waters have come up to his soul.[25]
For crowned with thorns
he was ordered to bend his back
under the burden of the cross
and to bear his own ignominy.
Led to the place of execution,
he was stripped of his garments
so that he seemed to be a leper
from the bruises and cuts in his flesh
that were visible over his back and sides
from the blows of the scourges.
And then transfixed
with nails,
he appeared to you as your beloved
cut through with wound upon wound
in order to heal you.
Who will grant me
that my request should come about
and that God will give me
what I long for,[26]
that having been totally transpierced
in both mind and flesh,
I may be fixed
with my beloved
to the yoke of the cross?

---

24. Rom 9:5; Isa. 1:6.
25. Ps. 68:2.
26. Job 6:8.

ST. BONAVENTURE

Jesus Linked with Thieves[27]

27. To increase the confusion, ignominy, shame and suffering, the innocent Lamb was lifted up on the cross as a spectacle, in the midst of thieves, outside the gate in the place of punishment for criminals on that solemn day at noon, while his friends wept and his enemies scoffed. For also *the passersby shook their heads* (Matt. 27:39), and those who were standing there were shouting, saying that *he saved others and* now *he cannot save himself* (Matt. 27:42). One thief did not refrain from this kind of mockery, while the most mild Lamb prayed out of the sweetness of his kindness to his Father for those who were crucifying him and deriding him; and to the thief who confessed and implored him, he promised paradise out of his most generous charity.

O words full of sweetness and forgiveness:
"Father, forgive them!"
O words full of love and grace:
"Today you will be with me
in paradise!"[28]
Breathe in peace now, O soul,
in hope of pardon,
however great a sinner you are,
if you do not shrink from following the footsteps
of the Lord God who is suffering for you,
"who in all his torments
did not once open his mouth
to say even the slightest word
of complaint or excuse or threat or abuse
against those accursed dogs.
Rather he poured upon his enemies
words of a new blessing
not heard since the beginning of the world."[29]

---

27. Cf. Matt. 27:38-44; Mark 15:27-32; Luke 23:35-43.
28. Luke 23:34, 43.
29. Pseudo-Anselm, *op. cit.*, 9; John 9:32.

Say, then, with much confidence:
"Have pity on me, O God,
have pity on me,
because my soul trusts in you."[30]
If only like the repentant thief
you would merit to hear
at the moment of death:
"Today you will be with me
in paradise."[31]

Jesus Given Gall to Drink[32]

28. *After this, Jesus, knowing that all things were now accomplished, that the Scripture might be fulfilled said, "I thirst"* (John 19:28). According to the testimony of John, who was present, after Jesus was given a drink of vinegar and gall on a sponge, he said: *"It is consummated"* (John 19:30). It was as if in the taste of vinegar and gall his bitter passion reached its fulness and completion. For since it was by tasting the sweetness of the forbidden tree that the prevaricator Adam became the cause of all our perdition, it was appropriate and fitting that a remedy for our salvation should be found in the opposite direction. While the hostile arrows of piercing suffering were increasing in each of his limbs, and his spirit was drinking in their poison (cf. Job 6:4), it was fitting that his mouth and tongue—the vehicles of food and speech—should by no means be spared in order that this prophecy might be fulfilled in our physician: *He has filled me with bitterness; he has inebriated me with wormwood* (Lam. 3:15); and that the following prophecy might be fulfilled in his most sweet and loving mother: *He has made me desolate and wasted with sorrow all the day long* (Lam. 1:13).

---

30. Ps. 56:2.
31. Luke 23:43.
32. Cf. Matt. 27:48; Mark 15:36; John 19:28-30.

What tongue can tell,
what intellect grasp
the heavy weight of your desolation,
blessed Virgin?
You were present at all these events,
standing close by and participating in them
in every way.
This blessed and most holy flesh—
which you so chastely conceived,
so sweetly nourished
and fed with your milk,
which you so often held on your lap,
and kissed with your lips—
you actually gazed upon
with your bodily eyes
now torn by the blows of the scourges,
now pierced by the points of the thorns,
now struck by the reed,
now beaten by hands and fists,
now pierced by nails and fixed to the wood of the cross,
and torn by its own weight as it hung there,
now mocked in every way,
finally made to drink gall and vinegar.
But with the eye of your mind
you saw that divine soul
filled with the gall of every form of bitterness,
now groaning in spirit,
now quaking with fear,
now wearied,
now in agony,
now in anxiety,
now in confusion,
now oppressed by sadness and sorrow
partly because of his most sensitive response
to bodily pain,

partly because of his most fervent zeal
for the divine honor taken away by sin,
partly because of his pity poured out upon wretched men,
partly because of his compassion for you,
his most sweet mother,
as the sword pierced the depths of your heart,
when with devoted eyes
he looked upon you standing before him
and spoke to you these loving words:
"*Woman, behold your son,*"[33]
in order to console in its trials your soul,
which he knew had been more deeply pierced
by a sword of compassion
than if you had suffered
in your own body.

EIGHTH FRUIT:
VICTORY IN THE CONFLICT OF DEATH

Jesus, Sun Dimmed in Death[34]

29.   Then when the innocent Lamb, who is the true Sun of justice, had hung upon the cross for the space of three hours, and when the visible sun, out of compassion for its Maker, had hidden the rays of its light, now that all things were consummated, at the ninth hour that Fountain of Life dried up. *With a loud cry and tears* (Heb. 5:7), Jesus, God and man, in order to manifest his feeling of pity and to declare the power of his divinity, commends his spirit to the hands of his Father and expires. Then *the veil of the temple was torn from top to bottom and the earth quaked and the rocks were rent and the tombs were opened* (Matt. 27:51-52). Then the centurion recognized that he was truly God. Then those who had come to a spectacle to jeer *returned,*

---

33. John 19:26.
34. Cf. Matt. 27:50-53; Mark 15:37-39; Luke 23:44-47; John 19:30.

beating their breasts (Luke 23:48). Then he who is *fairer in beauty than the sons of men* (Ps. 44:3), with his eyes clouding and his cheeks turning pale, appeared ugly for the sons of men, having been made a holocaust with a most sweet fragrance in view of his Father's glory in order to *avert his anger* from us (Ps. 84:4).

> O Lord, holy Father, *look down, then,*
> *from your sanctuary,*
> *from your lofty habitation in the heavens;*[35]
> *look*, I say, *upon the face of your Anointed;*[36]
> look upon this most holy Victim,
> which our High Priest offers to you
> for our sins
> and *be placated over your people's wantonness.* [37]
> And you also, redeemed man, consider
> who he is, how great he is, and what kind of a person he is
> who for you is hanging on the cross,
> whose death brings the dead to life,
> at whose passing away
> heaven and earth mourn and hard rocks crack
> as if out of natural compassion.
> O human heart,
> you are harder than any hardness of rocks,
> if at the recollection of such great expiation
> you are not struck with terror,
> nor moved with compassion
> nor shattered with compunction
> nor softened with devoted love.

Jesus Pierced with a Lance[38]

30. Then, in order that the Church might be formed out of the side of Christ sleeping on the cross and that the words of

---

35. Deut. 26:15.
36. Ps. 83:10.
37. Exod. 32:12.
38. Cf. John 19:31-37.

Scripture might be fulfilled which say: *They will look upon him whom they have pierced* (John 19:37; Zach. 12:10), the divine plan permitted that one of the soldiers should pierce open his sacred side with a lance. While blood mixed with water flowed, the price of our salvation was poured forth, which gushing from the secret fountain of the heart gave power to the sacraments of the Church to confer the life of grace and to become for those already living in Christ a draught of *the fountain* of living *water springing up into eternal life* (John 4:14). Behold how the spear thrown by the perfidy of Saul, that is, of the reprobate Jewish people, through the divine mercy *fastened in the wall without making a wound* (1 Kings 19:10) and made *a cleft in the rock and a hollow place in the cliff* as an abode for doves (Cant. 2:14).

Rise, therefore, beloved of Christ,
be like the dove
that makes its nest in the heights in the mouth of a cleft.[39]
There,
like *a sparrow that finds a home*,[40]
do not cease to keep watch;
there,
like the turtledove,
hide the offsprings of your chaste love;
there
apply your mouth
to draw water from the Savior's fountains[41]
for this is *the river*
arising from the midst of paradise
which, *divided into four branches*[42]
and flowing into devout hearts,
waters and makes fertile
the whole earth.

---

39. Jer. 48:28.
40. Ps. 83:4.
41. Isa. 12:3.
42. Gen. 2:10.

Jesus Dripping with Blood

31. Christ the Lord was stained with his own blood, which flowed profusely: first from the bloody sweat, then from the lashes and the thorns, then from the nails and finally from the lance. So that with God there might *be plenteous redemption* (Ps. 129:7), he wore a priestly robe of red; his *apparel* was truly *red and his garments like those of the wine presser* (Isa. 63:2). As in the case of Joseph who was thrown into an ancient cistern, his tunic was *dipped in the blood of a goat* (Gen. 37:31)—that is, because of the *likeness of sinful flesh* (Rom. 8:3)—and was sent to the Father for his recognition and acceptance.

> "Recognize, therefore, O most merciful Father,
> the tunic
> of your beloved son Joseph,
> whom the envy of his brothers in the flesh
> has devoured like *a wild beast*[43]
> and has trampled upon his garment in rage,
> befouling its beauty with the remains of blood,
> for it has left in it
> five lamentable gashes.
> For this is indeed, O Lord,
> the garment
> which your innocent Son willingly gave over
> into the hands of the Egyptian prostitute,
> that is to the Synagogue,
> choosing to be stripped of the mantle of his flesh
> and to descend into the prison of death
> rather than to seek temporal glory
> by acquiescing
> to the shouts of the adulterous mob."[44]
> For *when joy was set before him,*

---

43. Gen. 37:33.
44. Pseudo-Anselm, *op. cit.*, 9; cf. Gen. 39:7ff.

he endured a cross, despising the shame.[45]
But you also, my most merciful Lady,
behold
that most sacred garment of your beloved Son,
artistically woven by the Holy Spirit
from your most chaste body;
and together with him
beg forgiveness
for us who take refuge in you
that we may be found worthy
to flee from the wrath to come.[46]

Jesus Laid in the Tomb[47]

32. Finally a noble man, Joseph of Arimathea, came and with the permission of Pilate and the assistance of Nicodemus took the body of Christ down from the cross, embalmed it with spices, wrapped it in a cloth and buried it with all reverence in a new tomb which had been cut out of the rock for him in a nearby garden. Then, after the Lord was buried and soldiers were assigned to guard the tomb, those devoted and holy women who had followed him when he was alive, in order to render him service out of their dutiful piety now that he was dead, bought spices to anoint Jesus' most sacred body. Among them Mary Magdalene was borne along by such a burning in her heart, moved by such sweetness of piety and drawn by such strong bonds of love that, forgetting her feminine weakness, she was held back from visiting the tomb by neither the darkness of night nor the cruelty of the persecutors. Rather, she stood outside and bathed the tomb with her tears. Although the disciples had fled, she did not go away. Ablaze with the fire of divine love, she burned with such a powerful desire and was wounded with such

45. Heb. 12:2.
46. Matt. 3:7.
47. Cf. Matt. 27:57-66, 28:1; Mark 15:42-47, 16:1-2; Luke 23:50-56, 24:1; John 19:38-42, 20:1.

an impatient love that nothing had any taste for her except to be able to weep and to utter in truth those words of the Prophet: *My tears were my food day and night, as they say to me day after day: "Where is your God?"* (Ps. 41:4).

O my God, good Jesus,
although I am in every way without merit and unworthy,
grant to me,
who did not merit to be present at these events
in the body,
that I may ponder them faithfully
in my mind
and experience toward you,
my God crucified and put to death for me,
that feeling of compassion
which your innocent mother and the penitent Magdalene
experienced
at the very hour of your passion.

ON
THE MYSTERY
OF HIS GLORIFICATION

NINTH FRUIT:
THE NOVELTY OF HIS RESURRECTION

Jesus Triumphant in Death

33. Now that the combat of the passion was over, and the bloody dragon and raging lion thought that he had secured a victory by killing the Lamb, the power of the divinity began to shine forth in his soul as it descended into hell. By this power our strong *Lion of the tribe of Judah* (Apoc. 5:5), rising against the *strong man who was fully armed* (Luke 11:21), tore the prey away from him, broke down the gates of hell and bound the serpent. *Disarming the Principalities and Powers, he led them away boldly, displaying them openly in triumph in himself* (Col. 2:15). Then the *Leviathan was led about with a hook* (Job 40:25), his jaw pierced by Christ so that he who had no right over the Head which he had attacked, also lost what he had seemed to have over the body. Then the true Samson, as he died, laid prostrate an army of the enemy (cf. Judges 16:30). Then the Lamb without stain *by the blood of his Testament led forth the prisoners from the pit in which there was no water* (Zach. 9:11). Then the long-awaited brightness of a new light shone upon those *that dwelt in the region of the shadow of death* (Isa. 9:2).

Jesus Rising in Blessedness[1]

34. When the third day dawned of the Lord's sacred repose in the tomb, which in the cycle of the week is both the eighth and

---

1. Cf. Matt. 28:1-20; Mark 16:1-18; Luke 24:1-49; John 20:1-31, 21:1-25.

the first, Christ, *the power and wisdom of God* (1 Cor. 1:24), with the author of death lying prostrate, conquered even death itself and opened to us access to eternity, when he raised himself from the dead by his divine power in order *to make known to us the paths of life* (Ps. 15:11). Then *there was a great earthquake; for an angel of the Lord came down from heaven, with raiment like snow and his countenance like lightning* (Matt. 28:2-3). He appeared attractive to the devout and severe to the wicked; for he terrified the cruel soldiers and comforted the timid women, to whom the Lord himself first appeared after rising because their intense devotion so merited. Then he was seen by Peter, then by the disciples going to Emmaus, then by all the apostles, except Thomas. Later he presented himself to be touched by Thomas, who proclaimed his faith: *My Lord and my God* (John 20:28). And thus during forty days he appeared in many ways to his disciples, both eating and drinking with them; and he enlightened our faith with proofs and lifted up our hope with promises so as finally to enkindle our love with gifts from heaven.

Jesus, Extraordinary Beauty

35. This most beautiful *flower of the root of Jesse* (Isa. 11:1), which had blossomed in the incarnation and withered in the passion, thus blossomed again in the resurrection so as to become the beauty of all. For that most glorious body—subtle, agile and immortal—was clothed in glory so as to be truly more radiant than the sun, showing an example of the beauty destined for the risen human bodies. Concerning this the Savior himself said: *"Then the just will shine forth like the sun into the kingdom of their Father"* (Matt. 13:43), that is, in eternal beatitude. And if the just will shine forth like the sun, how great do you think is the radiance of the very Sun of justice himself? So great is it, I say, that it is *more beautiful than the sun and surpasses every constellation*

of the stars (Wisd. 7:29); compared to light, his beauty is deservedly judged to be preeminent.

> Happy the eyes that have seen!
> But you will be truly *happy*
> *if there will be remnants of your seed*
> *to see*[2]
> both interiorly and exteriorly
> that most desired splendor.

Jesus Given Dominion over the Earth

36. The Lord appeared to his disciples also in Galilee and declared that all power in heaven and earth had been given to him by the Father (cf. Matt. 28:16-20). In view of this he sent his disciples *into the whole world to preach the gospel to every creature* (Mark 16:15), promising salvation to believers, threatening damnation to unbelievers. *The Lord worked with them and confirmed the preaching by the signs that followed* (Mark 16:20) so that in the power of the name of Jesus Christ they might have command over all creatures and all diseases. And thus it was to be manifest to the whole world that Jesus Christ, the Son of the mighty Father, *lives and reigns* like another Joseph and *a true Savior* not only in *the land of Egypt* (Gen. 41:45, 45:26) but also *"in every place where* the eternal King *has dominion* (Ps. 102:22). At the command of the God of heaven he has been led forth from the prison of death and the underworld. And shorn of the fleece of mortality, he exchanged the clothing of flesh for the glory of immortality. Like a true Moses drawn out of the waters of mortality, he undermined the power of Pharaoh."[3] So exalted is his honor *that in his name every knee should bend of those in heaven, on earth and under the earth* (Phil. 2:10).

---

2. Tob. 13:20.
3. Pseudo-Anselm, *Meditationes*, 9; cf. Exod. 2:5.

TENTH FRUIT:
THE SUBLIMITY OF HIS ASCENSION

Jesus, Leader of His Army[4]

37. Forty days after the Lord's resurrection—and this fortieth day is not without mystical meaning—having eaten with his disciples, the benign Master climbed the Mount of Olives; and then *while they looked on, he lifted up his hands and was borne up into heaven* (Luke 24:50-51), and a cloud engulfed him (Acts 1:9) as he ascended, and he hid himself from the view of men. And so *ascending on high, he led captivity captive* (Ps. 67:19; cf. Mich. 2:13); and with the gates of heaven now open, he made a way for his followers and led the exiles into the kingdom. He made them fellow citizens with the angels and *members of God's household* (Eph. 2:19). Thus he repaired the fall of the angels, increased the honor of his eternal Father, manifested himself in triumph and proved that he is the Lord of Hosts.

Jesus Lifted Up to Heaven

38. While the angels sang and the saints rejoiced, the God and Lord of angels and men ascended *above the heaven of heavens* (Ps. 67:34), and he soared *on the wings of the wind* (Ps. 17:11) with the marvelous agility of his power and sat at the right hand of the Father, *having become so much superior to the angels as he inherited a more excellent name than they, and there he appeared before the face* of the most benign Father *to intercede for us* (Heb. 1:4, 9:24). *For it was fitting that we should have such a High Priest, holy, innocent, undefiled, set apart from sinners and become higher than the heavens* (Heb. 7:26), so that, seated at the right hand of Majesty, he might show to the glorious face of his Father the scars of the wounds which he suffered for us.

---

4. Cf. Acts 1:9-11.

Let every tongue give thanks to you,
Lord our Father,
for the unutterable gift
of your most abundant charity.
You have not spared the only Son of your heart,
but you have handed him over
to death
for all of us
that we might have so great and so faithful
an advocate
before your face in heaven.[5]

Jesus, Giver of the Spirit

39. When seven weeks had passed since the resurrection, on the fiftieth day, *when the disciples were gathered in one place with the women and Mary the mother of Jesus, suddenly there came a sound from heaven as of a violent wind blowing* (Acts 1:14, 2:1). The Spirit descended upon the group *of a hundred and twenty persons* (Acts 1:15) and *appeared in the form of tongues of fire* to give speech to the mouth, light to the intellect and ardor to the affection. *They were all filled with the Holy Spirit and began to speak in different languages* (Acts 2:4), as the prompting of the Holy Spirit dictated, who taught them all truth and inflamed them with all love and strengthened them in every virtue. For aided by his grace, illumined by his teaching and strengthened by his power, although they were few and simple, "they planted the Church with their own blood"[6] throughout the world, partly by their fiery words, partly by their perfect example, partly by their astonishing miracles. Purified, illumined and perfected by the power of the same Holy Spirit, the Church became lovable to her Spouse and his attendants for being exceedingly beautiful and *adorned with* a wonderful *variety* (Ps. 44:15); but to Satan and

---

5. Pseudo-Anselm, *op cit.*, 9; Rom. 8:32; cf. 1 John 2:1.
6. *Breviarium Romanum*, Commune apostolorum, noc. 3, resp. 1.

his angels she became *awe-inspiring like an army in battle array* (Cant. 6:10).

Jesus Freeing from Guilt

40. In this holy Church, which through the wonderful work of the Holy Spirit is diversified in a variety of forms throughout the world and yet is united in a single whole, there presides one High Priest, Christ, as supreme Hierarch. With a wonderful order, like that of the heavenly city, he dispenses offices in the Church and distributes charismatic gifts. For *he himself gave some men as apostles, some as prophets, others again as evangelists, others as pastors and teachers in order to perfect saints and to build up the body of Christ* (Eph. 4:11-12). Also according to the sevenfold grace of the Holy Spirit, he gave the sacraments as seven remedies against sickness. Through the administration of the sacraments he grants sanctifying grace and forgives sins, which are never taken away except within the faith and unity of Holy Mother Church. And since sins are cleansed in the fire of tribulation, therefore, just as God exposed Christ, the head of the Church, to the waves of suffering, so he permitted his body, that is, the Church, to suffer tribulation in order to be tested and purified until the end of the world.

So the patriarchs, so the prophets, so the apostles,
so the martyrs, confessors and virgins
and as many as have been pleasing to God
have passed through many tribulations
and remained faithful
and so will all the chosen members of Christ
until the day of judgment.

ELEVENTH FRUIT: THE EQUITY OF HIS JUDGMENT

Jesus, Truthful Witness

41. At the time of the future judgment, when God will judge the secrets of hearts, *fire will precede the judge; angels will be sent with trumpets; the elect will be gathered together from the four winds* (Ps. 96:3; Matt. 24:31; Mark 13:27); and all those who are in their tombs will rise by the power of the divine command and stand before his judgment seat (cf. 2 Thess. 1:7; Rom. 14:10).

> Then *things hidden in darkness*
> *will be illumined*;
> then *the counsels of hearts*
> *will be revealed*;[7]
> then the books of consciences will be opened
> and that book itself will be opened
> which is called *the book of life*.[8]
> Thus, altogether and in an instant,
> all the secrets of all
> will be revealed to all
> with such clear certainty
> that against the testimony of truth speaking in Christ
> and of each conscience giving similar testimony,
> not a single path will be open
> for denial, or defense or excuse or subterfuge,
> but each will receive *according to his deeds*.[9]
> "There is, then, a great necessity
> imposed upon us
> to be good,

---

7. 1 Cor. 4:5.
8. Apoc. 20:12.
9. Ps. 61:13; Rom. 2:6; Apoc. 2:23.

since all our actions are within the view
of the all-seeing Judge."[10]

Jesus, Wrathful Judge[11]

42. When the sign of the omnipotent Son of God appears in the clouds and the powers *of heaven are shaken* (Matt. 24:29) and fire engulfs the earth in the conflagration of the world and all the just are placed on the right and the wicked on the left, then the Judge of the universe will appear so wrathful to the reprobate that *they will say to the mountains and to the rocks: "Fall upon us and hide us from the face of him who sits upon the throne and from the wrath of the Lamb"* (Apoc. 6:16). *He shall don justice for a breastplate and shall wear sure judgment for a helmet. He shall take invincible equity as a shield and whet his dire anger for a spear, and the universe shall war with him against the foolhardy* (Wisd. 5:18-20); so that those who fought insolently against the Creator of all will then, by God's just judgment, be conquered by all creatures.

"On high
the wrathful Judge
will then appear;
below,
hell will open up
as a horrible chaos.
On the right
will be the accusing sins,
on the left
countless demons.
Thus surrounded,
where will the sinner flee?
Certainly, to hide will be impossible
and to be seen, intolerable.
For *if the just man scarcely will be saved,*

---

10. Boethius, *De consolatione philosophiae*, V, prosa 6.
11. Cf. Matt. 24:29-31 Mark 13:24-27; Luke 21:25-28.

where will the impious and sinner appear?"[12]
Do not, therefore, enter into judgment
with your servant,
O Lord![13]

Jesus, Glorious Conqueror[14]

43. Having condemned the reprobate to be burned in eternal flames and having gathered together as in a bundle all the enemies of Jesus Christ, the almighty power of God will cast them, in the flesh and in the spirit, into the everlasting voracity of the flames in which they will never be consumed but will burn and suffer eternally. *And the smoke of their torments goes up forever and ever* (Apoc. 14:11). Then *the beast and the false prophet and those who accepted its image shall be cast into the pool of fire and brimstone which was prepared for the devil and his angels* (Apoc. 19:20; Matt. 25:41). Then the elect *will go out to see the corpses* (Isa. 66:24)— dead by the death not indeed of nature but of penalty. Then the *just will bathe their hands in the blood of sinners* (Ps. 57:11). Then at last the victorious Lamb *will make his enemies his footstool* (Ps. 109:1) while the wicked *will go into the depths of the earth and will be delivered over to the sword and will be the prey of foxes* (Ps. 62:10-11), that is, of the demons who had seduced them through deceit.

Jesus, Adorned Spouse

44. Finally, when the face of the earth has been renewed, when *the light of the moon will be*
like the light of the sun
and the light of the sun will be seven times greater,
like the light of seven days,

---

12. Based on authentic Anselm, *Meditationes*, 1, and Pseudo-Bernard, *Tractatus de interiori domo*, c. 22, no. 46; 1 Pet. 4:18.
13. Ps. 142:1-2.
14. Cf. Matt. 13:24-30, 36-43.

that holy city of Jerusalem,
which *had come down from heaven*
like a bride adorned
now *prepared for the marriage of the Lamb*,[15]
clothed with a double stole,[16]
will be led into the palace of the heavenly court
and introduced into
that sacred and secret bridal chamber
and will be united to that heavenly Lamb
in so intense a covenant
that bride and groom will become
one spirit.[17]
Then Christ will be clothed
with all the beauty of the elect
as if *with a many-colored tunic*[18]
in which he will shine forth richly adorned
as if covered with all manner of precious stones.
Then the sweet wedding song will resound
and throughout all the quarters of Jerusalem
Alleluia will be sung!
Then *the virgins who were prudent and ready*
will enter into the nuptials
with the Spouse,
and with the door closed,[19]
will abide
in the beauty of peace
in the tabernacle of confidence
and in opulent repose.[20]

---

15. Isa. 30:26; Apoc. 21:10, 19:7.
16. Cf. Bonaventure, *Breviloquium*, VII, 7, no. 1; the double stole refers to the two rewards of paradise: the beatific vision and the glorification of the body.
17. 1 Cor. 6:17.
18. Gen. 37:3; cf. Ezech. 16:13.
19. Matt. 25:10.
20. Cf. Isa. 32:18.

TWELFTH FRUIT:
THE ETERNITY OF HIS KINGDOM

Jesus, King, Son of the King

45. The glory and nobility of God's eternal kingdom have to be estimated from the dignity of its King, since a king is not derived from a kingdom but a kingdom from a king. And he indeed is King who has *on his garment and on his thigh a name written: King of kings and Lord of lords* (Apoc. 19:16), whose *power is an everlasting power that shall not be taken away* (Dan. 7:14), whose kingdom will not be destroyed and whom *all tribes and peoples and tongues* (Apoc. 7:9) will serve throughout eternity. He is truly a *peaceable* (1 Par. 22:9) King, whose *countenance* both heaven and *all the earth desire to look upon* (3 Kings 10:24).

> O how glorious is the kingdom
> of this most excellent King
> where all the just reign with him!
> Its law is
> truth, peace, charity, life, eternity.
> It is not divided
> by the number of those who reign;
> nor lessened by being shared,
> nor disturbed by its multitude,
> nor disordered by its inequality of ranks,
> nor circumscribed by space,
> nor changed by motion,
> nor measured by time.

Jesus, Inscribed Book

46. For the glory of the kingdom to be perfect, there is required not only exalted power but also resplendent wisdom so that the government of the kingdom is directed not by arbitrary decision but by the brilliant rays of the eternal laws emanating

without deception from the light of wisdom. And this wisdom is written in Christ Jesus as in the book of life, in which God the Father has *hidden all the treasures of wisdom and knowledge* (Col. 2:3). Therefore, the only-begotten Son of God, as the uncreated Word, is the book of wisdom and the light that is full of living eternal principles in the mind of the supreme Craftsman, as the inspired Word in the angelic intellects and the blessed, as the incarnate Word in rational minds united with the flesh. Thus throughout the entire kingdom *the manifold wisdom of God* (Eph. 3:10) shines forth from him and in him, as in a mirror containing the beauty of all forms and lights and as in a book in which all things are written according to the deep secrets of God.

> O, if only I could find this book
> whose origin is eternal,
> whose essence is incorruptible,
> whose knowledge is life,
> whose script is indelible,
> whose study is desirable
> whose teaching is easy,
> whose knowledge is sweet,
> whose depth is inscrutable,
> whose words are ineffable;
> yet all are a single Word!
> Truly, whoever finds this book
> will *find life and will draw salvation
> from the Lord.*[21]

Jesus, Fountain-Ray of Light

47. In this eternal kingdom, *all good and perfect gifts come down* in plenty and abundance *from the Father of Lights* (James 1:17) through Jesus Christ, who is the superessential Ray and who, since he *is one, can do all things, and renews all things while*

21. Prov. 8:35.

perduring (Wisd. 7:27) himself. For he is *a pure effusion of the brightness of the power of the omnipotent God*, and therefore *nothing that is sullied can enter* (Wisd. 7:25) into this Fountain-Ray of light.

> You soul devoted to God,
> whoever you are,
> run
> with living desire
> to this Fountain of life and light
> and with the innermost power of your heart
> cry out to him:
> "O inaccessible beauty of the most high God
> and the pure brightness of the eternal light,
> life vivifying all life,
> light illuming every light,
> and keeping in perpetual splendor
> a thousand times a thousand lights
> brilliantly shining
> before the throne of your Divinity
> since the primeval dawn!
> O eternal and inaccessible,
> clear and sweet stream from the fountain
> hidden from the eyes of all mortals,
> whose depth is without bottom,
> whose height is without limit,
> whose breadth cannot be bounded,
> whose purity cannot be disturbed."[22]
> From this Fountain
> flows the stream of *the oil of gladness*,[23]
> which *gladdens the city of God*,[24]
> and the powerful fiery torrent,

---

22. Pseudo-Anselm, *op. cit.*, 9.
23. Ps. 44:8.
24. Ps. 45:5.

the *torrent*, I say, *of the pleasure* of God,[25]
from which the guests at the heavenly banquet
drink to joyful inebriation
and sing without ceasing
hymns of jubilation.

Anoint us
with this sacred oil
and refresh
with the longed-for waters of this torrent
the thirsting throat of our parched hearts
so that *amid shouts of joy and thanksgiving*[26]
we may sing to you
a canticle of praise,
proving by experience that
with you
is the fountain of life,
and in your light
we will see
light.[27]

Jesus, Desired End

48. It is true that the end of all desires is happiness, which is "a perfect state with the presence of all goods."[28] No one reaches this state except by an ultimate union with him who is the fountain and origin of goods that are both natural and gratuitous, both bodily and spiritual, both temporal and eternal. And this is the one who said of himself: "*I am the Alpha and the*

25. Ps. 35:9.
26. Ps. 41:5.
27. Ps. 35:10.
28. Boethius, *op. cit.*, III, prosa 2.

Omega, the beginning and the end" (Apoc. 1:8). As all things are produced through the Word eternally spoken, so all things are restored, advanced and completed through the Word united to flesh. Therefore he is truly and properly called Jesus, *because there is no other name under heaven given to men by which* one *can obtain salvation* (Acts 4:12).

> Believing, hoping and loving
> *with* my *whole heart, with* my *whole mind*
> *and with* my *whole strength,* [29]
> may I be carried
> to you, beloved Jesus,
> as to the goal of all things,
> because you alone are sufficient,
> you alone are good and pleasing
> to those who seek you and *love your name.* [30]
> "For you, my good Jesus,
> are the redeemer of the lost,
> the savior of the redeemed,
> the hope of exiles,
> the strength of laborers,
> the sweet solace of anguished spirits,
> the crown and imperial dignity of the triumphant,
> the unique reward and joy of all the citizens of heaven,
> the renowned offspring of the supreme God
> and the sublime fruit of the virginal womb,
> the abundant fountain of all graces,
> *of whose fulness we have all received.*"[31]

29. Matt. 22:37; Mark 12:30; Luke 10:27.
30. Ps. 5:12.
31. Pseudo-Anselm, *op. cit.,* 9; John 1:16.

Prayer

To Obtain the Seven Gifts of the Holy Spirit

49. We, therefore, pray
to the most kind Father
through you, his only-begotten Son,
who for us became man, was crucified and glorified,
that he send us
out of his treasures
the Spirit of sevenfold grace
who rested upon you in all fulness:
the Spirit, I say, of WISDOM,
that we may taste the life-giving flavors
of the fruit of the tree of life,
which you truly are;
the gift also of UNDERSTANDING,
by which the intentions of our mind are illumined;
the gift of COUNSEL,
by which we may follow in your footsteps
on the right paths;
the gift of FORTITUDE,
by which we may be able to weaken the violence
of our enemies' attacks;
the gift of KNOWLEDGE,
by which we may be filled with the brilliant light
of your sacred teaching
to distinguish good and evil;
the gift of PIETY,
by which we may acquire a merciful heart;
the gift of FEAR,
by which we may draw away from all evil
and be set at peace
by submitting in awe to your eternal majesty.
For you have wished

that we ask for these things
in that sacred prayer which you have taught us;
and now we ask to obtain them,
through your cross,
for the praise of your most holy name.
To you,
with the Father and the Holy Spirit,
be honor and glory,
thanksgiving, beauty and power,
forever and ever.
Amen.

HERE ENDS THE TREE OF LIFE

THE LIFE OF ST. FRANCIS
(LEGENDA MAIOR)

PROLOGUE

1. *In these last days*[1]
the grace of God our Savior has appeared[2]
in his servant Francis
to all who are truly humble and lovers of holy poverty.
In him
they can venerate God's superabundant mercy
and be taught by his example
to utterly *reject ungodliness and worldly passions*,[3]
to live in conformity with Christ
and to thirst after *blessed hope*[4] with unflagging desire.
He was *poor and lowly*,[5]
but *the Most High God looked upon* him[6]
with such condescension and kindness
that he not only *lifted him up in his need
from the dust*[7] of a worldly life,
but made him a practitioner, a leader and a herald
of Gospel perfection
and *set him up as a light*[8] for believers
so that by *bearing witness to the light*[9]
he might *prepare for the Lord
a way* of light and *peace*[10] into the hearts of his faithful.

---

1. Acts 2:17; Heb. 1:2.
2. Titus 2:11.
3. *Ibid.* 2:12.
4. *Ibid.* 2:13.
5. Isa. 66:2.
6. Job 36:22.
7. 1 Kings 2:8.
8. Isa. 49:6.
9. John 1:7.
10. Luke 1:76, 79.

Shining with the splendor of his life and teaching,
like the morning star in the midst of clouds,[11]
by his resplendent rays he guided into the light
those sitting in *darkness and in the shadow of death,*[12]
and like *the rainbow shining among clouds of glory*[13]
he made manifest in himself
the sign of the Lord's *covenant.*[14]
He *preached* to men
the Gospel of peace[15] and salvation,
being himself *the Angel* of true *peace.*[16]
Like John the Baptist
he was appointed by God *to prepare in the desert*[17]
a way of the highest poverty
and to *preach repentance*[18] by word and example.
First endowed with the gifts of divine grace,
he was then enriched
by the merit of unshakable virtue;
and *filled with the spirit*[19] of prophecy,
he was also assigned an angelic ministry
and was totally aflame with a Seraphic fire.
Like a hierarchic man[20]
he was lifted up in *a fiery chariot,*[21]

11. Ecclus. 50:6.
12. Luke 1:79.
13. Ecclus. 50:8.
14. Gen. 9:13; this is a reference to Francis' stigmata that manifested the cross, which is the sign of the New Covenant as the rainbow was the sign of the Old Covenant.
15. Rom. 10:15.
16. Isa. 33:7.
17. *Ibid.* 40:3.
18. Luke 24:47.
19. *Ibid.* 1:67.
20. The Latin is *vir hierarchicus*: the latter is a technical term in Bonaventure referring to the ordering of the soul according to the stages of the spiritual life: purgation, illumination and perfection. This hierarchical ordering of the soul reflects the angelic hierarchy and gives a basis for Bonaventure's association of Francis with angelic imagery. Cf. *The Soul's Journey into God*, IV, 3-4, pp. 89-91, and Bonaventure's treatise on this subject, *The Triple Way*.
21. Cf. 4 Kings 2:11; the Scripture reference here is to the prophet Elijah, who was taken to heaven in a fiery chariot. This is associated with the incident in Francis's life narrated in IV, 4, pp. 209-210.

as will be seen quite clearly in the course of his life;
therefore it can be reasonably proved
that he came *in the spirit and power of Elijah*.[22]
And so not without reason
is he considered to be symbolized by the image of the Angel
who ascends from the sunrise
bearing the seal of the living God,
in the true prophecy
of that other *friend of the Bridegroom*,[23]
John the Apostle and Evangelist.
For *"when the sixth seal was opened,"*[24]
John says in the Apocalypse,
"I saw another Angel
ascending from the rising of the sun,
having the seal of the living God."[25]

2. We can come to the conclusion, without any doubt,
that this messenger of God—
so worthy to be loved by Christ,
imitated by us and admired by the world—
was God's servant Francis,
if we consider the height
of his extraordinary sanctity.
For even while he lived among men,
he imitated angelic purity
so that he was held up as an example
for those who would be perfect followers of Christ.
We are led to hold this firmly and devoutly
because of his ministry
to call men to weep and mourn,
to shave their heads, and to put on sackcloth,[26]

22. Luke 1:17.
23. John 3:29.
24. Apoc. 6:12.
25. *Ibid*. 7:2.
26. Isa. 22:12.

and to mark with a Tau
the foreheads of men who moan and grieve,[27]
signing them with the cross of penance
and clothing them with his habit,
which is in the form of a cross.
But even more is this confirmed
with the irrefutable testimony of truth
by the *seal of the likeness*[28] of the living God,
namely of *Christ crucified,*[29]
which was imprinted on his body
not by natural forces or human skill
but by the wondrous power
of *the Spirit of the living God.*[30]

3. I feel that I am unworthy and unequal to the task of writing the life of a man so venerable and worthy of imitation. I would never have attempted it if the fervent desire of the friars had not aroused me, the unanimous urging of the General Chapter had not induced me[31] and the devotion which I am obliged to have toward our holy father had not compelled me. For when I was a boy, as I still vividly remember, I was snatched from the jaws of death by his invocation and merits. So if I remained silent and did not sing his praises, I fear that I would be rightly accused of the crime of ingratitude. I recognize that God saved my life through him, and I realize that I have experienced his power in my very person. This, then, is my principal reason for undertaking this task, that I may *gather*

---

27. Ezech. 9:4. The *Tau* is a letter of the Hebrew and Greek alphabets; its Greek form, which corresponds to the English capital T, was used as a variant form of the cross. Innocent III used this text of Ezechiel as the theme for the opening homily of the Fourth Lateran Council (1215), interpreting the marking with the Tau as a symbol of spiritual renewal in the Church. Francis seems to have been present on this occasion, and from that time used the Tau as his mark or signature. Cf. IV, 9, pp. 213-214; XI, note 17, p. 287.
28. Ezech. 28:12.
29. 1 Cor. 2:2; for Bonaventure's treatment of Francis's stigmata, cf. XIII, pp. 00.
30. 2 Cor. 3:3.
31. The General Chapter of Narbonne, 1260.

together the accounts of his virtues, his actions and his words—like so many *fragments*, partly forgotten and partly scattered—although I cannot accomplish this fully, *so that they may not be lost* (John 6:12) when those who lived with this servant of God die.

4. In order to have a clearer and more certain grasp of the authentic facts of his life, which I was to transmit to posterity, I visited the sites of the birth, life and death of this holy man. I had careful interviews with his companions who were still alive, especially those who had intimate knowledge of his holiness and were its principal followers. Because of their acknowledged truthfulness and their proven virtue, they can be trusted beyond any doubt. In describing what God graciously accomplished through his servant, I decided that I should avoid a cultivated literary style, since the reader's devotion profits more from simple rather than ornate expression. To avoid confusion I did not always weave the story together in chronological order. Rather, I strove to maintain a more thematic order, relating to the same theme events that happened at different times, and to different themes events that happened at the same time, as seemed appropriate.

5. The life of Francis—in its beginning, progress and end—is described in the following fifteen chapters:

CHAPTER ONE
  On his manner of life while in secular attire
CHAPTER TWO
  On his perfect conversion to God and his restoration of three churches
CHAPTER THREE
  On the foundation of the Order and the approval of the Rule
CHAPTER FOUR
  On the progress of the Order under his hand and the confirmation of the Rule

CHAPTER FIVE
On the austerity of his life and how creatures provided him comfort
CHAPTER SIX
On his humility and obedience and God's condescension to his slightest wish
CHAPTER SEVEN
On his love of poverty and the miraculous fulfillment of his needs
CHAPTER EIGHT
On his affectionate piety and how irrational creatures were affectionate toward him
CHAPTER NINE
On the fervor of his charity and his desire for martyrdom
CHAPTER TEN
On his zeal for prayer and the power of his prayer
CHAPTER ELEVEN
On his understanding of Scripture and his spirit of prophecy
CHAPTER TWELVE
On the efficacy of his preaching and his grace of healing
CHAPTER THIRTEEN
On his sacred stigmata
CHAPTER FOURTEEN
On his patience and his passing in death
CHAPTER FIFTEEN
On his canonization and the solemn transferal of his body

Finally, there is appended an account of miracles which took place after his happy death.[32]

HERE ENDS THE PROLOGUE

---

32. This account of miracles is not included in the present volume.

CHAPTER ONE

ON
SAINT FRANCIS'S
MANNER OF LIFE
WHILE IN SECULAR ATTIRE

1. *There was a man*
in the town of Assisi,
Francis *by name*,[1]
whose memory is held in benediction[2]
because God in his generosity
foreordained goodly blessings for him,[3]
mercifully snatching him from the dangers of the present life
and richly filling him with gifts of heavenly grace.
As a young boy,
he lived among *worldly sons of men*[4]
and was brought up in worldly ways.
After acquiring
a little knowledge of reading and writing,
he was assigned
to work in a lucrative merchant's business.
Yet with God's protection,
even among wanton youths,
he did not give himself over
to the drives of the flesh,
although he indulged himself in pleasures;

---

1. Job. 1:1.
2. Ecclus. 45:1.
3. Ps. 20:4.
4. *Ibid.* 61:10.

nor even among greedy merchants
did he place his hope in money or treasures[5]
although he was intent
on making a profit.[6]

God implanted in the heart of the youthful Francis a certain openhanded compassion for the poor. *Growing from his
infancy* (Job 31:18), this compassion had so filled his heart with
generosity that even at that time he determined not to be deaf
to the Gospel but *to give to everyone who begged* (Luke 6:30),
especially if he asked "for the love of God." On one occasion
when Francis was distracted by the press of business, contrary
to his custom, he sent away empty-handed a certain poor man
who had begged alms for the love of God. As soon as he came
to his senses, he ran after the man and gave him a generous
alms, promising God that from that moment onward, while he
had the means, he would never refuse those who begged from
him for the love of God. He kept this promise with untiring
fidelity until his death and merited an abundant increase of
grace and love for God. Afterwards, when he had perfectly *put
on Christ* (Gal. 3:27), he used to say that even while he was in
secular attire, he could scarcely ever hear any mention of the
love of God without being deeply moved in his heart.[7]

His gentleness, his refined manners, his patience, his
superhuman affability, his generosity beyond his means,
marked him as a young man of flourishing natural disposition.
This seemed to be a prelude to the even greater abundance of
God's blessings that would be showered on him in the future.
Indeed a certain man of Assisi, an exceptionally simple fellow

---

5. Ecclus. 31:8.
6. The major source of this paragraph is the *Vita prima S. Francisci* of Thomas of Celano,
1, with phrases taken also from 3 and *Celano's Vita secunda S. Francisci*, 7. Throughout we will
indicate the major and minor sources of Bonaventure's text with the abbreviations: I C, II C,
III C and Jul. for respectively Celano's *Vita prima*, *Vita secunda* and *Tractatus de miraculis*, and
the *Vita S. Francisci* of Julian of Speyer. Related sources from which Bonaventure did not draw
verbatim are indicated by *cf.*; for example, cf. here I C 23; II C 102.
7. Major sources: I C 17; II C 196; minor sources: I C 22; II C 5.

who, it is believed, was inspired by God, whenever he chanced to meet Francis going through the town, used to take off his cloak and spread it under his feet saying that Francis deserved every sign of respect since he was destined to do great things in the near future and would be magnificently honored by the entire body of the faithful.[8]

2. Up to this time, however, Francis was ignorant of God's plan for him. He was distracted by the external affairs of his father's business and drawn down toward earthly things by the corruption of human nature. As a result, he had not yet learned how to contemplate the things of heaven nor had he acquired a taste for the things of God. Since *affliction can enlighten* our spiritual *awareness* (Isa. 28:19), *the hand of the Lord came upon him* (Ezech. 1:3), *and the right hand of God effected a change in him* (Ps. 76:11). God afflicted his body with a prolonged illness in order to prepare his soul for the anointing of the Holy Spirit. After his strength was restored, when he had dressed as usual in his fine clothes, he met a certain knight who was of noble birth, but poor and badly clothed. Moved to compassion for his poverty, Francis took off his own garments and clothed the man on the spot. At one and the same time he fulfilled the two-fold duty of covering over the embarrassment of a noble knight and relieving the poverty of a poor man.[9]

3. The following night, when he had fallen asleep, God in his goodness showed him a large and splendid palace full of military weapons emblazoned with the insignia of Christ's cross. Thus God vividly indicated that the compassion he had exhibited toward the poor knight for love of the supreme King would be repaid with an incomparable reward. And so when Francis asked to whom these belonged, he received an answer from heaven that all these things were for him and his knights. When he awoke in the morning, he judged the strange vision to be an indication that he would have great prosperity; for he had

---

8. This incident is not found in Celano or Julian.
9. Major source: II C 5; minor sources: II C 4; I C 2; Jul. 2; I C 3.

no experience in interpreting divine mysteries nor did he know how to pass through visible images to grasp the invisible truth beyond. Therefore, still ignorant of God's plan, he decided to join a certain count in Apulia, hoping in his service to obtain the glory of knighthood, as his vision seemed to foretell.

He set out on his journey shortly afterwards; but when he had gone as far as the next town, he heard during the night the Lord address him in a familiar way, saying: "Francis, who can do more for you, a lord or a servant, a rich man or a poor man?" When Francis replied that a lord and a rich man could do more, he was at once asked: "Why, then, are you abandoning the Lord for a servant and the rich God for a poor man?" And Francis replied: *"Lord, what will you have me do?"* (Acts 9:6). *And the Lord answered him: "Return to your own land* (Gen. 32:9), because the vision which you have seen foretells a spiritual outcome which will be accomplished in you not by human but by divine planning." *In the morning* (John 21:4), then, he returned in haste to Assisi, joyous and free of care; already a model of obedience, he awaited the Lord's will.[10]

4. From that time on he withdrew from the bustle of public business and devoutly begged God in his goodness to show him what he should do. The flame of heavenly desire was fanned in him by his frequent prayer, and his desire for his heavenly home led him to *despise as nothing* (Cant. 8:7) all earthly things. He realized that he had found a *hidden treasure*, and like the wise merchant he planned *to sell all he had* and to buy the *pearl he had found* (Matt. 13:44-46). Nevertheless, how he should do this, he did not yet know; but it was being suggested to him inwardly that to be a spiritual merchant one must begin with contempt for the world and to be a knight of Christ one must begin with victory over one's self.[11]

5. One day while he was riding on horseback through the plain that lies below the town of Assisi, he came upon a leper.

---

10. Major sources: I C 5; II C 6; minor sources: I C 17; Jul. 3.
11. Major source: I C 6; minor source: Jul. 3.

This unforeseen encounter struck him with horror. But he recalled his resolution to be perfect and remembered that he must first conquer himself if he wanted to become a knight of Christ.[12] He slipped off his horse and ran to kiss the man. When the leper put out his hand as if to receive some alms, Francis gave him money and a kiss. Immediately mounting his horse, Francis looked all around; but although the open plain stretched clear in all directions, he could not see the leper anywhere. Filled with wonder and joy, he began devoutly to sing God's praises, resolving from this always to strive to do greater things in the future.[13]

After that he began to seek out solitary places, well suited for sorrow; and there he prayed incessantly with *unutterable groanings* (Rom. 8:26). After long and urgent prayer, he merited to be heard by the Lord. One day while he was praying in such a secluded spot and became totally absorbed in God through his extreme fervor, Jesus Christ appeared to him fastened to the cross. Francis's *soul melted* (Cant. 5:6) at the sight, and the memory of Christ's passion was so impressed on the innermost recesses of his heart that from that hour, whenever Christ's crucifixion came to his mind, he could scarcely contain his tears and sighs, as he later revealed to his companions when he was approaching the end of his life. Through this the man of God understood as addressed to himself the Gospel text: *If you wish to come after me, deny yourself and take up your cross and follow me* (Matt. 16:24).[14]

6. From that time on he clothed himself with a spirit of poverty, a sense of humility and a feeling of intimate devotion. Formerly he used to be horrified not only by close dealing with lepers but by their very sight, even from a distance; but now he

---

12. Cf. 2 Tim. 2:3.
13. Major source: II C 9; minor source: I C 16.
14. Major source II C 10-11; minor sources: II C 9; III C 2. In the present account Bonaventure uses phrases from Celano's version of the vision at San Damiano, II C 10-11, although this is a different incident. Cf. II, 1, p. 191.

rendered humble service to the lepers with human concern and devoted kindness in order that he might completely despise himself, because of Christ crucified, who according to the text of the prophet was despised *as a leper* (Isa. 53:3). He visited their houses frequently, generously distributed alms to them and with great compassion kissed their hands and their mouths.[15]

To beggars he wished to give not only his possessions but his very self. At times he took off his clothes, at times unstitched them, at times ripped them in pieces, in order to give them to beggars, when he had nothing else at hand. He came to the assistance of poor priests, reverently and devoutly, especially in adorning the altar. In this way he became a participator in the divine worship, while supplying the needs of its celebrants. During this period of time he made a pilgrimage to the shrine of St. Peter, where he saw a large number of the poor before the entrance of the church. Led partly by the sweetness of his devotion, partly by the love of poverty, he gave his own clothes to one of the neediest among them. Then he dressed in the poor man's rags and spent that day in the midst of the poor with an unaccustomed joy of spirit. This he did in order to spurn worldly glory and, by ascending in stages, to arrive at the perfection of the Gospel.[16]

He paid great attention
to the mortification of the flesh
so that he might carry externally in his body
the cross of Christ
which he carried internally in his heart.
Francis, the man of God,
did all these things
when he was not yet withdrawn
from the dress and life of the world.

---

15. Major sources: I C 17; II C 9; minor source: Jul. 12.
16. Major source: II C 8; minor source: I C 16.

CHAPTER TWO

ON
HIS PERFECT CONVERSION
TO GOD
AND HIS RESTORATION
OF THREE CHURCHES

1. Francis,
the servant of the Most High,
had no other teacher in these matters
except Christ,
whose kindness was shown once more
by visiting him with the sweetness of grace.

One day when Francis *went out to meditate in the fields* (Gen. 24:63), he walked beside the church of San Damiano which was threatening to collapse because of extreme age. Inspired by the Spirit, he went inside to pray. Prostrate before an image of the Crucified, he was filled with no little consolation as he prayed. While his tear-filled eyes were gazing at the Lord's cross, he heard with his bodily ears a voice coming from the cross, telling him three times: "Francis, go and repair my house which, as you see, is falling completely into ruin."

Trembling with fear, Francis was amazed at the sound of this astonishing voice, since he was alone in the church; and as he received in his heart the power of the divine words, he fell into a state of ecstasy. Returning finally to his senses, he prepared to obey, gathering himself together to carry out the command of repairing the church materially, although the principal intention of the words referred to that Church which *Christ purchased with his own blood* (Acts 20:28), as the Holy

Spirit taught him and as he himself later disclosed to the friars.[1]

He rose then, made the sign of the cross, and taking some cloth to sell, hurried off to the town called Foligno. There he sold all he had brought with him, and, lucky merchant that he was, even sold the horse he was riding. Returning to Assisi, he reverently entered the church which he had been commanded to repair. When he found the poor priest there, he greeted him with fitting reverence, offered him money for the repairs on the church and for the poor, and humbly requested that the priest allow him to stay with him for a time. The priest agreed to his staying there but would not accept the money out of fear of his parents. True despiser of money that he was, Francis threw it on a window sill, valuing it no more than if it were dust.[2]

2. When his father learned that the servant of God was staying with this priest, he was greatly disturbed and ran to the place. But Francis, upon hearing about the threats of those who were pursuing him and having a premonition that they were approaching, wished to *give place to wrath* (Rom. 12:19), and hid himself—being still untrained as an athlete of Christ—in a secret pit. There he remained in hiding for some days, imploring the Lord incessantly with a flood of tears to *deliver him from the hands of those who were persecuting his soul* (Ps. 30:16; 108:31; 141:7) and in his kindness to bring to realization the pious desires he had inspired. He was then filled with excessive joy and began to accuse himself of cowardice. He cast aside his fear, left the pit and took the road to the town of Assisi. When the townspeople saw his unkempt face and his changed mentality, they thought that he had gone out of his senses. They threw filth from the streets and stones at him, shouting insults at him, as if he were insane and out of his mind. But the Lord's servant passed through it as if he were deaf to it all, unbroken and unchanged by any of these insults. When his father heard

---
1. Major source: II C 10; minor sources: I C 8; II C 9; III C 2; II C 11.
2. Major source: I C 8-9; minor source: Jul. 6.

the shouting, he ran to him at once, not to save him but to destroy him. Casting aside all compassion, he dragged him home, tormenting him first with words, then with blows and chains. But this made Francis all the more eager and stronger to carry out what he had begun, as he recalled the words of the Gospel: *Blessed are they who suffer persecution for justice' sake, for theirs is the kingdom of heaven* (Matt. 5:10).[3]

3. After a little while, when his father went out of the country, his mother, who did not approve what her husband had done and had no hope of being able to soften her son's inflexible constancy, released him from his chains and permitted him to go away. He gave thanks to Almighty God and went back to the place where he had been before. Returning and not finding him at home, his father violently reproached his wife and in rage ran to that place. If he could not bring Francis back home, he would at least drive him out of the district. But strengthened by God, Francis went out on his own accord to meet his furious father, calling out in a clear voice that he cared nothing for his chains and blows. Besides, he stated that he would gladly undergo any evil for the name of Christ. When his father, therefore, saw that he could not bring him around, he turned his attention to getting his money back. When he finally found it thrown on the window sill, his rage was mitigated a little, and the thirst of his avarice was somewhat alleviated by the draught of money.[4]

4. Thereupon his carnally minded father led this child of grace, now stripped of his money, before the bishop of the town. He wanted to have Francis renounce into his hands his family possessions and return everything he had. A true lover of poverty, Francis showed himself eager to comply; he went before the bishop without delaying or hesitating. He did not wait for any words nor did he speak any, but immediately took off his clothes and gave them back to his father. Then it was

---

3. Major source: I C 10-12; minor source: Jul. 8.
4. Major source: I C 13-14; minor source: Jul. 8.

discovered that the man of God had a hairshirt next to his skin under his fine clothes. Moreover, drunk with remarkable fervor, he even took off his underwear, stripping himself completely naked before all. He said to his father: "Until now I have called you father here on earth, but now I can say without reservation, *Our Father who art in heaven* (Matt. 6:9), since I have placed all my treasure and all my hope in him." When the bishop saw this, he was amazed at such intense fervor in the man of God. He immediately stood up and in tears drew Francis into his arms, covering him with the mantle he was wearing, like the pious and good man that he was. He bade his servants give Francis something to cover his body. They brought him a poor, cheap cloak of a farmer who worked for the bishop. Francis accepted it gratefully and with his own hand marked a cross on it with a piece of chalk, thus designating it as the covering of a crucified man and a half-naked beggar.

Thus the servant of the Most High King
was left naked
so that he might follow
his naked crucified Lord, whom he loved.
Thus the cross strengthened him
to entrust his soul
to the wood of salvation
that would save him from the shipwreck of the world.[5]

5. Released now from the chains of all earthly desires, this despiser of the world left the town and in a carefree mood sought out a hidden place of solitude where alone and in silence he could hear the secrets God would convey to him. While Francis, the man of God, was making his way through a certain forest, merrily singing praises to the Lord in the French lan-

5. Cf. Wisd. 14:1-7. Major sources: I C 15; II C 12; minor sources: I C 13; II C 3; Jul. 10. Cf. II C 214; on the theme of nakedness, cf. XIV, 3-4, pp. 317-318.

guage, robbers suddenly rushed upon him from an ambush. When they asked in a brutal way who he was, the man of God, filled with confidence, replied with these prophetic words: "I am the herald of the great King." But they struck him and hurled him into a ditch filled with snow, saying: "Lie there, you hick herald of God!" When they went away, he jumped out of the ditch, and brimming over with joy, in a loud voice began to make the forest resound with the praises of the Creator of all.[6]

6. Coming to a certain neighboring monastery, he asked for alms like a beggar and received it—unrecognized and subjected to contempt. Setting out from there, he came to Gubbio, where he was recognized and welcomed by a former friend and given a poor little tunic, like one of Christ's little poor. From there the lover of complete humility went to the lepers and lived with them, serving them all most diligently for God's sake. He washed their feet, bandaged their ulcers, drew the pus from their wounds and washed out the diseased matter; he even kissed their ulcerous wounds out of his remarkable devotion, he who was soon to be a physician of the Gospel.[7] As a result, he received such power from the Lord that he had miraculous effectiveness in healing spiritual and physical illnesses. I will cite one case among many, which occurred after the fame of the man of God became more widely known. There was a man in the vicinity of Spoleto whose mouth and cheek were being eaten away by a certain horrible disease. He could not be helped by any medical treatment and went on a pilgrimage to implore the intercession of the holy apostles. On his way back from visiting their shrines, he happened to meet God's servant. When out of devotion he wanted to kiss Francis's footprints, that humble man, refusing to allow it, kissed the mouth of the one who wished to kiss his feet. In his remarkable compassion Francis, the servant of lepers, touched

---

6. Major source: I C 16; minor source: I C 91.
7. Cf. Luke 10:30-37. Major source: I C 16-17.

that horrible sore with his holy mouth, and suddenly every sign of the disease vanished and the sick man recovered the health he longed for. I do not know which of these we should admire more: the depth of his humility in such a compassionate kiss or his extraordinary power in such an amazing miracle.[8]

7. Grounded now in the humility of Christ, Francis recalled to mind the command enjoined upon him from the cross, to repair the church of San Damiano. As a truly obedient man, he returned to Assisi to obey the divine command at least by begging aid. Putting aside all embarrassment out of love of Christ poor and crucified, he begged from those among whom he used to show his wealth, and he loaded stones upon his body that was weakened by fasting. With God's help and the devoted assistance of the citizens, he completed repairs on the church. After this work, to prevent his body from becoming sluggish with laziness, he set himself to repair a certain church of St. Peter some distance from the town, because of the special devotion which, in his pure and sincere faith, he bore to the prince of the apostles.[9]

8. When he finally completed this church, he came to a place called the Portiuncula where there was a church dedicated to the Blessed Virgin Mother of God, built in ancient times but now deserted and cared for by no one. When the man of God saw how it was abandoned, he began to live there in order to repair it, moved by the fervent devotion he had toward the Lady of the world. According to the name of the church, which since ancient times was called St. Mary of the Angels, he felt that angels often visited there. So he took up residence there out of his reverence for the angels and his special love for the mother of Christ. The holy man loved this spot more than any other in the world. For here he began humbly, here he progressed steadily, here he ended happily. At his death he commended it to the friars as a place most dear to the Virgin.

---

8. This incident is not found in Celano or Julian.
9. Major sources: II C 13-14; I C 21.

Before his conversion, a certain friar, devoted to God, had a vision about this church which is worth relating. He saw a large group of men who had been struck blind, kneeling in a circle about this church, their faces turned to heaven. With uplifted hands and tearful voices, they were crying out to God, begging that he have pity on them and grant them sight. And behold, a splendrous light came down from heaven and spread over them all, giving to each his sight and the health they had longed for.

This is the place
where the Order of Friars Minor was begun
by Saint Francis
under the inspiration of divine revelation.
For at the bidding of divine providence
which guided Christ's servant in everything,
he physically repaired three churches
before he began the Order
and preached the Gospel.
This he did
not only
to ascend in an orderly progression
from the sensible realm to the intelligible,
from the lesser to the greater,
but also
to symbolize prophetically
in external actions perceived by the senses
what he would do in the future.
For like the three buildings he repaired,
so Christ's Church—
with its threefold victorious army
of those who are to be saved—[10]
was to be renewed under his leadership
in three ways:

10. This is an allusion to the three orders which Francis founded: the first order of Friars Minor; the second of Poor Clares; and the Third Order of those living in the world.

by the structure, rule and teaching
which he would provide.
And now we see
that this prophecy has been fulfilled.[11]

---

11. Major source: I C 21; II C 18-20; I C 37; minor source: Jul. 14.

CHAPTER THREE

ON
THE FOUNDATION
OF THE ORDER
AND THE APPROVAL
OF THE RULE

1. While her servant Francis
was living in the church of the Virgin Mother of God,
he prayed to her
who had conceived *the Word full of grace and truth*,[1]
imploring her with continuous sighs
to become his advocate.
Through the merits
of the Mother of Mercy,
he conceived and brought to birth
the spirit of the truth of the Gospel.

One day when he was devoutly hearing a Mass of the Apostles, the Gospel was read in which Christ sends forth his disciples to preach and explains to them the way of life according to the Gospel: that they *should not keep gold or silver or money in their belts, nor have a wallet for their journey, nor two tunics, nor shoes, nor staff* (Matt. 10:9). When he heard this, he grasped its meaning and committed it to memory. This lover of apostolic poverty was then filled with an indescribable joy and said: "This is what I want; this is what I long for with all my heart." He immediately took off his shoes from his feet, put aside his staff, cast away his wallet and money as if accursed, was content with one tunic and exchanged his leather belt for a piece of rope. He directed all his heart's desire to carry out what he had

---

1. John 1:14.

199

heard and to conform in every way to the rule of right living given to the apostles.[2]

2. Under divine inspiration the man of God now began to strive after Gospel perfection and invite others to penance. His words were not empty or joking, but full of the power of the Holy Spirit; they penetrated to the innermost depths of the heart, causing his hearers to be filled with amazement. In all his preaching, he proclaimed peace, saying: *"May the Lord give you peace"* (Matt. 10:12; Luke 10:5), as the greeting to the people at the beginning of his sermon. As he later testified, he had learned this greeting in a revelation from the Lord.[3] Hence, according to the words of a prophet and inspired by the spirit of the prophets, he proclaimed peace, preached salvation and by his salutary warnings united in a bond of true peace many who had previously been in opposition to Christ and far from salvation.[4]

3. When the truth of his simple teaching and his way of life became widely known, certain men began to be inspired to live a life of penance. Leaving everything, they joined him in his way of life and dress. The first among these was Bernard, a venerable man, who was made a *sharer* in a divine *vocation* (Heb. 3:1) and merited to be the firstborn son of our blessed father, both in priority of time and in the gift of holiness. When he discovered for himself the holiness of Christ's servant and decided to despise the world completely after his example, he sought his advice on how to carry this out. On hearing this, God's servant was filled with the consolation of the Holy Spirit over the conception of his first child. "We must ask God's advice about this," he said. In the morning they went to the church of Saint Nicholas, where they said some preliminary prayers; then Francis, who was devoted to the Trinity, opened the book of the Gospel three times, asking God to confirm

---

2. Major source: I C 22; minor sources: I C 21; II C 198; Jul. 15.
3. Cf. *Testamentum*, 5.
4. Cf. Isa. 52:7. Major source: Jul. 16; minor source: I C 23-24.

Bernard's plan with a threefold testimony. The book opened the first time to the text: *If you will be perfect, go, sell* all *that you have*, and *give to the poor* (Matt. 19:21). The second time to the text: *Take nothing on your journey* (Luke 9:3). And the third time to: *If anyone wishes to come after me, let him deny himself and take up his cross and follow me* (Matt. 16:24). "This is our life and our rule," the holy man said, "and the life and the rule of all who wish to join our company. *Go*, then, *if you wish to be perfect* (Matt. 19:21) and carry out what you have heard."[5]

4. Not long afterwards five other men were called by the same Spirit, and the number of Francis's sons reached six. The third among them was the holy father Giles,[6] a man indeed filled with God and worthy of his celebrated reputation. Although he was a simple and unlearned man, he later became famous for his practice of heroic virtue, as God's servant had prophesied, and was raised to the height of exalted contemplation. For through the passage of many years, he strove without ceasing to direct himself toward God; and he was so often rapt into God in ecstasy, as I myself have observed as an eyewitness, that he seemed to live among men more like an angel than a human being.[7]

5. Also at that time a certain priest of the town of Assisi, named Silvester, an upright man, was shown a vision by the Lord which should not be passed over in silence. Reacting in a purely human way, he had developed an abhorrence for the way Francis and his friars were going. But then he was visited by grace from heaven in order to save him from the danger of rash judgment. For he saw in a dream the whole town of Assisi encircled by a *huge dragon* (Dan. 14:22) which threatened to destroy the entire area by its enormous size. Then he saw coming from Francis's mouth a golden cross whose top touched

5. Major source: II C 15; minor sources: Jul. 17; I C 24, 92.
6. He died near Perugia on April 22, 1262, while Bonaventure was writing the present work.
7. Minor source: I C 25.

heaven and whose arms stretched far and wide and seemed to extend to the ends of the world. At the sight of its shining splendor, the foul and hideous dragon was put to flight. When he had seen this vision for the third time and realized that it was a divine revelation, he told it point by point to the man of God and his friars. Not long afterwards he left the world and followed in the footsteps of Christ with such perseverance that his life in the Order confirmed the authenticity of the vision which he had had in the world.[8]

6. On hearing of this vision, the man of God was not carried away by human glory; but recognizing God's goodness in his gifts, was more strongly inspired to put to flight our ancient enemy with his cunning and to preach the glory of the cross of Christ. One day while he was weeping as he *looked back over his past years in bitterness* (Isa. 38:15), the joy of the Holy Spirit came over him and he was assured that all of his sins had been completely forgiven. Then he was rapt in ecstasy and totally absorbed in a wonderful light, his heart was expanded and he clearly saw what would transpire for him and his sons in the future. After this he returned to the friars and said: *"Take strength*, my beloved ones, and *rejoice in the Lord* (Eph. 6:10; Phil. 3:1, 4:4). Do not be sad because you are few in number, nor afraid because of my simplicity or yours. For as the Lord has shown me in truth, God will make us grow into a great multitude and will cause us to expand in countless ways by the grace of his blessing.[9]

7. At the same time, another good man entered the Order, bringing the number of Francis's sons to seven. Then like a devoted father, Francis gathered all his sons around him and explained to them many things concerning the kingdom of God, contempt for the world, the renunciation of their own wills and the mortification of their bodies. Then he disclosed to

8. Major source: II C 109; but the dragon is not found in Celano's account of the vision. On Silvester, cf. VI, 9 and XII, 2, pp. 236, 294.

9. Major source: I C 26-27; minor source: Jul. 18.

them his plan to send them to the four corners of the world. For already the lowly and seemingly *sterile* simplicity of our holy father had *brought to birth* (1 Kings 2:5) seven sons. And now he wished to call all the faithful of the world to repentance and to bring them to birth in Christ the Lord. "Go," said the gentle father to his sons, "proclaim peace to men and *preach repentance for the forgiveness of sins* (Mark 1:4; Luke 3:3). Be patient in trials, watchful in prayer, strenuous in work, moderate in speech, reserved in manner and grateful for favors, because for all this an eternal kingdom is being prepared for you." The friars humbly cast themselves on the ground before God's servant and received the command of obedience in a spirit of joy. Then he said to each one of them individually: *"Cast your care upon the Lord and he will support you"* (Ps. 54:23). This is what he used to say whenever he sent a friar somewhere under obedience.

Francis knew he should give an example to others, and wanted to practice what he preached; so he himself set out in one direction with one of his companions. The remaining six he sent in the other three directions, thus forming the pattern of a cross. After a short time had passed, the loving father longed for the presence of his dear children; and since he could not summon them himself, he prayed that this should be done by God, who *gathers together the dispersed of Israel* (Ps. 146:2). It happened that, just as he wished, they all came together shortly afterwards quite unexpectedly and much to their surprise, through the kindness of divine providence, without being summoned in any human way. During those days four upright men joined them, increasing their number to twelve.[10]

8. Seeing that the number of friars was gradually increasing, Christ's servant wrote in simple words a rule of life for himself and his friars. He based it on the unshakable foundation of the observance of the Gospel and added a few other

---

10. Major source: I C 29-30; minor source: Jul. 19-20.

things that seemed necessary for their way of life in common. He very much wanted to have what he had written approved by the Supreme Pontiff; so he decided to go with his band of simple men before the presence of the Apostolic See, placing his trust solely in God's guidance. From on high God looked with favor upon his desire and comforted the souls of his companions who were frightened at the thought of their simplicity, by showing him the following vision. It seemed to him that he was walking along a certain road beside which stood a very tall tree. Drawing near, he stood under it and marveled at its height. Suddenly he was lifted up by divine power to such a height that he was able to touch the top of the tree and very easily bend it down to the ground. Filled with God, he realized that the vision was a prophecy of how the Apostolic See, with all its dignity, would show him condescension; and he was overjoyed. He encouraged his friars in the Lord and set out with them on the journey.[11]

9. When he arrived in Rome, he was led into the presence of the Supreme Pontiff. The Vicar of Christ was in the Lateran Palace, walking in a place called the Hall of the Mirror, occupied in deep meditation. Knowing nothing of Christ's servant, he sent him away indignantly. Francis left humbly, and the next night God showed the Supreme Pontiff the following vision. He saw a palm tree sprout between his feet and grow gradually until it became a beautiful tree. As he wondered what this vision might mean, the divine light impressed upon the mind of the Vicar of Christ that this palm tree symbolized the poor man whom he had sent away the previous day. The next morning he commanded his servants to search the city for the poor man. When they found him near the Lateran at St. Anthony's hospice, he ordered him brought to his presence without delay.[12]

---

11. Major source: I C 32-33; minor source: Jul. 21.
12. The above paragraph, except for the first sentence, was added to Bonaventure's text by Jerome of Ascoli, Minister General of the Order, 1274-1279, and later Pope Nicholas IV. He learned of it from Cardinal Riccardo degli Annibaldi, a relative of Innocent III; cf. *Chron. 24 General.* in *Analecta franciscana*, III, 365.

When he was led before the Supreme Pontiff, Francis explained his plan, humbly and urgently imploring him to approve the rule of life mentioned above. Now the Vicar of Christ, Innocent III, was a man famous for his wisdom; and when he saw in the man of God such remarkable purity and simplicity of heart, such firmness of purpose and such fiery ardor of will, he was inclined to give his assent to the request. Yet he hesitated to do what Christ's little poor man asked because it seemed to some of the cardinals to be something novel and difficult beyond human powers. There was among the cardinals a most venerable man, John of St. Paul, bishop of Sabina, a lover of holiness and helper of Christ's poor. Inspired by the Holy Spirit, he said to the Supreme Pontiff and his brother cardinals: "If we refuse the request of this poor man as novel or too difficult, when all he asks is to be allowed to lead the Gospel life, we must be on our guard lest we commit an offense against Christ's Gospel. For if anyone says that there is something novel or irrational or impossible to observe in this man's desire to live according to the perfection of the Gospel, he is guilty of blasphemy against Christ, the author of the Gospel." At this observation, the successor of the Apostle Peter turned to the poor man of Christ and said: "My son, pray to Christ that he may show us his will through you. When we know this with more certainty, we can give our approval to your pious desires with more assurance."[13]

10. The servant of Almighty God totally gave himself to prayer, and through his devout supplications obtained for himself knowledge of what he should say outwardly and for the pope what he should think inwardly. Francis told the pope a parable, which he had learned from God, about a rich king who voluntarily married a poor but beautiful woman. She bore him children who resembled the king and for this reason could be brought up at his table. Then Francis added by way of interpretation: "The sons and heirs of the eternal King should

---

13. Major source: I C 33, 32; minor sources: Jul. 21; II C 16.

not fear that they will die of hunger. They have been born of a poor mother by the power of the Holy Spirit in the image of Christ the King, and they will be begotten by the spirit of poverty in our poor little Order. For if the King of heaven promises his followers an *eternal kingdom* (2 Pet. 1:11; cf. Matt. 19:28ff.), he will certainly supply them with those things that he gives to the *good and the bad* alike" (Matt. 5:45). When the Vicar of Christ had listened to this parable and its interpretation, he was quite amazed and recognized without the slightest doubt that here Christ had spoken through man. And he affirmed that a vision which he had recently received from heaven through the inspiration of the divine Spirit would be fulfilled in this man. He had seen in a dream, as he recounted, that a little poor man, insignificant and despised, was holding up on his back the Lateran basilica which was about to collapse. "This is certainly the man," he said, "who by his work and teaching will hold up the Church of Christ." Filled with reverence for Francis, he was favorably inclined toward everything he asked and always held Christ's servant in special affection. Then he granted what was requested and promised to grant even more in the future. He approved the rule and gave them a mission to preach penance, and he had small tonsures shaved on the laymen among Francis's companions so that they could freely preach the *word of God* (Luke 11:28).[14]

---

14. Major source: II C 16-17; minor source: Jul. 21.

CHAPTER FOUR

ON
THE PROGRESS OF
THE ORDER UNDER HIS HAND
AND
THE CONFIRMATION OF THE RULE

1. Strengthened by God's grace and the pope's approval, Francis with great confidence took the road toward the valley of Spoleto, where he intended to preach and to live the Gospel of Christ. On the way he discussed with his companions how they should sincerely keep the rule which they had taken upon themselves, how they should proceed in all *holiness* and *justice before* God (Luke 1:75), how they should improve themselves and be an example for others. It was already late in the day as they continued their long discussion. Fatigued from their prolonged activity and feeling hungry, they stopped at an isolated spot. When there seemed to be no way for them to get the food they needed, God's providence immediately came to their aid. For suddenly a man appeared carrying bread in his hand, which he gave to Christ's little poor and then suddenly disappeared. They had no idea where he came from or where he went. From this the poor friars realized that while in the company of the man of God they would be given assistance from heaven and so they were refreshed more by the gift of God's generosity than by the food they had received for their bodies. Moreover, filled with divine consolation, they firmly resolved and irrevocably committed themselves never to turn back from the promise they had made to holy poverty, in spite of any pressure from lack of food or other trials.[1]

2. When they arrived at the valley of Spoleto full of their

---

1. Major source: I C 34; minor sources: II C 17; Jul. 22; I C 35.

holy plans, they began to discuss whether they should live among the people or go off into places of solitude. But Christ's servant Francis did not place his trust in his own efforts or those of his companions; rather he sought to discern God's will in this matter by earnest prayer. Then, enlightened by a revelation from heaven, he realized that he was sent by the Lord to win for Christ the souls which the devil was trying to snatch away. Therefore he chose to live for all men rather than for himself alone, drawn by the example of the one who deigned *to die for all* (2 Cor. 5:15).[2]

3. Then with his companions the man of God took shelter in an abandoned hut near the town of Assisi,[3] where they barely subsisted according to the rule of holy poverty in much labor and want, drawing their nourishment more from *the bread of tears* (Ps. 79:6) than from the delights of bodily food. They spent their time there praying incessantly, devoting themselves to mental rather than vocal prayer because they did not yet have liturgical books from which to chant the canonical hours. In place of these they had the book of Christ's cross which they studied continually day and night, taught by the example and words of their father who spoke to them constantly about the cross of Christ. When the friars asked him to teach them to pray, he said: "When you pray, say *'Our Father . . .'* (Luke 11:2) and 'We adore you, O Christ, in all your churches in the whole world and we bless you because by your holy cross you have redeemed the world.'" He also taught them to praise God in all creatures and from all creatures, to honor priests with special reverence and to firmly believe and simply profess the true faith as held and taught by the Holy Roman Church. The friars followed his teaching in every detail; and before every church and crucifix which they saw even from a distance, they

---

2. Major source: I C 35; minor source: Jul. 23.
3. At Rivo Torto, on the road between Spoleto and Perugia.

humbly prostrated themselves and prayed according to the form he had taught them.[4]

4. While the friars were still staying in the place already mentioned, one Saturday the holy man went to the town of Assisi to preach in the cathedral on Sunday morning, as was his custom. The devoted man of God spent the night in prayer, as he usually did, in a hut situated in the garden of the canons, separated physically from the friars. At about midnight while some of the friars were resting and others continued to pray, behold, a fiery chariot of wonderful brilliance entered through the door of the house and turned here and there three times through the house. A globe of light rested above it which shone like the sun and lit up the night. Those who were awake were dumbfounded, and those who were sleeping woke up terrified. They felt the brightness light up their hearts no less than their bodies, and the conscience of each was laid bare to the others by the strength of that marvelous light. As they looked into each other's hearts, they all realized together that their holy father, who was *absent physically*, was *present in spirit* (1 Cor. 5:3), transfigured in this image. And they realized that by supernatural power the Lord had shown him to them in this glowing *chariot of fire* (4 Kings 2:11), radiant with heavenly splendor and inflamed with burning ardor so that they might follow him like *true Israelites* (John 1:47). Like a second Elijah, God had made him *a chariot and charioteer* for spiritual men (4 Kings 2:12). Certainly we can believe that God *opened the eyes* (John 9:32) of these simple men at the prayers of Francis so that they might see *the wonders of God* (Acts 2:11; Ecclus. 18:5) just as he had once *opened the eyes* of the servant of Elisha so that he could see *the mountain full of horses and chariots of fire round about the prophet* (4 Kings 6:17). When the holy man returned to the friars, he

---

4. Major sources: I C 42; I C 45; minor sources: I C 40; II C 91; I C 45; Jul. 27; I C 80-81; I C 62, 41; Jul. 27. Cf. *Testamentum*, 1.

began to probe the secrets of their consciences, to draw courage for them from this wonderful vision and to make many predictions about the growth of the Order. When he disclosed many things that transcended human understanding, the friars realized the *Spirit of the Lord had come to rest* (Isa. 11:2) upon him in such fulness that it was absolutely safe for them to follow his life and teaching.[5]

5. After this, under the guidance of heavenly grace, the shepherd Francis led the *little flock* (Luke 12:32) of twelve friars to St. Mary of the Portiuncula, so that there, where the Order of Friars Minor had had its beginning by the merits of the mother of God, it might also begin to grow with her assistance. There, also, he became a herald of the Gospel. He went *about the towns and villages proclaiming the kingdom of God not in words taught by human wisdom, but in the power of the Spirit* (Matt. 9:35; Luke 9:60; 1 Cor. 2:4, 13). To those who saw him, he seemed to be a man of another world as, with his mind and face always turned toward heaven, he tried to draw them all on high. As a result, the vineyard of Christ began to sprout shoots with the fragrance of the Lord and to bring forth abundant fruit, producing blossoms *of sweetness, of honor and goodness* (Ecclus. 24:23).[6]

6. Set on fire by the fervor of his preaching, a great number of people bound themselves by new laws of penance according to the rule which they received from the man of God. Christ's servant decided to name this way of life the Order of the Brothers of Penance. As the road of penance is common to all who are striving toward heaven, so this way of life admits clerics and laity, single and married of both sexes.[7] How meritorious it is before God is clear from the numerous miracles performed by some of its members. Young women,

---

5. Major source: I C 47; minor sources: Jul. 29; I C 48.
6. Major source: I C 36-37; minor source: Jul. 21.
7. A reference to the emergence of the Third Order; cf. II, 8, n. 10, p. 197; also I C 37 and Jul. 23.

too, were drawn to perpetual celibacy, among whom was the maiden Clare, who was especially dear to God.

She was the first tender sprout
among these
and gave forth fragrance
like a bright white flower
that blossoms in springtime,
and she shone
like a radiant star.
Now she is glorified
in heaven
and venerated in a fitting manner
by the Church on earth,
she who was the daughter in Christ
of our holy father Francis, the little poor man,
and the mother of the Poor Clares.[8]

7. Many people also, not only stirred by devotion but inflamed by a desire for the perfection of Christ, despised the emptiness of worldly things and followed in the footsteps of Francis. Their numbers increased daily and quickly reached *to the ends of the earth.*[9]

Holy poverty,
which was all they had to meet their expenses,
made them prompt for obedience,
robust for work and free for travel.
Because they possessed nothing that belonged to the world,
they were attached to nothing and feared to lose nothing.
They were safe everywhere,
not held back by fear, nor distracted by care;

---

8. The Latin term is *Pauperes Dominae*, Poor Ladies, the official name of the Second Order; we have translated it here by the popular title *Poor Clares*. On Clare and her nuns, cf. I C 18-20 and Jul. 13; also XII, 2, p. 294. Minor sources for no. 6 are Jul. 23 and II C 109.
9. Ps. 18:15.

they lived with untroubled minds,
and, without any anxiety,
looked forward to the morrow
and to finding a lodging for the night.
In different parts of the world
many insults were hurled against them
as persons unknown and despised.
But their love of the Gospel of Christ
had made them so patient
that they sought
to be where they would suffer physical persecution
rather than where their holiness was recognized
and they could glory in worldly honor.
Their very poverty
seemed to them overflowing abundance
since, according to the advice of the wise man,
they were content *with a minimum
as if it were much.* [10]

When some of the friars went to the lands of the infidels, a
certain Saracen, moved by compassion, once offered them
money for the food they needed. When they refused to accept
it the man was amazed, seeing that they were without means.
Realizing they did not want to possess money because they had
become poor out of love of God, he felt so attracted to them
that he offered to *provide for their needs* (3 Kings 4:7) as long as he
had something to give.

O inestimable value of poverty,
whose marvelous power moved
the fierce heart of a barbarian
to such sweet compassion!
What a horrible and unspeakable crime

---

10. Ecclus. 29:30. Major source: I C 39-40; minor sources: I C 37, 41.

212

> that a Christian should *trample underfoot*
> this noble *pearl*[11]
> which a Saracen held in such veneration![12]

8. At that time a certain religious of the Order of the Crosiers,[13] Morico by name, was suffering from such a grave and prolonged illness in a hospital near Assisi that the doctors had already despaired of his life. In his need, he turned to the man of God, urgently entreating him through a messenger to intercede for him before the Lord. Our blessed father kindly consented and said a prayer for him. Then he took some bread crumbs and mixed them with oil taken from a lamp that burned before the altar of the Virgin. He made a kind of pill out of them and sent it to the sick man through the hands of the friars, saying: "Take this medicine to our brother Morico. By means of it Christ's power will not only restore him to full health but will make him a sturdy warrior and enlist him in our forces permanently." When the sick man took the medicine which had been prepared under the inspiration of the Holy Spirit, he was cured immediately. God gave him such strength of mind and body that when a little later he entered the holy man's Order, he wore only a single tunic, under which for a long time he wore a hairshirt next to his skin. He was satisfied with uncooked food such as herbs, vegetables and fruit and for many years never tasted bread or wine, yet remained strong and in good health.

9. As the merits of virtue increased in Christ's little poor men, their good reputation spread all about and attracted a great number of people from different parts of the world to come and see our holy father. Among them was a spirited

---

11. Matt. 7:6.

12. This incident is not found in Celano or Julian.

13. The Latin term is *Ordo Cruciferorum*, the title of the religious order known as the Crosiers or Religious of the Holy Cross. This incident is not found in Celano or Julian.

composer of worldly songs, who had been crowned by the Emperor[14] and was therefore called the King of Verses. He decided to visit the man of God, who despised the things of the world. When he found him preaching in a monastery in the village of San Severino, *the hand of the Lord came upon* him (Ezech. 1:3); and he saw Francis, the preacher of Christ's cross, signed with a cross, in the form of two flashing swords, one of which stretched from his head to his feet, the other crossed his chest from one hand to the other. He did not know Christ's servant by sight, but quickly recognized him once he had been pointed out by so great a miracle. Dumbfounded at the vision, he immediately began to resolve to do better. He was struck in his conscience by the power of the saint's words, as if pierced by a spiritual sword coming from his mouth. He completely despised his worldly popularity and joined our blessed father by making a religious profession. When the holy man saw that he had been completely converted from the restlessness of the world to the peace of Christ, he called him Brother Pacificus. Afterwards he advanced in holiness; and before he went to France as provincial minister—indeed he was the first to hold that office there[15]—he merited to see a second vision: a great Tau on Francis's forehead, which shone in a variety of colors and caused his face to glow with wonderful beauty. The holy man venerated this symbol with great affection, often spoke highly of it and signed it with his own hand at the end of the letters which he sent, as if his whole desire were *to mark with a Tau the foreheads of men* who have been truly converted to Jesus Christ and *who moan and grieve*, according to the text of the Prophet (Ezech. 9:4).[16]

10. As the number of friars increased with the passing of time, Francis began to summon them, like a solicitous

---

14. Either Frederick Barbarossa or Henry VI; certainly not Frederick II, who did not bear the imperial title until 1220.

15. He held this office from 1217 to 1223 or 1224.

16. Major source: II C 106; on the sign Tau, cf. prol., 2, n. 27, p. 182; also p. 287, n. 17.

shepherd, to a general chapter at St. Mary of the Portiuncula, so as to allot to each a portion of obedience *in the land of their poverty*, according to *the measuring-cord of divine distribution* (Gen. 41:52; Ps. 77:54). Although there was a complete lack of all necessities and sometimes the friars numbered more than five thousand, nevertheless with the assistance of divine mercy, they had adequate food, enjoyed physical health and over-flowed with spiritual joy.

Francis could not be physically present at the provincial chapters, but he was present in spirit through his solicitous care in governing, his insistent prayers and his effective bless-ing. Occasionally, however, he did appear visibly by God's miraculous power. For at the chapter of Arles that outstanding preacher Anthony,[17] who is now a glorious confessor of Christ, was preaching to the friars on the inscription on the cross: *Jesus of Nazareth, King of the Jews* (John 19:19). A certain friar of proven virtue, Monaldus by name, was moved by divine inspi-ration to look toward the door of the chapter and saw with his bodily eyes blessed Francis lifted up in midair, his arms ex-tended as though on a cross, and blessing the friars. All the friars felt themselves filled with such unusual inner consolation that it was clear the Spirit *was giving* them certain *testimony* (John 1:7) that their holy father had been really present. In addition to these evident signs, it was later confirmed by the external testimony of the words of the holy father himself. We can indeed believe that the almighty power of God, which allowed the holy bishop Ambrose to attend the burial of the glorious St. Martin and to honor that holy prelate with his holy presence, also allowed his servant Francis to be present at the preaching of his true herald Anthony in order to attest to the truth of his words, especially those concerning Christ's cross, which Francis both carried and served.[18]

---

17. This is Anthony of Padua, the widely venerated saint of the early Franciscan Order.
18. Major source: I C 48.

11. When the Order was already widely spread and Francis was considering having the rule which had been approved by Innocent permanently confirmed by his successor Honorius, he was advised by the following revelation from God. It seemed to him that he had to gather some tiny bread crumbs from the ground and distribute them to many hungry friars who were standing around him. He was afraid to distribute such small crumbs lest they should fall from his hands. Then a voice spoke to him from above: "Francis, make one host out of all these crumbs and give it to those who want to eat it." When he did this, whoever did not receive it devoutly or despised the gift they had received suddenly appeared covered with leprosy. In the morning the holy man told all this to his companions, regretting that he did not understand the meaning of the vision. On the following day, while he was keeping watch in prayer, he heard a voice coming down from heaven, saying: "Francis the crumbs of last night are the words of the Gospel, the host is the rule and the leprosy is wickedness."[19]

Since the profusion of texts from the Gospel had lengthened the rule unduly, Francis wished to condense it into a more concentrated form as the vision he was shown had commanded. Led by the Holy Spirit, he went up to a certain mountain with two of his companions where he fasted on bread and water and dictated the rule as the Holy Spirit suggested to him in prayer. When he came down from the mountain, he gave the rule to his vicar to keep.[20] But after a few days had elapsed, the vicar claimed that he had lost it by an oversight. A second time the holy man went off to a place of solitude and at once rewrote the rule just as before, as if he were taking the words from the mouth of God. And he obtained confirmation for it, as he had desired, from the Lord Pope Honorius, in the

---

19. Major source: II C 209.
20. Brother Elias of Cortona, the controversial vicar to Francis and Minister General of the Order.

eighth year of his pontificate.[21]

Fervently exhorting the friars
to observe this rule,
Francis used to say
that nothing of what he had placed there
came from his own efforts
but that he dictated everything
just as it had been revealed by God.[22]
To confirm this with greater certainty
by God's own testimony,
when only a few days had passed,[23]
the stigmata of our Lord Jesus
were imprinted upon him
by the finger of the *living God*,[24]
as the bull or seal
of Christ, the Supreme Pontiff,
for the complete confirmation of the rule
and approval of its author,
as will be described below,
after our exposition of his virtues.[25]

---

21. Honorius III was pope from 1216-1227; he confirmed the Second Rule of Francis in a bull dated November 29, 1223. This incident on the writing of the rule and its approbation by Honorius III are not found in Celano or Julian.

22. Cf. *Testamentum*, 8.

23. Bonaventure uses the expression *paucis diebus*, literally *a few days*; but actually eight and a half months separated the approval of the Rule from the impression of the stigma, and presumably the time-lapse between the latter and the composition of the Rule was even longer.

24. Apoc. 7:2.

25. Cf. XIII, 3-8, pp. 305-311.

CHAPTER FIVE

ON
THE AUSTERITY OF HIS LIFE
AND
HOW CREATURES PROVIDED HIM
COMFORT

1. When Francis the man of God saw
that many were being inspired
by his example
to carry the cross of Christ with fervent spirit,
he himself like a good leader of Christ's army
was encouraged to reach the palm of victory[1]
through the height of heroic virtue.
He directed his attention to this text of the Apostle:
Those who belong to Christ
have crucified their flesh
with its passions and desires.[2]

In order to carry in his own body the armor of the cross,
he held in check his sensual appetites with such a rigid discipline that he scarcely took what was necessary for the sustenance of nature. He used to say that it would be difficult to
satisfy the needs of the body without giving in to the earth-
bound inclinations of the senses. Therefore when he was in
good health, he scarcely ever allowed himself cooked food; and
on the rare occasions when he did so, he either mixed it with
ashes or made its flavor tasteless, usually by adding water.
About his drinking wine, what shall I say since he would
scarcely drink even enough water when he was burning with
thirst? He discovered more effective methods of abstinence and

---

1. Cf. Apoc. 7:9.
2. Gal. 5:24.

218

daily improved in their exercise. Although he had already attained the height of perfection, he used to try new ways of punishing his sensual desires by afflicting his body, as if he were always beginning again.

When he went out among men, he conformed himself to his hosts in the food he ate because of the Gospel text (Luke 10:7).[3] But when he returned home, he kept strictly his sparse and rigid abstinence. Thus he was austere toward himself but considerate toward his neighbor. Making himself obedient to the Gospel of Christ in everything, he gave an edifying example not only when he abstained but also when he ate. More often than not, the bare ground was a bed for his weary body; and he often used to sleep sitting up, with a piece of wood or a stone for a pillow. Clothed in a single poor little tunic, he served the Lord in *cold and nakedness* (2 Cor. 11:27).[4]

2. Once when he was asked how he could protect himself against the bite of the winter's frost with such thin clothing, he answered with a burning spirit: "If we were touched within by the flame of desire for our heavenly home, we would easily endure that exterior cold." In the matter of clothes, he had a horror for softness and loved coarseness, claiming that John the Baptist had been praised by the Lord for this (Matt. 11:8; Luke 7:25). If he felt the softness of a tunic that had been given to him, he used to sew pieces of cord on the inside because he used to say, according to the statement of Truth itself (Matt. 11:8), that we should look for soft clothes not in the huts of the poor but in the palaces of princes. For his own certain experience had taught him that demons were terrified by harshness but were inspired to tempt one more strongly by what is pleasant and soft.

One night, contrary to his custom, he had allowed a feather pillow to be placed under his head because of an illness in his head and eyes. The devil got into it, gave him no rest

---

3. Cf. *Regula I*, c. 9 and *Regula II*, c. 3.
4. Major source: I C 51; minor sources: I C 52; Jul. 31. Cf. II C 12.

until morning and in many ways disturbed him from praying, until finally Francis called a companion and had him take the pillow with the devil in it far away out of his cell. But when the friar went out of the cell with the pillow, he lost the strength and use of his limbs, until at the sound of the holy father's voice, who was aware of this in spirit, his former strength of heart and body was fully restored to him.[5]

3. *He stood* unbending in the discipline with which he *watched over* (Isa. 21:8) himself, and he took the greatest care to preserve purity of soul and body. Around the beginning of his conversion, in wintertime he often plunged into a ditch full of icy water in order to perfectly subjugate the enemy within and preserve the white robe of purity from the flames of sensual pleasure. He used to say that it should be incomparably more tolerable for a spiritual man to endure great cold in his flesh rather than to feel even slightly the heat of carnal lust in his heart.[6]

4. One night when he was praying in his cell at the hermitage of Sarteano, the ancient enemy called him three times: "Francis, Francis, Francis!" When Francis replied and asked what he wanted, he continued deceitfully: "There is no sinner in the world whom God will not forgive if he is converted; but whoever kills himself by harsh penance will never find mercy for all eternity." At once the treachery of the enemy was revealed to the man of God: how the devil was trying to lead him back to lukewarmness. This was shown by what followed. For immediately after this, a temptation of the flesh seized him, inspired by the one *whose breath sets coals afire* (Job 41:12). When that lover of chastity felt it coming, he took off his clothes and began to lash himself very heavily with a cord, saying: "There, Brother Ass, this is how you ought to be treated, to bear the whip like this. The habit serves the religious state and presents a symbol of holiness. A lustful man has no right to steal it. If

---

5. Major source: II C 64.
6. Major source: I C 42; minor source: Jul. 24.

you want to go that way, then go!" Even more inspired by a wonderful fervor of spirit, he opened his cell and went out into the garden and plunged his poor naked body into the deep snow. Then with handfuls of snow he began to form seven snowmen, which he presented to himself, saying to his body: "Look, this larger one is your wife; those four are your two sons and two daughters; the other two are a servant and a maid whom you should have to serve you. Hurry, then, and clothe them since they are dying of cold. But if it is too much for you to care for so many, then take care to serve one Master!" At that the tempter went away conquered, and the holy man returned to his cell in victory. While he froze outwardly for penance's sake, he so quenched the fire of passion within that he hardly felt anything of that sort from that time on. A certain friar who was praying at the time saw in the bright moonlight everything that happened. When the man of God discovered that the friar had seen all of this that night, he gave him an account of the temptation and commanded him to tell no living person what he had seen as long as Francis himself lived.[7]

5. He taught that not only the vices of the flesh should be mortified and fleshly impulses curbed but also that the exterior senses, through which death enters the soul, should be guarded with the greatest diligence. He solicitously commanded the friars to avoid familiarity with women, whether by sight or by conversation, which have often led many to a fall. He affirmed that through this sort of thing a weak spirit is often broken and a strong spirit weakened. He said that it is about as easy for one who has much contact with women—unless he be a man of the most proven virtue—to avoid contamination from them as *to walk in fire and not to burn one's feet* (Prov. 6:28). He himself so *turned aside his eyes lest they see vanity* of this kind (Ps. 118:37) that he scarcely recognized any woman by her face, as he once said to a companion. For he did not think it was safe to drink into

---

7. Major source: II C 116-117.

one's interior such images of woman's form, which could re-kindle the fire in an already tamed flesh or stain the brightness of a pure heart. He used to say that conversation with a woman was frivolous except only for confession or very brief instruction,[8] according to what their salvation requires and respectability allows. "What business," he asked, "should a religious transact with a woman except when she makes a devout request for holy penance or for advice concerning a better life? Out of too much self-confidence one is less on guard against the enemy, and if the devil can claim as his own even one hair from a man, he will soon make it grow into a beam."[9]

6. He taught the friars to flee with all their might from idleness, the cesspool of all evil thoughts;[10] and he demonstrated to them by his own example that they should master their rebellious and lazy flesh by constant discipline and useful work. He used to call his body Brother Ass, for he felt it should be subjected to heavy labor, beaten frequently with whips and fed with the poorest food. If he saw that an idle and vagrant friar wanted to be fed by the labor of others, he thought he should be called Brother Fly, because he did nothing good himself but poisoned the good done by others and so rendered himself useless and obnoxious to all. On account of this he once said: "I want my friars to work and to be kept busy lest by giving themselves to idleness their hearts and tongues wander to unlawful things." He strongly wished that the friars observe the silence recommended by the Gospel, that is, to abstain carefully at all times from *every idle word* that they would have *to render an account of on the day of judgment* (Matt. 12:37).[11] But if he found a friar given to empty babbling, he used to reprimand him sharply, affirming that a modest silence is the guardian of a

8. Cf. *Regula I*, c. 12.
9. Major sources: II C 112, 114; minor sources: I C 43; II C 113.
10. Cf. *Regula I*, c. 7; *Regula II*, c. 5; *Testamentum*, 4; cf. II C 159-162.
11. Cf. *Regula I*, c. 11; *De religiosa habitatione in eremo*, 40; *Admonitiones*, c. 22; *Regula II*, c. 3; cf. II C 19.

pure heart and no small virtue itself, in view of the fact that *death and life* are said to be *in the power of the tongue* (Prov. 18:21), not so much because of taste but because of speech.[12]

7. Although he energetically urged the friars to lead an austere life, he was not pleased by an over-strict severity that did not *put on a heart* of compassion (Col. 3:12) and was not seasoned with the salt of discretion. One night a friar was tormented with hunger because of his excessive fasting and was unable to get any rest. When the devoted shepherd realized that danger threatened one of his sheep, he called the friar and put some bread before him. Then, to take away his embarrassment, Francis himself began to eat first and affectionately invited him to eat. The friar overcame his embarrassment and took the food, overjoyed that through the discreet condescension of his shepherd he had avoided harm to his body and received an edifying example of no small proportion. When morning came, the man of God called the friars together and told them what had happened during the night, adding this advice: "Brothers, in this incident let the charity and not the food be an example to you." He taught them besides to follow prudence as the charioteer of the virtues, not the prudence which the flesh recommends, but the prudence taught by Christ, whose most holy life expressed for us the model of perfection.[13]

<blockquote>

8. Encompassed by the weakness of the flesh,
   man cannot follow
the spotless crucified Lamb so perfectly
   as to avoid contacting any filth.
      Therefore Francis taught
that those who strive after the perfect life
   should cleanse themselves daily
      with streams of tears.

</blockquote>

---

12. Minor sources: II C 129, 75, 161, 160.
13. Major source: II C 22; minor source: II C 21.

Although he had already attained extraordinary purity
of heart and body,
he did not cease to cleanse the eyes of his soul
with a continuous flood of tears,
unconcerned about the loss of his bodily sight.
When he had incurred a very serious eye illness
from his continuous weeping,
and a doctor advised him to restrain his tears
if he wanted to avoid losing his sight,
the holy man answered:
"Brother doctor,
we should not stave off
a visitation of heavenly light even a little
because of love of the light,
which we have in common with flies.
For the body receives the gift of light
for the sake of the spirit
and not the spirit for the sake of the body."
He preferred to lose his sight
rather than to repress the devotion of his spirit
and hold back the tears
which cleansed his interior vision
so that he could see God.[14]

9. Once he was advised by doctors and strongly urged by
the friars to allow himself to be cauterized. The man of God
agreed humbly because he realized that it would be at once
good for his health and harsh on his body. So a surgeon was
called and when he came, he placed an iron in the fire for
performing the cauterization. But Christ's servant encouraged
his body which was now struck with horror and began to speak
to the fire as a friend: "My brother fire, whose beauty is the
envy of all other creatures, the Most High has created you

---

14. This incident is not found in Celano or Julian, but Francis's eye ailment is treated in
I C 98, 101, 105, 108; II C 44, 92-93, 126.

strong, beautiful and useful. Be kind to me in this hour, be courteous! I beseech the great Lord who created you to temper your heat for me so that you will burn gently and I can endure it." When he had finished his prayer, he made the sign of the cross over the instrument that glowed with fire, and he waited unafraid. The iron was plunged hissing into the sensitive flesh and was drawn from his ear to his eyebrow in the process of cauterizing. How much pain the fire caused, the holy man himself expressed: "Praise the Most High," he said to the friars, "because I tell you truly, I felt neither the heat of the fire nor any pain in my flesh." And turning to the doctor, he said: "If my flesh is not well cauterized, then do it again!" The experienced doctor marveled at such strength of spirit in his weak body, and he proclaimed it a divine miracle, saying: "I say to you, brothers, *I have seen wonderful things today* (Luke 5:26).

> Francis had reached such purity
> that his body was in remarkable harmony
> with his spirit
> and his spirit with God.
> As a result God ordained
> that *creation which serves its Maker*[15]
> should be subject in an extraordinary way
> to his will and command.[16]

10. Another time when he was suffering from a very serious illness at the hermitage of Sant' Urbano, feeling his physical weakness, he asked for a drink of wine. He was told that there was no wine to give him; so he ordered water and when it was brought, he blessed it with the sign of the cross. At once what had been pure water was changed into the best wine; and what the poverty of this deserted place could not provide was

---

15. Wisd. 16:24.
16. Major source: II C 166; minor source: Jul. 64; cf. I C 97; II C 129.

obtained by the purity of the holy man. With the taste of this wine, he immediately regained his health so easily that the newness of the taste and the recovery of his health, by supernaturally renewing the drink and the one who drank, confirmed by a double testimony that he had perfectly put off *the old man* and put on the *new* (Col. 3:9-10).[17]

11. Not only did creation serve God's servant at his beck and call, but the Creator's providence itself everywhere inclined itself to his good pleasure. One time when his body was weighed down by many forms of illness, he had the desire to hear some music to awaken and delight his spirit. But since it was considered inappropriate that this should be done for him by human musicians, angels came to indulge the holy man's wish. One night when he was watching and meditating about the Lord, he suddenly heard the sound of a lute playing wonderful harmony and a very sweet melody. No one was seen, but he was aware that the musician was moving back and forth by the fluctuation of the sound. With his spirit directed to God, Francis enjoyed so thoroughly the beauty of that sweet sounding song that he thought he had been transported to another world. This did not remain hidden from the friars who were close to him, for they often used to see clear indications that he was *visited by the Lord* (Luke 1:68; 7:16), who gave him such overwhelming and frequent consolation that he could not hide it completely.[18]

12. At another time when the man of God and a companion were walking on the banks of the Po while on a journey of preaching between Lombardy and the Marches of Treviso, they were overtaken by the darkness of night. The road was exposed to many great dangers because of the darkness, the river and some swamps. His companion said to the holy man: "Pray, father, that we may be saved from these threatening

---

17. Major sources: III C 17; I C 61.
18. Major source: II C 126; minor source: I C 61.

dangers!" Full of confidence, the man of God answered him: "*God has the power* (Luke 3:8), if it pleases him in his sweetness, to disperse this darkness and give us the benefit of light." Scarcely had he finished speaking when, behold, such a great light began to shine around them with a heavenly radiance that they could see in clear light not only the road, but also many other things all around, although the night remained dark elsewhere. By the guidance of this light they were led physically and comforted spiritually; singing hymns of praise to God they arrived safely at their lodging, which was quite a stretch of road away.[19]

Consider carefully
the marvelous purity and the degree of virtue
that Francis attained.
At his mere wish
fire tempered its heat,
water changed its taste,
an angelic melody brought him comfort
and a divine light gave him guidance.
Thus it is proven
that all of creation came to the service
of the sanctified senses
of this holy man.

---

19. This incident is not found in Celano or Julian.

CHAPTER SIX

ON
HIS HUMILITY AND OBEDIENCE
AND
GOD'S CONDESCENSION TO HIS
SLIGHTEST WISH

1. Humility,
the guardian and the ornament
of all the virtues,
had filled the man of God in copious abundance.
In his own estimation
he was nothing but a sinner,
although in truth he was
a resplendent mirror
of all holiness.
He strove to build himself up
upon this virtue
like an architect laying the foundations,[1]
for he had learned this
from Christ.
He used to say that it was for this reason
that the Son of God came down
from the height of his Father's bosom
to our lowly estate
so that our Lord and Teacher might teach humility
in both word and example.
Therefore as Christ's disciple,
he strove to appear worthless
in his own eyes and those of others,
recalling what had been said

---

1. 1 Cor. 3:10; Heb. 6:1.

by his supreme Teacher:
What is highly esteemed among men
is an abomination before God.[2]
He often used to make this statement:
"What a man is in God's eyes,
that he is
and nothing more."[3]
Therefore, judging that it was foolish
to be elated by worldly approval,
he rejoiced in insults
and was saddened by praise.
He preferred to hear himself
blamed rather than praised,
knowing that blame would lead him
to amend his life,
while praise would drive him to a fall.
And so when people extolled the merits
of his holiness,
he commanded one of the friars
to do the opposite
and to impress upon his ears
insulting words.
When that friar,
although unwilling, called him
boorish and mercenary, unskilled and useless,
he would reply
with inner joy shining on his face:
"May the Lord bless you,
my beloved son,
for it is you that speak the very truth
and what the son of Peter Bernardone should hear."[4]

---

2. Luke 16:15.
3. *Admonitiones*, 20.
4. Major sources: II C 140; I C 53; minor sources: II C 26; I C 4; Jul. 33.

2. In order to render himself contemptible to others, he did not spare himself the embarrassment of bringing up his own faults when he preached before all the people. Once it happened that when he was weighed down with sickness, he relaxed a little the rigor of his abstinence in order to recover his health. When his strength of body returned, he was aroused to insult his own body out of true self-contempt: "It is not right," he said, "that the people should believe I am abstaining while, in fact, I eat meat on the sly." Inflamed with the spirit of true humility, he called the people together in the square of the town of Assisi and solemnly entered the principal church with many of the friars whom he had brought with him. With a rope tied around his neck and stripped to his underwear, he had himself dragged before the eyes of all to the stone where criminals received their punishment. He climbed up upon the stone and preached with much vigor and spirit although he was suffering from a fever and the weather was bitter cold. He asserted to all his hearers that he should not be honored as a spiritual man but rather he should be despised by all as a carnal man and a glutton. Therefore those who had gathered there were amazed at so great a spectacle. They were well aware of his austerity, and so their hearts were struck with compunction; but they professed that his humility was easier to admire than to imitate. Although this incident seemed to be more a *portent* like that of the Prophet (Isa. 20:3)[5] than an example, nevertheless it was a lesson in true humility instructing the follower of Christ that he should despise the fame of transitory praise, suppress the arrogance of bloated bragging and reject the lies of deceptive pretense.[6]

3. He often did many things like this so that outwardly he might become *like a discarded utensil* (Ps. 30:13) while inwardly possessing the spirit of holiness. He strove to hide the gifts of

---

5. The text of Isaiah reads: *My servant Isaiah has walked naked and barefoot for three years as a sign and a portent against Egypt and Ethiopia.*
6. Major source: I C 52; minor sources: I C 54, 53.

his Lord in the secret recesses of his heart, not wanting them to be exposed to praise, which could be an occasion of a fall. For often when he was praised by the crowds, he would answer like this: "I could still have sons and daughters; don't praise me as if I were secure! No one should be praised whose end is still uncertain." This is what he would say to those who praised him, and to himself he would say: "If the Most High had given so much to a brigand, he would be more grateful than you, Francis." He often used to tell the friars: "No one should flatter himself for doing anything a sinner can also do. A sinner," he said, "can fast, pray, weep and mortify his flesh. This one thing he cannot do: be faithful to his Lord. Therefore we should glory in this: if we give back to the Lord the glory that is his, if we serve him faithfully and ascribe to him whatever he gives to us."[7]

4. In order to profit in many ways like the merchant in the Gospel and to use all the present time to gain merit, he wanted to be a subject rather than a superior, to obey rather than command. Therefore he relinquished his office as general[8] and looked for a guardian whose will he would obey in all things.[9] He used to say that the fruits of holy obedience are so abundant that for those who submit their necks to its yoke not an hour passes without making a profit. Therefore he used to always promise and observe obedience to whatever friar went with him on journeys. Once he said to his companions: "Among the many other things that the kindness of God has generously bestowed upon me, it has granted me this grace: that I would obey a novice of one hour, if he were given to me as my guardian, as diligently as I would obey the oldest and most discreet friar. A subject," he said, "should not consider the man in his superior but rather Christ, for whose love he is a subject. The more contemptible the superior, the more pleas-

---

7. Major source: II C 133-134; minor source: Jul. 33.
8. Out of humility Francis resigned the office of Minister General, probably at the General Chapter of 1220; cf. II C 143.
9. Cf. *Testamentum*, 6; guardian, in Latin *guardianus*, is the term for the local superior

ing is the humility of the one who obeys."

On one occasion when he was asked who should be considered truly obedient, he gave as an example the comparison with a dead body. "Take a corpse," he said, "and put it where you will! You will see that it does not resist being moved, nor murmur about its position nor protest when it is cast aside. If it is placed on a throne, it will not raise its eyes up, but cast them down. If it is clothed in purple, it will look twice as pale. This," he said, "is a truly obedient man. He does not judge why he is moved; he does not care where he is placed; he does not insist on being transferred. If he is raised to an office, he retains his customary humility. The more he is honored, the more unworthy he considers himself."[10]

5. Once he told his companion: "I would not seem to myself to be a Friar Minor unless I were in the state I will describe to you. Suppose, as superior of the friars, I go to the chapter, preach and admonish the friars and at the end they answer back: 'You are not suitable for us because you are illiterate, without eloquence and an ignorant simpleton.' Finally I am thrown out with reproaches and despised by all. I tell you that if I did not listen to these words with the same expression on my face, with the same joy and with the same determination for holiness, I am in no way a Friar Minor." And he added: "In the office of superior there is danger of a fall, in praise a precipice and in the humility of being a subject profit for the soul. Why, then, do we direct our attention to the dangers rather than to profit, when it is to gain profit that we have been given time?"[11]

For this reason
Francis,

---

among Franciscans. The term *prior* seemed to Francis incompatible with the humility of a Friar Minor; cf. *Regula I*, 6: "Let none receive the name *prior*, but let them be called *lesser brothers* [*fratres minores*], and wash each other's feet."

10. Major source: II C 151-152.

11. Major source: II C 145.

the model of humility,
wanted his friars to be called Minor[12]
and the superiors of his Order to be called servants,[13]
in order to use the very words of the Gospel[14]
which he had promised to observe
and in order that his followers
might learn from this very name
that they had come to the school
of the humble Christ
to learn humility.
Jesus Christ,
the teacher of humility,
instructed his disciples in true humility
by saying: *"Whoever wishes to become great among you,
let him be your servant;
and whoever wishes to be first among you
will be your slave."*[15]

When the cardinal of Ostia, the chief protector and pro-moter of the Order of Friars Minor (who afterwards, as the holy man had prophesied,[16] was elevated to the honor of the supreme pontificate, and was called Gregory IX) asked him whether he would allow his friars to be promoted to ecclesiastical offices, he responded: "Lord, my brothers are called Minors so that they will not presume to become great men. If you want them to bear fruit in the Church of God, hold them and preserve them in the state to which they have been called, and by no means permit them to rise to ecclesiastical offices."[17]

6. Because he preferred humility to honors both in him-

---

12. *Regula I*, 6-7; *Regula II*, 1.
13. The Latin term is *minister*, which is usually translated as *minister* but which, in fact, means *servant*; cf. *Regula I*, 4-5; *Regula II*, 2, 10.
14. Matt. 25:45: *Amen I say to you, as long as you did not do it for one of these least ones, you did not do it for me.* For the phrase *for one of these least ones* the Latin Vulgate has *uni de minoribus his.*
15. Matt. 20:26-27; cf. *Regula I*, 5. Minor source: I C 38; cf. I C 30, 34; II C 21.
16. Cardinal Hugolino; cf. I C 75, 100-101; II C 25.
17. Major source: II C 148; minor source: Jul. 65.

self and in all his subjects, God, the lover of the humble, judged him worthy of the highest honors. This was shown in a vision from heaven to one of the friars, a man of outstanding virtue and devotion. When he was in the company of the man of God and was praying fervently with him in a deserted church, he was rapt in ecstasy and saw among the many thrones in heaven one more honorable than the rest, ornamented with precious stones and shining with the fulness of glory. He marveled within himself at the splendor of this lofty throne and began to wonder anxiously who would be raised to it. In the midst of these thoughts he heard a voice saying to him: "This throne belonged to one of the fallen angels[18] and now is reserved for the humble Francis." At length, when the friar came back to himself from his ecstasy, he followed the blessed man as usual when he left the church. As they went along the road talking together about God, the friar, not unmindful of his vision, skillfully asked Francis what he thought of himself. The humble servant of Christ said to him: "I see myself as the greatest of sinners." When the friar said to the contrary that he could not say or feel that with a good conscience, Francis continued: "If Christ had shown as much mercy to the greatest criminal, I am convinced that he would be much more grateful to God than I." At hearing such remarkable humility, the friar was convinced of the truth of his vision, knowing from the testimony of the Gospel (Matt. 23:12; Luke 1:52) that the truly humble will be exalted to the height of glory from which the proud have been cast out.[19]

7. Another time, when he was praying in an abandoned church at Monte Casale in the province of Massa, he learned through the spirit that sacred relics had been left there. When he sadly reflected that they had been for a long time deprived of the honor due to them, he ordered the friars to bring them with reverence to their place. But when Francis for some rea-

---

18. Cf. Isa. 14:9-15; Apoc. 12:7-9.
19. Major source: II C 123; minor source: II C 122.

son had gone away, his sons forgot about his command and neglected the merit of obedience. One day when they wanted to celebrate the sacred mysteries and removed the cover from the altar, they were astonished to find some very beautiful and fragrant bones. What they were looking upon were the relics which had been brought there by God's power, not by human hands. When the man devoted to God returned a little later, he began to diligently inquire if what he had ordered about the relics had been carried out. Humbly confessing the guilt of their neglected obedience, the friars merited pardon along with a penance. And the holy man said: "Blessed be my Lord and God who carried out himself what you should have done."

> Consider diligently
> the care of divine providence for our dust,
> and the excellence of the virtue
> of the humble Francis
> in the eyes of God.
> For when men neglected his commands,
> God himself
> obeyed his wishes.[20]

8. One time when he came to Imola, he went to the bishop of the town and humbly asked his permission to call the people together and preach to them. The bishop replied harshly: "My preaching should be quite enough for them, brother." This truly humble man bowed his head and went away, but in less than an hour he came back. The bishop was annoyed and asked him what he was looking for a second time. Then Francis replied with a humble heart and a humble tone of voice: "My lord, if a father throws his son out one door, he has to come in another." Conquered by this humility, the bishop embraced him enthusiastically and said: "From now on you

---

20. Major source: II C 202.

and all your friars may preach in my diocese with my general permission, because your holy humility has won this."[21]

9. It happened once that he came to Arezzo at a time when the whole city was shaken by civil war and was on the brink of destruction. Given hospitality in the outskirts, he saw over the city devils rejoicing and inflaming the troubled citizens to mutual slaughter. In order to put to flight those seditious spiritual powers, he sent Brother Silvester, a man of dove-like simplicity, before him like a herald, saying: "Go before the gate of the city and on the part of Almighty God command the devils to leave immediately!" This truly obedient man hastened to carry out his father's orders and *singing psalms of praise before the face* of the Lord (Ps. 94:2), he began to shout out forcefully before the gate of the city: "On the part of Almighty God and at the command of his servant Francis, depart far from here, all you devils." At once the city returned to peace and all the citizens reformed their civil statutes very peacefully. Once the raging pride of the devils, which had surrounded the city like a siege, had been driven out, the wisdom of a poor man, namely the humility of Francis, entered in, brought back peace and saved the city. By his lofty virtue of humble obedience, he had gained such powerful control over those rebellious and obstinate spirits that he could repress their ferocious brashness and drive back their savage violence.[22]

10. The proud demons flee from the lofty virtues of the humble unless occasionally the divine goodness should permit the demons *to buffet* them in order to protect their humility, as the Apostle Paul writes about himself (2 Cor. 12:7) and Francis learned through his own experience. Once he had been asked by Lord Leo, cardinal of the church of the Holy Cross, to stay for a little while with him in Rome and he humbly accepted out

---

21. Major source: II C 147.
22. Major source: II C 108.

of respect and affection. The first night he spent there, when he wanted to rest after his prayer, the devils came upon the soldier of Christ and attacked him fiercely. They beat him severely for a long time and in the end left him half dead. As they departed, the man of God called his companion and, when he came, told him what had happened, adding: "Brother, I believe that the devils can do nothing that God's providence does not allow. Therefore they attacked me so fiercely now because my staying in the court of great personages does not present a good example. My friars who live in poor places, hearing that I am staying with cardinals, will perhaps suspect that I am involved in worldly affairs, puffed up by honors and wallowing in pleasure. Therefore I judge that it is better for one who is set as an example to avoid courts and to live humbly among the humble in humble places, in order to strengthen those who are bearing severe poverty by bearing the same himself." In the morning, then, they went to the cardinal, excused themselves humbly and said goodbye.[23]

11. The holy man abhorred pride, the source of all evil, and disobedience, its worst offspring, but he welcomed the humility of repentance with no less intensity. It happened once that a friar who had done something against the law of obedience was brought to him to be punished according to justice. Seeing that the friar showed clear signs of being truly sorry, the man of God was drawn to be easy on him out of love of humility. However, lest this easy forgiveness be an incentive for others to fail in their duty, he ordered that the friar's hood be taken off and thrown into the fire so that all could see what and how harsh a punishment the offense of disobedience deserved. When the hood had been within the fire for a while, he ordered that it be taken out of the flames and returned to the humbly repentant friar. What a marvel! The hood was taken out of the middle of the flames, but showed no trace of a burn.

---

23. Major source: II C 119-120.

Thus with this one miracle God showed his approval both of the holy man's virtue and of the humility of repentance.[24]

Francis's humility, therefore,
is worthy of imitation.
It merited such marvelous honor
even on earth
that it inclined God to his wishes
and changed the attitude of men,
repulsed the obstinacy of demons
at his command,
and held in check voracious flames
at his mere nod.
Truly this is the humility
which exalts those who possess it,
while it shows reverence to all
and deserves honor from all.

---

24. Major source: II C 154.

CHAPTER SEVEN

ON
HIS LOVE OF POVERTY
AND
THE MIRACULOUS FULFILLMENT OF HIS
NEEDS

1. Among the gifts of grace
which Francis received
from God the generous Giver,
he merited
as a special privilege
to grow in the riches of simplicity
through his love
of the highest poverty.[1]
The holy man saw
that poverty was the close companion
of the Son of God,
and now that it was rejected by the whole world,
he was eager to espouse it
in everlasting love.[2]
For the sake of poverty
he not only *left his father and mother,*[3]
but also gave away
everything he had.
No one was so greedy for gold
as he was for poverty;
nor was anyone so anxious
to guard his treasure
as he was in guarding

---

1. Cf. *Regula II*, 6.
2. Jer. 31:3.
3. Gen. 2:24; Mark 10:7.

this pearl of the Gospel.[4]
In this especially would his sight be offended
if he saw in the friars
anything which did not accord completely
with poverty.
Indeed, from the beginning of his religious life
until his death,
his only riches were
a tunic, a cord and underclothes;
and with this much
he was content.
He used to frequently call to mind with tears
the poverty of Jesus Christ and his mother,
claiming that it was
the queen of the virtues
because it shone forth so preeminently
in the *King of Kings*[5] and in the Queen, his mother.

When the friars asked him at a gathering what virtue does
more to make one a friend of Christ, he replied as if opening up
the hidden depths of his heart: "Know, brothers, that poverty
is the special way to salvation, as the stimulus of humility and
the root of perfection, whose fruit is manifold but hidden. This
is the Gospel's treasure *hidden in a field* (Matt. 13:44); to buy this
we should sell everything, and in comparison to this we should
spurn everything we cannot sell."[6]

2. Whoever desires to attain the height of poverty should
renounce in some way not only worldly wisdom but also learning, that having renounced such a possession, he *might enter into
the mighty works of the Lord* (Ps. 70:15-16) and offer himself
naked to the arms of the Crucified. No one can be said to have
perfectly renounced the world if he still keeps the purse of his

---

4. Cf. Matt. 13:45-46.
5. 1 Tim. 6:15; Apoc. 19:16.
6. Major sources: II C 55, 200; minor source: I C 76; cf. I C 84; II C 17, 199.

own opinion in the hidden recesses of his heart.

When speaking about poverty, he often proposed to the friars this text of the Gospel: *The foxes have their holes and the birds of the air their nests, but the Son of Man has nowhere to lay his head* (Matt. 8:20; Luke 9:58). For this reason he instructed the friars to build poor houses like those of the poor and to live in these not as their own, but like *pilgrims and strangers* in the house of another (1 Pet. 2:11).[7] For he used to say that the law of pilgrims was to take shelter under another's roof, to thirst for their homeland and to travel peacefully. Sometimes he ordered the friars to tear down a house they had built or to move out of it if he noticed something contrary to Gospel poverty either because they had appropriated it as their possession or because it was too sumptuous. He used to say that poverty was the foundation of the Order, on which the entire structure of their religious life so basically depended that it would stand firm if poverty were firm and collapse completely if poverty were undermined.[8]

3. He taught, as he had learned from a revelation, that one entering the holy Order should begin from this text of the Gospel: *If you wish to be perfect, go, sell all that you have, and give to the poor* (Matt. 19:21).[9] Only those who had given away all possessions and retained absolutely nothing did he admit to the Order, both on account of the text of the Gospel and lest scandal should arise over any possessions kept back.[10] Thus when a man asked to be received into the Order in the Marches of Ancona, the true patriarch of the poor replied: "If you want to join Christ's poor, distribute what you have to the poor of the world." When he heard this, the man went off and, led by a carnal love, left his goods to his relatives, giving nothing to the poor. When the holy man heard him tell of this, he reproached

---

7. Cf. *Regula II*, 6.
8. Major sources: II C 194, 140, 56, 59; cf. II C 57, 58, 59.
9. Cf. *Testamentum*, 3; *Regula I*, 1-2; *Regula II*, 1-2.
10. We have translated by *possessions* the Latin term *loculus*, which means *moneybag* and which suggests the moneybag of Judas (John 12:6, 13:29).

him harshly and said: "Go on your way, Brother Fly, because you have not yet *left your home and your kindred* (Gen. 12:1). You gave your goods to your relatives and you have cheated the poor; you are not worthy of the holy poor. You have begun with the flesh; you have laid a ruinous foundation for a spiritual structure." That *carnal man* (1 Cor. 2:14) returned to his relatives and reclaimed his goods, which he did not want to give to the poor, and so very quickly abandoned his virtuous intention.[11]

4. Another time there was such a lack of resources at St. Mary of the Portiuncula that it was impossible to provide for the needs of the friars who were visiting there. Francis's vicar came to him, pointed out the destitution of the friars and asked permission to keep aside some of the goods of the novices when they entered so that the friars could have something to fall back on in case of necessity. Not without heavenly guidance, Francis said to him: "Let it be far from us, dearest brother, to sin against the rule for the sake of any man. I prefer that you strip the altar of the glorious Virgin, when necessity requires it, than to tamper even a little with the vow of poverty and the observance of the Gospel. The Blessed Virgin will be more pleased to have her altar stripped and the Gospel counsel observed perfectly rather than to have her altar adorned and her Son's counsel neglected when we have promised to keep it."[12]

5. One time when the man of God was going through Apulia near Bari with a companion, he found on the road a large purse, of the type they call *funda*,[13] apparently bursting with money. His companion advised him and nagged him to pick up the purse from the ground and give the money to the poor. The man of God refused, claiming there was a trick of the devil in this purse they had found and that the friar was recommending something sinful rather than meritorious,

---

11. Major sources: II C 80-81; minor source: II C 78.
12. Major source: II C 67.
13. The Latin term *funda* literally means a sling and might be translated as *money belt*.

namely to take what belonged to another and give it away. They left the place and hurried to finish the journey they had begun. But the friar was not yet satisfied, deluded as he was by a false sense of charity; he kept bothering the man of God as if the latter had no concern to relieve the destitution of the poor. Finally the patient man agreed to return to the place—not to carry out the friar's wish, but to uncover the devil's trickery. So he returned to the purse with the friar and with a young man who was on the road. After praying, he commanded his companion to pick it up. The friar was dumbfounded and trembled, for now he had a premonition of some diabolic manifestation. Nevertheless, because of the command of holy obedience, he drove away the doubt in his heart and stretched out his hand toward the purse; and behold, a large snake jumped out of the purse and suddenly disappeared along with it, showing the friar that this was the deception of the devil. The enemy's trickery and cunning were grasped, and the holy man said to his companion: "To the servants of God, brother, money is the very devil and a poisonous snake."[14]

6. After this a remarkable thing happened to the holy man when he was going to the city of Siena on some necessary business. In a great plain between Campiglia and San Quirico he was met by three poor women who were exactly alike in height, age and appearance. They offered him the gift of a new salutation, saying: "Welcome, Lady Poverty!" When he heard this, the true lover of poverty was filled with unspeakable joy because there was nothing in him that he would rather have people acknowledge than what these women singled out.

They suddenly disappeared,
and when his companions considered
their remarkable similarity,
their novel greeting,

---

14. Major source: II C 68.

their strange meeting and disappearance,
they concluded
not without reason
that this had some mystical meaning
for the holy man.
It seemed that these three poor women
who were so alike in appearance,
who gave such an unusual greeting
and disappeared so suddenly,
appropriately showed that the beauty of Gospel perfection,
in poverty, chastity and obedience,
shone forth all perfectly equal
in the man of God
although he had chosen to glory above all
in the privilege of poverty
which he used to call
his mother, his bride and his lady.
It was in poverty that he desired
to surpass others
because from it he had learned
to regard himself
inferior to all.

Therefore whenever he saw anyone more poorly dressed
than he, Francis immediately censured himself and roused
himself to imitate him, as if he were competing in a rivalry over
poverty and feared to be beaten by another. It once happened
that he met a poor man on the road and when he saw how
ragged he was, his heart was struck, and he said to his companion sorrowfully: "This man's need puts us to shame, because
we have chosen poverty as our wealth; and see, it shines more
clearly in him."[15]

7. For love of holy poverty, God's servant more gladly

15. Major sources: II C 93, 83-84; cf. I C 51; II C 55, 70, 72, 82, 84, 215.

used the alms that had been begged from door to door than those that had been spontaneously offered. If he were invited by distinguished personages and they served a better table than usual in his honor, he would first beg some pieces of bread from the neighboring houses and then sit down at table, thus enriched by his poverty. He did this once when he had been invited by the lord bishop of Ostia,[16] who held Christ's poor man in special affection. The bishop complained that Francis had disparaged the honor shown him by going out after alms when he was to share his hospitality at table. God's servant replied: "My lord, I have shown you great honor in honoring a greater Lord. For the Lord is pleased with poverty and especially with that poverty which involves voluntary begging for Christ. This is the royal dignity which the Lord Jesus assumed when he *became poor* for us that he might enrich us by *his poverty* (2 Cor. 8:9) and establish us as heirs and kings of *the kingdom of heaven* if we are truly *poor in spirit* (Matt. 5:3). I do not wish to relinquish this royal dignity for a fief of false riches loaned to you for only an hour."[17]

8. Sometimes he would exhort the friars to beg for alms with words such as these: "Go forth because in this last hour the Friars Minor have been given to the world that through them the elect might have the opportunity to fulfill what will be commended by the Judge as they hear those most sweet words: '*As long as you have done it to one of these, the least of my brothers, you did it to me* '" (Matt. 25:40). Therefore he used to say that it was a delight to beg with the title of Friars Minor, which the Teacher of Gospel truth had so clearly expressed by his own mouth when rewarding the just.[18] When there was an opportunity, he used to go begging on the principal feasts, saying that the prophecy *Man will eat the bread of Angels* (Ps. 77:25) is fulfilled in

---

16. Cardinal Hugolino; cf. VI, 5, n. 16, p. 233.

17. Major sources: II C 72-73; cf. I C 101.

18. The Latin text of the Gospel uses the term *minimus*, the superlative of *parum*, meaning small or little, whose comparative form is *minor*, the source of the name Friar Minor. Cf. VI, 5, n. 14, p. 233.

the holy poor. For he said that it is indeed the bread of angels that has been begged for the love of God and has been given for his love at the inspiration of the angels and gathered from door to door by holy poverty.[19]

9. Once on an Easter Sunday he was staying at a hermitage that was so far from any houses that he could not conveniently go begging. And so in remembrance of him who appeared that very day in the guise of a pilgrim to his disciples on the road to Emmaus, Francis then begged alms from the friars themselves, like a pilgrim and beggar. When he had received it humbly, he informed them with holy eloquence that they should pass through the desert of the world like *pilgrims and strangers* (1 Pet. 2:11) and like true Hebrews continually celebrate in poverty of spirit the Lord's Pasch, that is his passing over *from this world to the Father* (John 13:1).

Since, when he begged alms,
he was motivated
not by greed for profit but by liberty of spirit,
God *the Father of the poor*[20]
seemed to have special care for him.

10. Once when this servant of the Lord was very ill at Nocera, he was brought back to Assisi by a formal embassy sent for that purpose out of devotion by the townspeople. While they were taking Christ's servant back, they came to a poor little village by the name of Satriano. Since their hunger and the hour called for food, they went out; but, finding nothing for sale, they returned empty-handed. The holy man told them: "You found nothing because you trust more in your flies than in God." (For he called coins flies.) "Go back," he said, "to the houses which you have visited and humbly ask for an alms, offering God's love in place of money. Do not consider this

---

19. Cf. *Testamentum*, 4. Major source: II C 71. Cf. I C 26, 35; II C 17.
20. Job 29:16. Major source: II C 61; cf. I C 76.

shameful or cheap out of false esteem, because after man's sin that great Almsgiver has bestowed all things as alms to both the worthy and the unworthy, out of his abundant kindness." The knights put aside their embarrassment, readily begged for alms and bought more with the love of God than with money. Their hearts struck with compunction by God, the poor villagers generously gave not only what they had but also themselves. And so it happened that Francis's wealthy poverty supplied the need which money could not alleviate.[21]

11. At the time when he was lying ill in a hermitage near Rieti, a doctor visited him often to care for him. Since the poor man of Christ was unable to pay him adequately for his services, the most generous God made up for the poor man and repaid the doctor for his devoted care with the following favor, so that he would not go without payment in the present life. The doctor's new house, which he had just spent all his money building, was threatened with collapse because of a wide crack in the wall, which reached *from the top to the bottom* (Matt. 27:51)—a collapse which seemed unavoidable by human means. Fully trusting in the merits of the holy man and out of the devotion of his great faith, he asked Francis's companions to give him something which the man of God had touched with his hands. After many requests he obtained a small amount of his hair which he placed one evening in the crack in the wall. When he rose in the morning, he found that the crack had been so firmly closed that he could not pull out the hairs he had placed there nor could he find any trace of the crack. And so it happened that because he had dutifully ministered to the body of God's servant in its state of collapse, he avoided the danger of the collapse of his house.[22]

12. Another time the man of God wanted to go to a hermitage where he could spend more time in contemplation. Because he was weak, he rode on an ass that belonged to a cer-

---

21. Major source: II C 77.
22. This incident is not found in Celano or Julian; minor source: II C 44.

tain poor man. Since it was summertime and the man had to climb up the mountain following after God's servant, he became fatigued by the long and grueling journey. Weakened by a burning thirst, he began to cry out urgently to the saint: "Look, I'll die of thirst if I don't get a drink immediately." Without delay the man of God jumped off the ass, knelt on the ground, stretched forth his hands to heaven and did not cease praying until he knew that he had been heard. Finally, when he finished his prayer, he told the man: "Hurry to that rock and you will find running water which this very hour Christ has mercifully drawn out of the rock for you to drink." How amazing is God's condescension, which bows so easily to his servants! A thirsty man drank *water from the rock* (Ps. 77:16) by the power of another's prayer and took a drink from *the solid stone* (Deut. 32:13). There was no stream of water there before, nor could any be found since, although a careful search was made.[23]

13. How Christ multiplied food at sea through the merits of his poor man will be noted below.[24] Here let it suffice to mention that with only a small amount of food which he had been given as alms, he saved the sailors from the danger of starvation and death for a number of days. From this one could clearly see that just as the servant of Almighty God was like Moses in drawing *water from the rock* (Ps. 77:16; Exod. 17:1-7) so he was like Elisha in the multiplication of provisions (4 Kings 4:1ff.).[25]

Therefore, let all distrust be far
from Christ's poor.
For if Francis's poverty was so abundantly sufficient
that it supplied by miraculous power
the needs of those who came to his aid,

---

23. Major sources: II C 46; III C 15.
24. IX, 5, pp. 266-267.
25. Major source: I C 55; minor source: Jul. 34.

providing food, drink and housing
when money, skill and natural means were lacking,
how much more will it merit
those things that are given to all
in the usual plan of divine providence.
If a dry rock gave drink abundantly
to a poor man who was thirsty
at the word of another poor man,
nothing at all
will refuse its service
to those who have left all
for the Maker of all.

CHAPTER EIGHT

ON
HIS AFFECTIONATE PIETY
AND
HOW IRRATIONAL CREATURES
WERE AFFECTIONATE TOWARD HIM

1. True *piety*,[1]
which according to the Apostle
is helpful *for all things*,
had so filled Francis's heart
and penetrated its depths
that it seemed to have appropriated the man of God
completely into its dominion.
This is what
drew him up to God
through devotion,
transformed him into Christ
through compassion,
attracted him to his neighbor
through condescension
and symbolically showed a return
to the state of original innocence
through universal reconciliation
with each and every thing.
Through this virtue
he was attracted to all things
in spiritual love,
especially to souls redeemed by the precious blood
of Jesus Christ.

---

1. The Latin term is *pietas*, which has a broader scope than the English "piety"; in the context of this chapter it includes love, devotion, affection, reverence, kindness, fidelity and compassion. The Pauline reference is to I Tim. 4:8.

When he saw them being stained
by the filth of sin,
he grieved with such tender pity
that he seemed like a mother
who was daily in labor pains
bringing them to birth in Christ.
This was his principal reason
for reverencing the ministers
of the word of God,
because with their devoted concern
for the conversion of sinners
they *raise up seed for their* dead *brother*,[2]
namely Christ, crucified for us,
and guide them
with their concerned devotion.
He firmly held
that such work of mercy
was more acceptable
to *the Father of mercies*[3]
than any sacrifice,
especially if this eagerness arose
out of perfect charity
more by example than by word,
more by tear-filled prayer
than by long-winded sermons.[4]

2. He used to say that we should feel sorry for a preacher, as for a man without real piety, who in his preaching does not seek the salvation of souls but his own praise or who destroys with the evil of his life what he builds up with the truth of his teaching. He said that a simple tongue-tied friar should be preferred to such a preacher because he called others to good

---

2. Deut. 25:5, 7; Matt. 22:24.
3. 2 Cor. 1:3.
4. Minor source: II C 172.

by his good example. And so he explained the text *So that the barren has borne many* (1 Kings 2:5) as follows: "*The barren woman*," he said, "is that poor little friar who does not have the duty of bringing forth children in the Church. He will *bring forth many* at the judgment because those he is now converting to Christ by his private prayers, the Judge will ascribe to his glory. The continuation of the text, *she that has many children will be weakened* (1 Kings 2:5), means that a vain and loquacious preacher who now rejoices over the many as if he had brought them forth by his own power will then realize that he had nothing of his own involved with them."[5]

3. He longed with heartfelt piety and burned with ardent zeal for the salvation of souls. He used to say that he *was filled with the sweetest fragrance* (Exod. 29:18) and anointed with *precious ointment* (John 12:3) when he heard that many were being converted to the way of truth by the fragrant reputation of the holy friars in the distant regions of the world. When he heard of such things, he rejoiced in spirit, and heaped his most desirable blessings upon those friars who by word or deed led sinners to the love of Christ. Thus also the ones who dishonored the religious life by their evil deeds incurred his severest curse: "May you, most holy Lord, and the whole celestial court, and I too, your little one, curse them who disrupt and destroy by their bad example what you have built up and do not cease to build up through the holy friars of this Order" He was often so deeply saddened by scandal given to the weak that he felt he would be overcome unless he had been supported by God's merciful consolation. Once when he was disturbed by certain instances of bad example and anxiously prayed to the merciful Father for his sons, he received this response from the Lord: "What's all this worry, you poor bit of a man? Did I so make you the shepherd of my Order that you can forget that it is I who am its principal protector? I chose you for this because

---

5. Major source: II C 164.

you are a simple man and what I would do in you would be ascribed to divine grace and not to human effort. I have called the friars, I will preserve and feed them; and if some fall away, I will call others—indeed, even if they are yet unborn, I will have them born. No matter how severely this poor little Order is shaken, it will always remain safe by my grace."[6]

4. He abhorred like a snakebite the vice of detraction, as a foe to the source of piety and grace; and he firmly held it to be a devastating plague and an abomination to God's mercy because the detractor feeds on the blood of the souls which he kills with *the sword of his tongue* (Ps. 56:5). Once when he heard a friar blacken the reputation of another, he turned to his vicar and said: "Arise, arise, examine diligently and if you find that the friar accused is innocent, make an example of the accuser by correcting him severely." Sometimes he decreed that a friar who had stripped another friar of his good name should be stripped of his habit and that he should not be allowed to raise his eyes to God until he first did his best to restore what he had taken away. He used to say that the impiety of detractors is a much greater sin than that of robbers; for the law of Christ, which is fulfilled in the observance of piety, obliges us to desire the well-being of the soul more than the body.[7]

5. He responded with a remarkably tender compassion to those suffering from any bodily affliction. If he saw signs of poverty in anyone or signs of deprivation, he referred them to Christ in the sweetness of his pious heart. He had an inborn kindness[8] which was doubled by the kindness of Christ infused in him from above. Therefore his soul melted at the sight of the poor and infirm, and to those to whom he could not extend a helping hand he extended his affection. Once it happened that one of the friars responded gruffly to a beggar who had asked for an alms at an inconvenient time. When the devoted lover of

---

6. Major source: II C 155, 156, 157, 158.
7. Major source: II C 182; cf. *Regula I*, 11; *Admonitiones*, 25; II C 183.
8. Cf. I, 1, p. 186.

the poor heard this, he ordered the friar to strip himself, cast himself at the beggar's feet, confess his guilt and beg for his prayers and forgiveness. When he had done this humbly, the father added sweetly: "When you see a poor man, my brother, an image of the Lord and his poor mother is being placed before you. Likewise in the case of the sick, consider the physical weakness which the Lord took upon himself." That most Christian pauper saw Christ's image in all the poor; and when he met them, he not only generously gave them even the necessities of life that had been given to him, but he believed that these should be given them as if theirs by right. It happened once that a poor man met him on his return from Siena, when because of an illness he was wearing a short mantle over his habit. When his kind eye observed the man's misery, he said to his companion: "We should return this mantle to this poor man because it is his. For we got it on loan until we should find someone poorer than ourselves." But his companion, considering the need of his devoted father, obstinately refused, lest Francis provide for another by neglecting himself. But Francis said: "I believe that the great Almsgiver will charge me with theft if I do not give what I have to one who needs it more." Therefore concerning all that was given him to relieve the needs of his body, he was accustomed to ask the permission of the donors to give it away if he should meet someone in greater need. He spared nothing at all, neither mantles, tunics nor books; not even decorations from the altar—all these he gave to the poor when he could, in order to fulfill his obligation of piety. When he met the poor along the road carrying heavy burdens, he often took the load on his own weak shoulders.[9]

6. When he considered the primordial source of all things, he was filled with even more abundant piety, calling creatures, no matter how small, by the name of brother or sister, because

---

9. Major sources: II C 83; I C 76; II C 85, 87; I C 76; minor sources: II C 8, 77. Cf. II C 86, 88, 89, 90, 92, 196; I C 79; also VII, 1, pp. 239-240.

he knew they had the same source as himself.[10] However, he embraced more affectionately and sweetly those creatures which present a natural reflection of Christ's merciful gentleness and represent him in Scriptural symbolism. He often paid to ransom lambs that were being led to their death, remembering that most gentle Lamb who willed to be *led to slaughter* (Isa. 53:7) to pay the ransom of sinners.

One time when God's servant was lodging at the monastery of San Verecondo in the diocese of Gubbio, a sheep gave birth to a little lamb during the night. There was a ferocious sow there, which did not spare the life of the innocent lamb, but killed it with her ravenous bite. When he heard of this, the devoted father was moved by wonderful compassion and, remembering the Lamb without stain, grieved in the presence of all over the death of the little lamb, saying: "Alas, brother lamb, innocent animal, you represent Christ to men. A curse on that impious beast that killed you; may no man or beast ever eat of her." Remarkably, the evil sow immediately became ill and after paying for her deed with three days of bodily punishment she finally suffered avenging death. She was thrown into the monastery ditch and lay there for a long time dried up like a board, and did not serve as food for any hungry animal.

Let the impiety of men, therefore,
be warned
how great a punishment will be inflicted on it
at the end of time,
if the cruelty of an animal
was punished
with so horrible a death.
Let also the devotion of the faithful consider
that the marvelous power and abundant sweetness

---

10. This is an application of Bonaventure's exemplarism, whereby creatures reflect God, a theme developed throughout *The Soul's Journey into God*.

of the piety of God's servant
was so great
that it was acknowledged in their own way
even by animals.[11]

7. When Francis was traveling near the city of Siena, he came upon a large flock of sheep in a pasture. When he greeted them kindly, as he was accustomed to do, they all stopped grazing and ran to him, lifting their heads and fixing their eyes on him. They gave him such a welcome that the shepherds and the friars were amazed to see the lambs and even the rams frisking about him in such an extraordinary way.

Another time at St. Mary of the Portiuncula the man of God was offered a sheep, which he gratefully accepted in his love of that innocence and simplicity which the sheep by its nature reflects. The pious man admonished the little sheep to praise God attentively and to avoid giving any offense to the friars. The sheep carefully observed his instructions, as if it recognized the piety of the man of God. For when it heard the friars chanting in choir, it would enter the church, genuflect without instructions from anyone, and bleat before the altar of the Virgin, the mother of the Lamb, as if it wished to greet her. Besides, when the most sacred body of Christ was elevated at mass, it would bow down on bended knees as if this reverent animal were reproaching those who were not devout and inviting the devout to reverence the sacrament.

Once in Rome he had with him a little lamb out of reverence for the most gentle Lamb of God. At his departure he left it in the care of the noble matron, the Lady Jacoba of Settesoli.[12] Now the lamb went with the lady to church, standing reverently by her side as her inseparable companion, as if it had

---

11. Major sources: I C 80-81, 77, 79; II C 111. Cf. I C 77, 80-81; II C 165, and IX, 1, pp. 262-263.

12. A noble Roman lady, widow of Graziano Frangipani, Lord of the Septizonium; she was a close friend of Francis, (who called her "Brother Jacoba"), and was summoned to his deathbed. Cf. III C 37-38-39.

been trained in spiritual matters by the saint. If the lady was late in rising in the morning, the lamb rose and nudged her with its horns and woke her with its bleating, urging her with its nods and gestures to hurry to the church. On account of this, the lamb, which was Francis's disciple and had now become a master of devotion, was held by the lady as an object of wonder and love.[13]

8. Another time at Greccio a live hare was offered to the man of God, which he placed on the ground and let it free to go where it wished. But when the kind father called, it ran and jumped into his arms. He fondled it with warm affection and seemed to pity it like a mother. After warning it gently not to let itself be caught again, he let it go free. But as often as he placed it on the ground to run away, it always came back to the father's arms, as if in some secret way it perceived the kind feeling he had for it. Finally, at the father's command, the friars carried it away to a safer place far from the haunts of men.

In the same way on an island in the lake of Perugia[14] a rabbit was caught and offered to the man of God. Although it fled from everyone else, it entrusted itself to his hands and his heart as if to the security of its home. When he was hurrying across the Lake of Rieti to the hermitage of Greccio, out of devotion a fisherman offered him a waterfowl. He took it gladly and opened his hands to let it go, but it did not want to. He prayed for a long time with his eyes turned to heaven. After more than an hour, he came back to himself as if from another realm and gently told the bird again to go away and praise God. Having received his permission with a blessing, the bird expressed its joy in the movements of its body, and flew away. On the same lake in a similar way he was offered a large live fish which he addressed as brother in his usual way and put it back into the water by the boat. The fish played about in the

---

13. Major source: III C 31. The two incidents of a lamb are not found in Celano or Julian.
14. Lago Trasimeno.

water in front of the man of God; and as if it were attracted by his love, it would not go away from the ship until it received from him his permission with a blessing.[15]

9. Another time when he was walking with a friar through the marshes of Venice, he came upon a large flock of birds singing among the reeds. When he saw them, he said to his companion: "Our sisters the birds are praising their Creator; so we should go in among them and chant the Lord's praises and the canonical hours." When they had entered among them, the birds did not move from the place; and on account of the noise the birds were making, they could not hear each other saying the hours. The saint turned to the birds and said: "Sister birds, stop singing until we have done our duty of praising God!" At once they were silent and remained in silence as long as it took the friars to say the hours at length and to finish their praises. Then the holy man of God gave them permission to sing again. When the man of God gave them permission, they immediately resumed singing in their usual way.[16]

A cricket used to perch on a figtree beside the cell of the man of God at St. Mary of the Portiuncula and sing, arousing with its songs the Lord's servant to sing more frequently the divine praises, for he had learned to marvel at the Creator's magnificence even in insignificant creatures. He called it one day, and it flew upon his hand as if it had been taught by God. He said to it: "Sing, my sister cricket, praise the Lord Creator with your joyful song!" It obeyed without delay and began to sing; nor did it stop until at his command it flew back to its usual place. There it remained for eight days, coming each day, singing and returning, all at his command. Finally the man of God said to his companions: "Let us give our sister cricket permission to go away now, for she has cheered us enough with her singing and has aroused us to praise God over

15. Major sources: III C 29; I C 60; III C 30, 23-24; minor source: Jul. 40.
16. This incident is not found in Celano or Julian.

the space of eight days." With his permission, it departed and never appeared there again, as if it did not dare to disobey his command in the slightest way.[17]

10. When he was ill at Siena, a nobleman sent him a live pheasant he had recently caught. The moment it saw and heard the holy man, it was drawn to him with such affection that it would in no way allow itself to be separated from him. Many times it was placed outside the friars' place in the vineyard so that it could go away if it wanted. But every time it ran right back to the father as if it had always been reared by him. Then it was given to a man who used to visit God's servant out of devotion but it absolutely refused to eat, as if it were upset at being out of the sight of the devoted father. It was finally brought back to God's servant, and as soon as it saw him, showed signs of joy and ate heartily.[18]

When he went to the hermitage of La Verna to observe a forty-day fast in honor of the Archangel Michael,[19] birds of different kinds flew around his cell, with melodious singing and joyful movements, as if rejoicing at his arrival, and seemed to be inviting and enticing the devoted father to stay. When he saw this, he said to his companion: "I see, brother, that it is God's will that we stay here for some time, for our sisters the birds seem so delighted at our presence."[20] When he extended his stay there, a falcon that had built its nest there became deeply attached to him as a friend. For at the hour of the night when the holy man used to rise for the divine office, the falcon always came to wake him by making noise and singing. This pleased God's servant very much because the falcon was so solicitous toward him that it shook out of him all sluggish laziness. But when Christ's servant was more than usually weighed down with illness, the falcon had pity and did not

---

17. Major source: III C 27; minor source III C 20.
18. Major source: III C 26.
19. Cf. IX, 3 and XIII, 1, pp. 264-265, 303-304.
20. This incident is not found in Celano or Julian.

impose such early vigils on him. As if instructed by God, about dawn it would ring the bell of its voice with a light touch.[21]

There certainly seems to have been
a divine prophecy
both in the joy of the different kinds of birds
and in the song of the falcon—
a prophecy
of the time when
this praiser and worshiper of God
would be lifted up
on the wings of contemplation
and there would be exalted
with a Seraphic vision.[22]

11. Once when he was staying in the hermitage at Greccio, the local inhabitants were being troubled by many evils. For a pack of ravenous wolves were devouring not only animals but even men, and every year hail storms were devastating the fields and vineyards. When the herald of the holy Gospel preached to these people who were thus afflicted, he said to them: "For the honor and praise of Almighty God I promise you that all this pestilence will depart and the Lord will look kindly upon you and give you an increase of temporal goods if you believe me and show mercy to yourselves by making a good confession and *bring forth fruits worthy of repentance* (Matt. 3:8). Again I announce to you that if you are ungrateful for his gifts and *return to your vomit* (Prov. 26:11), the plague will be renewed, punishment will be doubled and even greater *wrath will rage* against you" (Jos. 22:18). The people did penance at his exhortation, and from that hour, the damage ceased, the dangers passed and neither the wolves nor the hail caused any further trouble. Furthermore, what is even greater, if hail came

---

21. Major source: III C 25.
22. Cf. XIII, 1-3, pp. 303-306.

over the fields of their neighbors and approached their borders,
it either stopped there or was diverted to another area.[23]

The hail kept the pact
of God's servant
and so too did the wolves;
nor did they try to rage anymore
contrary to the law of piety
against men who had been converted to piety,
as long as, according to their agreement,
the people did not act impiously
against God's most pious laws.
Therefore, we should respond piously
to the piety
of this blessed man,
which had such remarkable
sweetness and power
that it subdued ferocious beasts,
tamed the wild,
trained the tame
and bent to his obedience
the brute beasts that had rebelled
against fallen mankind.
Truly this is the virtue
that unites all creatures in brotherhood
and is helpful *for all things*
since it has the promise of the present life,
and of the life to come.[24]

---

23. Major source: II C 35-36.
24. 1 Tim. 4:8.

CHAPTER NINE

ON
THE FERVOR OF HIS CHARITY
AND
HIS DESIRE FOR MARTYRDOM

1. Who can describe
the fervent charity
which burned within Francis, the *friend of the Bridegroom*?[1]
Like a glowing coal,
he seemed totally absorbed
in the flame of divine love.
Whenever he heard of the love of God,[2]
he was at once excited, moved and inflamed
as if an inner chord of his heart
had been plucked by the plectrum
of the external voice.
He used to say
that to offer the love of God in exchange for an alms
was a noble prodigality
and that those who valued it less than money
were most foolish,
because the incalculable price of divine love alone
was sufficient to purchase
the kingdom of heaven.
And he used to say
that greatly should the love be loved
of him who loved us so greatly.
Aroused by all things to the love of God,
he *rejoiced* in all *the works of the Lord's hands*[3]

---

1. John 3:29.
2. Cf. I, 1, p. 186; VII, 8-10, pp. 245-246.
3. Ps. 91:5.

and from these joy-producing manifestations
he rose to their life-giving
principle and cause.
In beautiful things
he saw Beauty itself
and through his *vestiges* imprinted on creation
he followed his Beloved everywhere,[4]
making from all things a ladder
by which he could climb up
and embrace him *who is utterly desirable.*[5]
With a feeling of unprecedented devotion
he savored
in each and every creature—
as in so many rivulets—
that Goodness
which is their fountain-source.
And he perceived a heavenly harmony
in the consonance
of powers and activities
God has given them,
and like the prophet David
sweetly exhorted them to praise the Lord.[6]

2. Jesus Christ crucified always *rested like a bundle of myrrh in the bosom* of Francis's soul (Cant. 1:12), and he longed to be totally transformed into him by the fire of ecstatic love. As a sign of his special devotion to him, Francis spent the time from the feast of the Epiphany through forty successive days—that period when Christ was hidden in the desert—secluded in a lonely place, shut up in a cell, with as little food and drink as possible, fasting, praying and praising God without interrup-

---

4. Job 23:11; Cant. 5:17.
5. Cant. 5:16.
6. Cf. Ps. 148:1-14. Bonaventure seems to be alluding here to Francis's *Canticle of Brother Sun.* Major sources: I C 80; II C 196, 165. Cf. also VIII, 6, p. 254-255.

tion.[7] He was drawn to Christ with such fervent love, and *the Beloved* (Cant. 1:12) returned such intimate love to him that God's servant always seemed to feel the presence of his Savior before his eyes, as he once intimately revealed to his companions. His very marrow burned with love for the sacrament of the Lord's Body and he was overcome by wonder at such loving condescension and such condescending love. He received Holy Communion often and so devoutly that he made others devout also, for at the sweet taste of the *spotless Lamb* (1 Pet. 1:19) he was often rapt in ecstasy as if drunk in the Spirit.[8]

3. He embraced the mother of the Lord Jesus with an indescribable love because she had made the Lord of Majesty our brother and because through her we *have obtained mercy* (1 Pet. 2:10). After Christ he put all his trust in her and made her his advocate and that of his friars. In her honor he used to fast with great devotion from the feast of the Apostles Peter and Paul to the feast of the Assumption.[9] He was joined in a bond of inseparable love to the angels who burn with a marvelous fire to be rapt out of themselves into God and to inflame the souls of the elect. Out of devotion to the angels he used to spend the forty days after the Assumption of the glorious Virgin in fasting and continual prayer.[10] Because of the ardent zeal he had for the salvation of all, he was devoted with a special love to blessed Michael the Archangel in view of his ministry of presenting souls to God.

In remembering all the saints who are like *fiery stones* (Ezech. 28:14, 16), he burned with a divine fire, and embraced

7. Cf. Matt. 4:1ff. The Rules (*Regula I*, 3; *Regula II*, 3) suggest this extra Lent as a commendable but optional practice. It is reckoned from the Epiphany because Christ was taken by the Spirit to the desert immediately after his baptism, which is commemorated on that feast. Cf. also II C 59.

8. Major source: II C 201. Cf. also II C 95. The metaphor of drunkenness in the Spirit is from St. Ambrose's hymn *Splendor paternae gloriae* (original version), sung on Monday at Lauds.

9. From June 29 to August 15.

10. From August 15 to September 29. It was while keeping this Lent of St. Michael that Francis received the stigmata. Cf. XIII, 1, p. 304; cf. also VIII, 10, p. 259.

with great devotion all the apostles, especially Peter and Paul, because of the ardent love they had toward Christ. Out of reverence and love for them he dedicated to the Lord a special fast of forty days.

The poor man of Christ
had only *two mites*,[11]
namely his body and his soul,
which he could give away in generous charity.
But out of love of Christ
he offered them so continuously
that he seemed to be constantly immolating
his body
through the rigor of fasting
and his spirit
through the ardor of his desire,
sacrificing a *holocaust* in the outer courtyard
and burning *incense*
in the interior of the temple.[12]

4. The ecstatic devotion of his charity so bore him aloft into the divine that his loving kindness was enlarged and extended to all who shared with him in nature and grace. Since his heartfelt devotedness had made him a brother to all other creatures, it is no wonder that the charity of Christ made him more than a brother to those who are stamped with the image of their Creator and *redeemed with the blood* of their Maker (Apoc. 5:9).[13] He would not consider himself a friend of Christ unless he cared for the souls whom Christ redeemed. He used to say that nothing should be preferred to the salvation of souls, offering as the supreme proof of this the fact that it was for souls that the only-begotten Son of God deigned to hang on the

---

11. Mark 12:42.
12. Exod. 30:1, 27-28. Major sources: II C 198, 197.
13. Cf. VIII, 1, p. 250-251.

cross. This is the reason for his struggles in prayer, his untiring preaching tours and his lack of measure in giving example.

Therefore when he was reproached for his excessive severity toward himself, he would reply that he was given as an example for others. For although his innocent flesh, which always of its own accord subjected itself to the spirit, had no need for any penitential scourging, he nevertheless inflicted punishment and burdens on it as an example, *keeping to the hard paths* (Ps. 16:4) for the sake of others. For he used to say: "*If I speak with the tongues of men and angels, but have not charity* and do not show examples of virtue to my neighbors, it is little use to them and *nothing* to myself" (1 Cor. 13:1-3).[14]

5. In the fervent fire
of his charity
he strove to emulate
the glorious triumph of the holy martyrs
in whom
the flame of love could not be extinguished
nor courage be weakened.
Set on fire, therefore,
by that perfect charity *which drives out fear*,[15]
he longed to offer to the Lord
his own life as a *living sacrifice*[16]
in the flames of martyrdom
so that he might repay Christ,
who died for us,
and inspire others to divine love.

In the sixth year of his conversion, burning with a desire of martyrdom, he decided to cross the sea to the regions of Syria in order to preach penance and the Christian faith to the

14. Major source: II C 172-173.
15. 1 John 4:18.
16. Rom. 12:1.

Saracens and other infidels. When he had boarded a ship to go
there, he was driven by contrary winds to land in the region of
Dalmatia. He spent some time there and could not find a ship
that would cross the sea at that time. Feeling that he had been
cheated of his desire, he begged some sailors who were going to
Ancona to take him with them for the love of God. When they
obstinately refused because he could not pay his expenses, the
man of God, trusting completely in the Lord's goodness,
stowed away on the boat with his companion. A certain man
came on board, sent by God for his poor man, as it is believed,
who brought with him the necessary provisions. He called one
of the crew who feared God and told him: "Keep all these
things faithfully for the poor friars who are hiding on board
and give them to them in a friendly fashion when they need
them." And it so happened that, when the crew could not land
anywhere for a number of days because of the force of the
winds, they ate all their provisions and all that was left over
was the alms supernaturally given to the poor Francis.[17] Although this was only a very small amount, by God's power it
was multiplied so much that while they were delayed at sea for
many days by the continuing storm, it fully provided for their
needs all the way to Ancona. Therefore when the sailors saw
that they had escaped many threats of death, as men who had
experienced the horrible dangers of the sea and *had seen the
wonderful works of the Lord in the deep* (Ps. 106:24), they thanked
Almighty God, who always shows himself wonderful and lovable in his friends and servants.[18]

6. When he left the coast, he began to walk over the land
and to sow in it the seed of salvation, reaping a fruitful harvest.
But the fruit of martyrdom had so attracted his heart that he
desired a precious death for the sake of Christ more intensely
than all the merits from the virtues. So he took the road to
Morocco in order to preach the Gospel of Christ to the

---

17. Cf. VII, 13, p. 248-249.
18. Major source: I C 55; minor source: Jul. 34. Cf. *Regula II*, 12.

Miramamolin[19] and his people, hoping to attain in this way the palm of martyrdom he so strongly desired. He was carried along with such a great desire that although he was physically weak, he used to run ahead of his companion on the trip in his haste to achieve his purpose, flying along, as if drunk in spirit. But when he had gone as far as Spain, by God's design, which had more important things in store for him, he was overtaken by a serious illness which hindered him from achieving what he desired. Realizing, then, that his physical life was still necessary for the children he had begotten, the man of God, although he considered death as *gain* for himself (Phil. 1:21), returned to *feed the sheep* entrusted to his care (John 21:17).[20]

7. The ardor of his charity urged his spirit on toward martyrdom, and he tried to set out to the infidels yet a third time, hoping to shed his blood for the spread of the faith in the Trinity. In the 13th year of his conversion, he traveled to the regions of Syria, constantly exposing himself to many dangers in order to reach the presence of the Soldan of Babylon.[21] For at that time there was a fierce war between the Christians and the Saracens,[22] with their camps situated in close quarters opposite each other in the field so that there was no way of passing from one to the other without danger of death. A cruel edict had been issued by the Soldan that whoever would bring back the head of a Christian would receive as a reward a gold piece.[23] But Francis, the intrepid knight of Christ, hoping to be able to achieve his purpose, decided to make the journey, not terrified by the fear of death, but rather drawn by desire for it.

---

19. The medieval European designation for the Almohad sovereign of Morocco; it is a corruption of the Arabic *Amiru'l muminin*, commander of the faithful.

20. Major source: I C 56; minor sources: Jul. 35-36; I C 37.

21. *Syria* was often used as a general name for the Levant. The *soldan of Babylon* was actually the ruler of Egypt (*Babylon* was the name given to modern Cairo) whose power extended also over the Holy Land except for the small enclaves still held by the Crusaders.

22. The fifth Crusade, which for tactical reasons attacked Egypt rather than Palestine. The Crusaders were at this time besieging Damietta, on the delta of the Nile.

23. In the original *Byzantinum aureum*. The gold *byzant* or *bezant* was a current coin all over Christendom and Islam.

After praying, *strengthened* by *the Lord* (1 Kings 30:6), he confidently chanted the verse of the Prophet: *"Even if I should walk in the midst of the shadow of death, I shall not fear evil because you are with me"* (Ps. 22:4).[24]

8. He took with him as his companion a friar named Illuminato, a virtuous and enlightened man. When he had begun his journey, he came upon two lambs. Overjoyed to see them, the holy man said to his companion: *"Trust in the Lord* (Ecclus. 11:22), brother, for the Gospel text is being fulfilled in us: *Behold, I am sending you forth like sheep in the midst of wolves"* (Matt. 10:16). When they proceeded farther, the Saracen sentries fell upon them like wolves swiftly overtaking sheep, savagely seized the servants of God and cruelly and contemptuously dragged them away, insulting them, beating them and putting them in chains. Finally, after they had been maltreated in many ways and were exhausted, by divine providence they were led to the Soldan, just as the man of God wished. When that ruler inquired by whom, why and how they had been sent and how they got there, Francis, Christ's servant, answered with an intrepid heart that he had been sent not by man but by the Most High God in order to point out to him and his people the way of salvation and to announce the Gospel of truth. He preached to the Soldan the Triune God and the one Savior of all, Jesus Christ, with such constancy of mind, such courage of soul and such fervor of spirit that the words of the Gospel were clearly and truly fulfilled in him: *I will give you utterance and wisdom which all your adversaries will not be able to resist or answer back* (Luke 21:15).

When the Soldan saw this admirable fervor of spirit and courage in the man of God, he willingly listened to him and earnestly invited him to stay longer with him. Inspired from heaven, Christ's servant said: "If you wish to be converted to Christ along with your people, I will most gladly stay with you

---

24. Major source: I C 57.

for love of him. But if you hesitate to abandon the law of Mahomet for the faith of Christ, then command that an enormous fire be lit and I will walk into the fire along with your priests so that you will recognize which faith deserves to be held as the holier and more certain." The Soldan answered him: "I do not believe that any of my priests would be willing to expose himself to the fire to defend his faith or to undergo any kind of torment." For he had seen immediately one of his priests, a man full of authority and years, slipping away from his view when he heard Francis's words. The saint said to the Soldan: "If you wish to promise that if I come out of the fire unharmed, you and your people will come over to the worship of Christ, then I will enter the fire alone. And if I shall be burned, you must attribute it to my sins. But if God's power protects me, you will acknowledge *Christ the power and wisdom of God* as *true God* and the *Savior* of all" (1 Cor. 1:24; John 17:3, 4:42). The Soldan replied that he did not dare to accept this choice because he feared a revolt among his people. Nevertheless he offered Francis many valuable gifts, which the man of God, greedy not for worldly possessions but the salvation of souls, spurned as if they were dirt.[25] Seeing that the holy man so completely despised worldly possessions, the Soldan was filled with admiration, and developed an even greater respect for him. Although he refused, or perhaps did not dare, to come over to the Christian faith, he nevertheless devoutly asked Christ's servant to accept the gifts and give them to the Christian poor or to churches for the Soldan's salvation. But Francis would in no way accept them because he was accustomed to flee from the burden of money and he did not see that true piety had taken root in the Soldan's soul.[26]

9. When he saw that he was making no progress in con-

---

25. Cf. II, 1, p. 192.
26. Major source: I C 57; minor source: Jul. 36. The incidents of the two sheep and of the proposed ordeal by fire are not in any of Bonaventure's sources; he may have obtained them orally from brother Illuminato.

verting these people and that he could not *achieve his purpose* (2 Tim. 3:10), namely martyrdom, he went back to the lands of the faithful, as he was advised by a divine revelation.

> Thus by the kindness of God
> and the merits of the virtue of the holy man,
> it came about
> mercifully and remarkably
> that the friend of Christ
> sought with all his strength
> to die for him
> and yet could not achieve it.
> Thus he was not deprived
> of the merit of his desired martyrdom
> and was spared
> to be honored in the future
> with a unique privilege.
> Thus it came about
> that the divine fire
> burned still more perfectly in his heart
> so that later it steamed forth clearly
> in his flesh.
> O truly blessed man,
> whose flesh,
> although not cut down by a tyrant's steel,
> was yet not deprived
> of bearing a likeness of *the Lamb that was slain*![27]
> O, truly and fully blessed man, I say,
> whose life
> "the persecutor's sword did not take away,
> and who yet did not lose the palm of martyrdom"![28]

---

27. Apoc. 5:12.
28. *Breviarium Romanum*, antiphon at second Vespers for the feast of St. Martin of Tours. Minor source: I C 57.

CHAPTER TEN

ON
HIS ZEAL FOR PRAYER
AND
THE POWER OF HIS PRAYER

1. Realizing that while he was *in the body*
he was *exiled from the Lord*,[1]
since he was made totally insensible
to earthly desires
through his *love of Christ*,[2]
the servant of Christ Francis
strove to keep his spirit
in the presence of God,
by praying without ceasing[3]
so that he might not be without the comfort
of his *Beloved*.[4]
Prayer was a delight
to this contemplative
who had already become
a fellow citizen of the angels
and who, making the rounds of the heavenly mansions,
sought with burning desire
that Beloved[5]
from whom he was separated
only by the wall of the flesh.
Prayer was a support
to this worker;

1. 2 Cor. 5:6, 8.
2. 2 Cor. 5:14.
3. 1 Thes. 5:17.
4. Cant. 2:3.
5. Cant. 3:1-2.

for in everything which he did,
distrusting his own effort
and trusting in God's loving concern,
he cast his care completely *upon the Lord*[6]
in urgent prayers to him.
He used to state firmly
that the grace of prayer
was to be desired above all else
by a religious man,
believing that without it no one could prosper in God's service.
He used whatever means he could
to arouse his friars
to be zealous in prayer.[7]
For whether walking or sitting,
inside or outside,
working or resting,
he was so intent on prayer
that he seemed to have dedicated to it
not only his heart and body
but also all his effort and time.[8]

2. He was accustomed not to pass over negligently any visitation of the Spirit. When it was granted, he followed it and as long as the Lord allowed, he enjoyed the sweetness offered him. When he was on a journey and felt the breathing of the divine Spirit, letting his companions go on ahead, he would stand still and render this new inspiration fruitful, not *receiving the grace in vain* (2 Cor. 6:1). Many times he was lifted up in ecstatic contemplation so that, rapt out of himself and experiencing what is beyond human understanding, he was unaware of what went on about him. Once when he was traveling

---

6. Ps. 54:23.
7. Cf. IV, 3, p. 208-209.
8. Major source: II C 94; minor source I C 71. Cf. *Regula I*, 3, 23; *Regula II*, 3, 5; *De religiosa habitatione in eremo*, 1-3.

through Borgo San Sepolcro, a heavily populated town, and was riding on an ass because of physical weakness, crowds rushed to meet him out of devotion. He was pulled and held back by them, pushed and touched all over; yet he seemed insensible to it all and noticed nothing at all of what was going on around him, as if he were a lifeless corpse. Long after he had passed the town and left the crowds, he came to a house of lepers; and that contemplator of heavenly things, as if returning from far away, solicitously inquired when they would be approaching Borgo San Sepolcro. His mind was so fixed on heavenly splendors that he was not aware of the varieties of place, time and people that he passed. That this happened to him often was confirmed by the repeated experience of his companions.[9]

3. He had learned in prayer that the presence of the Holy Spirit for which he longed was granted more intimately to those who invoke him, the more the Holy Spirit found them withdrawn from the noise of worldly affairs. Therefore seeking out lonely places,[10] he used to go to deserted areas and abandoned churches to pray at night. There he often endured horrible struggles with devils who fought with him physically, trying to distract him from his commitment to prayer. But armed with heavenly weapons, the more vehemently he was attacked by the enemy, the more courageous he became in practicing virtue and the more fervent in prayer, saying confidently to Christ:[11] *"Under the shadow of your wings, protect me from the face of the wicked who have attacked me"* (Ps. 16:8-9). To the devils he said: "Do whatever you want to me, you malicious and deceitful spirits! For you cannot do anything except insofar as God relaxes his hold on you. And I am ready and happy to endure everything that his hand should decide to let

---

9. Major sources: II C 95, 98.
10. Cf. VI, 6-7, pp. 234-235.
11. Cf. VI, 10, p. 236-237.

loose on me." Such firmness of mind the devils could not bear, and they retreated in confusion.[12]

4. When the man of God was left alone and at peace, he would fill the groves with sighs, sprinkle the ground with tears, strike his breast with his fist and having found there a kind of secret hiding place, would converse with his Lord. There he would answer his Judge, there he would entreat his Father, there he would entertain his Friend; and there also on several occasions the friars who were devoutly observing him heard him groan aloud, imploring the divine mercy for sinners and weeping for the Lord's passion[13] as if it were there before his eyes. There he was seen praying at night, with his hands outstretched in the form of a cross, his whole body lifted up from the ground and surrounded by a sort of shining cloud. The extraordinary illumination around his body was a witness to the wonderful light that shone within his soul. There also, as is proven by certain evidence, the *unknown and hidden secrets of* divine *wisdom* were opened up to him (Ps. 50:8), although he never spoke of them outside except when *the love of Christ urged* him (2 Cor. 5:14) and the good of his neighbor demanded. For he used to say: "It happens that if a person loses some priceless thing for the sake of a small gain, he easily provokes the one who gave it not to give again."

When he returned from his private prayers, by which he was changed almost into another man, he used to expend the greatest effort to be like the others so that what he might show outwardly would not *deprive* him *of* his inner *reward* (Ecclus. 2:8) because of the glow of human attention. When he was suddenly moved in public by a visitation from the Lord, he would always put something between himself and the bystanders, lest he make common the sight of the Bridegroom's intimate embraces. When he prayed with the friars, he completely

---

12. Major sources: I C 71-72; II C 122. Cf. I C 91, 94, 103; II C 94.
13. Cf. I, 5, p. 189.

avoided all spluttering, groaning, deep sighs or external movements, either because he loved to keep secrecy or because he had withdrawn into his interior and was totally carried into God. He often told his companions: "When a servant of God receives a divine visitation in prayer, he should say: 'Lord, you have sent this consolation from heaven to me an unworthy sinner and I entrust it to your keeping because I feel that I am a robber of your treasure.' When he returns from his prayer, he should show himself as a poor man and a sinner, as if he had obtained no new grace."[14]

5. Once when the man of God was praying at the Portiuncula, it happened that the bishop of Assisi came to visit him as he often did. As soon as he entered the friars' place, he went more abruptly than he should to the cell where Christ's servant was praying, and after knocking at the door, was about to enter when he put his head in and saw the saint praying. Suddenly the bishop began to tremble, his limbs stiffened, he lost his voice and all at once by the will of God he was cast outside with force and driven some distance backward. Shaken, the bishop hurried to the friars, and when God had restored his speech, with his first words and as best he could he confessed his fault.

Another time it happened that the abbot of the monastery of St. Justin in the diocese of Perugia met Christ's servant on the road. When he saw him, the devout abbot quickly got down from his horse to show reverence to the man of God and to confer with him a bit on the welfare of his soul. Finally, after a pleasant conversation, the abbot, as he was leaving, humbly asked Francis to pray for him. The beloved man of God replied: "I will be happy to pray for you." When the abbot had gone a little way, the faithful Francis said to his companion: "Wait a little, brother, because I wish to pay the debt as I promised." As Francis prayed, suddenly the abbot felt in his

---

14. Major sources: II C 95, 11, 99, 94. Cf. II C 52-53, 127; *Admonitiones*, 22, 28; I C 98; II C 135, 137, 139.

spirit an unusual warmth and sweetness such as he had never before experienced, so much so that he was rapt in ecstasy and totally lost himself in God. He remained so for a short while, and when he came back to himself, recognized the power of St. Francis in prayer. After that he always burned with a greater love for the Order and related the event to many as a miracle.[15]

6. The holy man was accustomed to recite the canonical hours with no less reverence than devotion. For although he suffered from an illness of the eyes, stomach, spleen and liver, nevertheless he did not want to lean against a wall while he chanted the psalms; but he said the complete hours standing erect[16] and with head uncovered, not letting his eyes wander around and not clipping the syllables short. If he were on a journey, he would stop at the right time and never omitted this reverent and holy practice because of rain. For he used to say: "If the body requires quiet to eat its food, which along with itself will become the food of worms, with what peace and tranquillity should not the soul receive the food of life?"

He thought that he had seriously offended if, when he was at prayer, his mind wandered over vain imaginations. When something like this happened, he did not wait to confess it so that he could atone for it immediately. He so put his zeal into practice that he rarely was bothered by "flies" of this kind.

One Lent he was whittling a little cup to occupy his spare moments and to prevent them from being wasted. When he was reciting Terce, it came to his mind and distracted him a little. Moved by fervor of spirit, he burned the cup in the fire, saying: "I will sacrifice this to the Lord, whose sacrifice it has impeded."

He used to say the psalms with such attention of mind and spirit, as if he had God present. When the Lord's name oc-

---

15. Major sources: II C 100-101.
16. The usual custom is to sit for the psalms and readings and stand for the hymns, canticles and collects, but until recent times the Franciscan custom was to chant the whole office standing.

curred in the psalms, he seemed to lick his lips because of its sweetness. He wanted to honor with special reverence the Lord's name not only when thought but also when spoken and written. He once persuaded the friars to gather all pieces of paper wherever found and to place them in a clean place so that if that sacred name happened to be written there, it would not be trodden underfoot. When he pronounced or heard the name "Jesus," he was filled with joy interiorly and seemed to be altered exteriorly as if some honey-sweet flavor had transformed his taste or some harmonious sound had transformed his hearing.[17]

7. It happened in the third year before his death that he decided, in order to arouse devotion, to celebrate at Greccio with the greatest possible solemnity the memory of the birth of the Child Jesus. So that this would not be considered a type of novelty, he petitioned for and obtained permission from the Supreme Pontiff.[18] He had a crib prepared, hay carried in and an ox and an ass led to the place. The friars are summoned, the people come, the forest resounds with their voices and that venerable night is rendered brilliant and solemn by a multitude of bright lights and by resonant and harmonious hymns of praise. The man of God stands before the crib, filled with affection, bathed in tears and overflowing with joy. A solemn Mass is celebrated over the crib, with Francis as deacon chanting the holy Gospel. Then he preaches to the people standing about concerning the birth of the poor King, whom, when he wished to name him, he called in his tender love, the Child of Bethlehem.

A certain virtuous and truthful knight, Sir John of Greccio, who had abandoned worldly military activity out of love of Christ and had become an intimate friend of the man of God, claimed that he saw a beautiful little boy asleep in the crib and

---

17. Major sources: II C 96-97; I C 82; minor source: I C 115. Cf. II C 70, 197; I C 86; II C 199; I C 45.

18. This detail is added by Bonaventure to his sources.

that the blessed father Francis embraced it in both of his arms
and seemed to wake it from sleep.

Not only does the holiness of the witness
make credible
this vision of the devout knight,
but also the truth it expresses
proves its validity
and the subsequent miracles confirm it.
For Francis's example
when considered by the world
is capable of arousing
the hearts of those who are sluggish
in the faith of Christ.
The hay from the crib
was kept by the people
and miraculously cured sick animals
and drove away different kinds of pestilence.
Thus God glorified his servant in every way
and demonstrated the efficacy
of his holy prayer
by the evident signs
of wonderful miracles.[19]

19. Major sources: I C 84-85-86-87; minor source: Jul. 54-55.

CHAPTER ELEVEN

ON
HIS UNDERSTANDING OF SCRIPTURE
AND
HIS SPIRIT OF PROPHECY

1. His unwearied application to prayer
along with his continual exercise of virtue
had led the man of God
to such serenity of mind
that although he had no skill in Sacred Scripture
acquired through study,[1]
his intellect,
illumined by the brilliance of eternal light,
probed the depths[2] of Scripture
with remarkable acumen.
Free from all stain,
his genius penetrated the hidden depths of the mysteries,
and where the scholarship of the teacher
stands outside,
the affection of the lover
entered within.

At times he would read the sacred books, and what he had once put in his mind he imprinted firmly on his memory. It was not in vain that this attentive mind grasped something he heard, for he would meditate on it with love and continued devotion. Once the friars asked him whether he was pleased that the learned men who had by that time been received into the Order should devote themselves to the study of Sacred Scripture. He

---

1. Cf. I, 1, p. 185.
2. Job 28:11.

replied: "I am indeed pleased, as long as they do not neglect application to prayer, after the example of Christ, of whom we read that he prayed more than he read,[3] and as long as they study not only in order to know what they should say but in order to practice what they have heard and when they have put it into practice themselves to propose it to others likewise. I want my friars," he said, "to be disciples of the Gospel and to progress in knowledge of the truth in such a way as to increase in pure simplicity without separating the simplicity of the dove from the wisdom of the serpent which our eminent Teacher joined together in a statement from his own blessed lips."[4]

2. Francis was once consulted at Siena by a religious who was a doctor of theology about certain questions that were difficult to understand.[5] He brought to light the secrets of divine wisdom with such clarity in teaching that the learned man was absolutely dumbfounded and responded with admiration: "Truly the theology of this holy father, borne aloft, as it were, on the wings of purity and contemplation, is a soaring eagle; but our learning crawls on its belly on the ground." Although he was *unskilled in speaking* (2 Cor. 11:6), he was filled with knowledge and explained doubtful questions and *brought hidden things to light* (Job 28:11). Nor should it sound odd that the holy man should have received from God an understanding of the Scriptures, since through his perfect imitation of Christ he carried into practice the truth described in them and, through the abundant anointing of the Holy Spirit, had their Teacher within himself in his heart (cf. 1 John 2:20).[6]

3. The spirit of prophecy, too, so shone forth in him that he foresaw the future and had knowledge of the secrets of the heart. He was aware of things absent as if they were present, and he miraculously appeared present to those who were ab-

---

3. On Christ's prayer, cf. Matt. 14:23, 19:13; Mark 1:35; Luke 5:16, 6:12. On his reading, cf. Luke 4:16, 2:46.
4. Matt. 10:16. Major sources: II C 102, 195. Cf. II C 102, 163, 189, 194; I C 57; II C 91, 195, 102; *Regula II*, 5.
5. The source indicates that this theologian was a Dominican.
6. Major sources: II C 103, 102.

sent. At the time when the Christian army was besieging Damietta, the man of God was there, armed with faith and not weapons.[7] When on the day of the battle he heard that the Christians were preparing to fight, Christ's servant sighed heavily and said to his companion: "The Lord has shown me that if the battle takes place, it will not go well for the Christians. But if I tell them this, I will be considered a fool. If I remain silent, I will not escape my conscience. What therefore seems best to you?" His companion replied: "Brother, consider it unimportant to be judged by men, for this won't be the first time you pass for a fool. Unburden your conscience, and fear God rather than men." When he heard this, the herald of Christ jumped to his feet and went to the Christians with his salutary warnings, forbidding the battle and announcing their defeat. They took his truth for a fairy tale, hardened their hearts and refused to turn back. They advanced and engaged the enemy in battle, with the result that the whole Christian army was turned to flight, bearing away disgrace rather than triumph. The Christian forces suffered such heavy losses that there were about six thousand dead or captured. From this it was abundantly clear that the wisdom of this poor man was not to be scorned, since *sometimes the soul of a just man will declare truths more clearly than seven sentinels searching the horizon from a height* (Ecclus. 37:18).[8]

4. Another time, after his return from overseas, he went to Celano to preach; and a certain knight invited him to dinner with humble devotion and with great insistence. So he came to the knight's home and the whole family rejoiced at the coming of the poor guests. Before they took any food, the saint offered prayers and praise to God as was his custom, standing with his eyes raised to heaven. When he finished his prayer, he called his kind host aside and confidentially told him: "Look, brother

7. Cf. IX, 7, p. 268.
8. Major sources: II C 27, 30.

host, conquered by your prayers, I have entered your house to eat. Now heed my warnings quickly because you will not dine here but elsewhere. Confess your sins right now, contrite with the sorrow of true repentance; and let nothing remain in you that you do not reveal in a true confession. The Lord will reward you today because you have received his poor with such devotion." The man heeded the saint's words at once; and laying bare all of his sins in confession to Francis's companion, *he put his house in order* (Isa. 38:1) and did everything in his power to prepare for death. At length they went to the table; and while the others began to eat, suddenly their host breathed forth his spirit, carried away by sudden death as the man of God had foretold. So it happened that in recompense for the kindness of his hospitality *he received a prophet's reward because he had received a prophet*, according to the word of Truth (Matt. 10:41). Through the holy man's prophecy, that devout knight prepared himself for a sudden death so that, protected by the armor of repentance, he escaped perpetual damnation and entered into *the eternal dwellings* (Luke 16:9).[9]

5. At the time when the holy man was lying ill at Rieti, a canon by the name of Gedeon, a dissolute and worldly man, became seriously ill and took to his bed. He had himself carried to Francis and, together with those present, he tearfully begged to be blessed with the sign of the cross. Francis answered: "Since you lived in the past according to the desires of the flesh, not fearing God's judgments, how will I make the sign of the cross over you? However, because of the devout requests of those pleading for you, I will make the sign of the cross over you in the name of the Lord. Nevertheless, realize that you will suffer more seriously if, after being delivered, you return *to your vomit* (Prov. 26:11).[10] Because of the sin of ingratitude *worse things than before* (Matt. 12:45) are inflicted." The moment

9. Major source: III C 41; minor source: II C 31.
10. Cf. VIᴵI, 11, p. 260.

he made the sign of the cross over him, the man who had lain there crippled arose healthy and broke out in praise of God, saying: "I am freed." But the bones of his loins made a noise which many heard as if dry sticks were being broken with the hand. After a short time had elapsed, forgetful of God, he gave his body again to impurity. One evening when he had dined at the home of another canon and was sleeping there that night, suddenly the roof of the house fell down on them all. The others escaped death and only that wretched man was trapped and killed. Therefore by the just judgment of God, *the last state of that man became worse than the first* (Matt. 12:45) on account of his vice of ingratitude and his contempt for God, when he should have been grateful for the forgiveness he had received. A crime that is repeated is doubly offensive.[11]

6. Another time, a noble woman, devoted to God, came to the saint to explain her trouble to him and ask for help. She had a very cruel husband who opposed her serving Christ. So she begged the saint to pray for him so that God in his goodness would soften his heart. When he heard this, he said to her: "Go in peace, and without any doubt be assured that your husband will soon be a comfort to you." And he added: "Tell him on God's part and my own, that now is the time of mercy, and afterwards of justice." After receiving a blessing, the woman went home, found her husband and delivered the message. *The Holy Spirit came upon* him (Acts 10:44) making him a new man and inducing him to answer with gentleness: "My lady, let us serve the Lord and save our souls." At the suggestion of his holy wife, they lived a celibate life for many years and both passed away to the Lord on the same day.

The power of the prophetic spirit
in the man of God
was certainly extraordinary,

---

11. Major source: II C 41.

which restored vigor to dried-up limbs
and impressed piety on hardened hearts.
The lucidity of his spirit
was no less an object of wonder;
for he could foresee future events
and even probe the secrets of conscience,
as if he were another Elisha,
who had acquired the two-fold spirit of Elijah.[12]

7. On one occasion he told a friend at Siena what would happen to him at the end of his life. Now when the learned man mentioned above,[13] who consulted him at one time about the Scriptures, heard of this, he asked the holy father in doubt whether he had really said what the man had claimed. Francis not only confirmed that he had said this but besides foretold to this learned man who was so eager to know another's future the circumstances of his own end. To impress this with greater certainty on his heart, Francis miraculously revealed to him a certain secret scruple of conscience which the man had and which he had never disclosed to any living person; and he relieved him of it by his sound advice. The truth of all this was confirmed by the fact that this religious eventually died just as Christ's servant had foretold.[14]

8. When he was returning from overseas with Brother Leonard of Assisi as his companion, it happened that he was riding for a while on a donkey because he was fatigued and weary. But his companion, following along behind, was not a little weary himself and giving in to human weakness began to say within himself: "His parents and mine never played together as equals. And look—he is riding and I am on foot leading his donkey." While he was thinking this, the holy man all at once got down from the donkey and said: "Brother, it is

---

12. Cf. 4 Kings 2:9ff. Major source: II C 38.
13. Cf. XI, 2, p. 281.
14. This incident is not found in Celano or Julian.

not right that I should ride and you should go on foot, for in the world you were more noble and more powerful than I." The friar was dumbfounded at this and blushed, realizing he had been caught. He fell at Francis's feet and, bathed in tears, exposed his thought naked to the saint and begged his forgiveness.[15]

9. A certain friar, devoted to God and to Christ's servant, frequently turned over in his heart the idea that whoever was held in the holy man's intimate affection would be worthy of God's grace and whomever he excluded from his intimacy would not be regarded among the elect by God. He was obsessed by the repeated pressure of this thought and intensely longed for the intimate friendship of the man of God, but never revealed the secret of his heart to anyone. The devoted father called him and spoke sweetly to him as follows: "Let no thought trouble you, my son, because among those who are especially dear to me I hold you most dear, and I gladly lavish upon you my friendship and love." The friar was amazed at this and became even more devoted to Francis. He not only grew in his love for the holy man, but also through the grace of the Holy Spirit he was filled with still greater gifts.

While Francis was staying on Mount La Verna, secluded in his cell, one of his companions[16] greatly desired to have some of the Lord's words briefly noted down and written in the saint's own hand. By this means he believed he would escape from a serious temptation that was vexing him, not of the flesh but of the spirit, or at very least that he would bear it more easily. Languishing with this desire, he was in a state of internal anxiety because, overcome with embarrassment, he did not dare to disclose the matter to the venerable father. But what man did not tell Francis the Holy Spirit revealed to him. He ordered this previously mentioned friar to bring him some ink

15. Major source: II C 31.
16. Brother Leo.

and paper; and he wrote down the Praises of the Lord in his own hand as the friar desired and, finally, a blessing for him, saying: "Take this slip of paper and guard it carefully until the day of your death."[17] The friar took the gift he so much desired and immediately his temptation was put to flight. The writing was preserved and, since it later worked miracles, it became a witness to the power of Francis.[18]

10. There was a certain friar, eminent in holiness and outstanding in his manner of life, as far as it seemed outwardly, but who did everything very much in his own way. He spent all his time in prayer and observed silence with such strictness that he used to confess not with words but with signs. It happened that the holy father came to that place, saw the friar and spoke to the other friars about him. When they all commended and praised him highly, the man of God replied: "Brothers, let him alone and do not praise to me what the devil has wrought in him. Know in truth that it is a temptation of the devil and a fraudulent deception." The friars took this harshly, judging that it was impossible that contrivances of fraud could paint themselves over with so many signs of perfection. But not many days later this friar left the Order, and the brilliance of the interior insight with which the man of God perceived the secrets of his heart became abundantly clear.

In this way
Francis foretold with unchanging truth
the fall
of many who seemed to stand firm
and the conversion to Christ
of many who were perverse.

---

17. On one side of this slip of paper Francis wrote the *Praises of God*, and on the other the Aaronic blessing (Num. 6:24-26) now commonly known as the *Blessing of St. Francis*, with the added line *May the Lord bless you, Brother Leo*, and the Tau as signature.

18. The original sheet in the handwriting of St. Francis (with a few lines of authentication in that of Brother Leo) is still preserved today in a reliquiary in the Basilica of St. Francis at Assisi. Major sources: I C 49-50; II C 49.

He seemed to have approached
in contemplation
the mirror of the eternal light,[19]
in whose marvelous splendor
the gaze of his mind saw
things that happened at a physical distance
as if they were present.[20]

11. Once while his vicar[21] was holding a chapter, Francis was praying in his cell, as the *go-between and mediator* (Deut. 5:5) between the friars and God. One of them, hiding behind the mantle of some excuse, would not submit himself to the discipline of obedience. Seeing this in spirit, the holy man called one of the friars and said to him: "Brother, I saw the devil on the back of that disobedient friar, holding him tightly by the neck. Driven by such a rider, he had spurned the bridle of obedience and was giving rein to his own inclination. But when I prayed to God for the friar, the devil suddenly went away in confusion. Go and tell the friar to submit his neck to the yoke of holy obedience without delay!" Admonished by this intermediary, the friar immediately was converted to God and cast himself humbly at the feet of the vicar.[22]

12. Another time it happened that two friars came from a distance to the hermitage of Greccio to see the man of God and to receive his blessing which they had desired for a long time. When they came and did not find him, because he had already withdrawn and gone to his cell, they went away quite desolate. And behold, as they were leaving, although he could not have known anything of their arrival or departure through any human perception, he came out of his cell contrary to his custom, shouted after them and blessed them in Christ's name

---

19. Wisd. 7:26.
20. Major sources: II C 28; I C 48. Cf. II C 27, 54.
21. Elias.
22. Major source: II C 34.

with the sign of the cross, just as they had desired.[23]

13. Two friars once came from the Terra di Lavoro, the elder of whom had given much scandal to the younger. When they reached the father, he asked the younger friar how his companion had behaved toward him on the way. The friar replied: "Quite well"; but Francis said: "Be careful, brother, not to tell a lie under the pretext of humility. For I know, I know; but wait a little and you will see." The friar was amazed at how he could have known in spirit what had happened at a distance. Now not many days after, the one who had given scandal to his brother left the Order in contempt and went out into the world. He did not ask the father's forgiveness nor accept the discipline of correction as he should. In that single fall, two things shone forth clearly: the equity of the divine judgment and the penetrating power of the spirit of prophecy.[24]

14. How he appeared as present
to those who were absent,
through God's power,
becomes evidently clear
from what was said above,
if we recall to mind
how he appeared to the friars,
although absent,
transfigured in a fiery chariot,[25]
and how he presented himself
at the Chapter of Arles
in the image of a cross.[26]
We ought to believe
that this was done by divine providence
so that from his miraculous appearance in bodily presence

---

23. Major source: II C 45.
24. Major source: II C 39.
25. Cf. IV, 4, p. 209-210.
26. Cf. IV, 10, p. 215.

it might clearly shine forth
how present and open his spirit was
to the light of *eternal wisdom*,
which is mobile beyond all motion,
reaching everywhere because of its purity.
And spreading through the nations
into holy souls
it makes them prophets and friends of God.[27]
The exalted Teacher
is accustomed to open his mysteries
to the simple and the *little ones*[28]
as was first seen
in the case of David, the most distinguished of the prophets,
and afterwards in Peter, the prince of the apostles,
and finally in Francis, the little poor man of Christ.
Although these were simple men[29]
unskilled in learning,
they were made illustrious
by the teaching of the Holy Spirit.[30]
One was a shepherd
who *pastured the Synagogue,*
the flock[31] God had led out of Egypt;[32]
the other was a fisherman
who *filled the net* of the Church[33]
with many kinds of believers.
The last was a *merchant*
who *bought the pearl* of the Gospel life,
selling and giving away *all he had*
for the sake of Christ.[34]

27. Wisd. 7:24, 27.
28. Prov. 3:32; Matt. 11:25.
29. Cf. Acts 4:13.
30. Cf. John 16:13; Acts 13:9.
31. Cf. John 21:15; 1 Pet. 5:2.
32. Cf. 1 Kings 16:11-12; 2 Kings 5:2.
33. Cf. Matt. 13:47-48.
34. Cf. Matt. 13:44-46. Cf. also I C 25.

CHAPTER TWELVE

ON
THE EFFICACY OF HIS PREACHING
AND
HIS GRACE OF HEALING

1. Francis,
the truly faithful servant and minister of Christ,
in order to do everything
faithfully and perfectly,
used to direct his efforts chiefly
to the exercise of those virtues
which by the inspiration of the Holy Spirit
he knew pleased God more.
In this matter it happened
that he fell into a great struggle
over a doubt which,
after many days of prayer,
he proposed for resolution
to the friars who were close to him.
"What do you think, brothers,
what do you judge better?
That I should spend my time in prayer
or that I should go about preaching?
I am a poor little man,
simple and *unskilled in speech*;[1]
I have received a greater grace of prayer than of speaking.
Also in prayer there seems to be a profit
and the accumulation of graces,
but in preaching
the distribution of gifts already received from heaven.

---

1. 2 Cor. 11:6.

In prayer
our interior affections are purified
and we are united
with the one, 'true and highest good'[2]
as well as strengthened in virtue;
in preaching,
we get dust on our spiritual feet,[3]
distraction over many things and relaxation of discipline.
Finally, in prayer
we address God,
listen to him
and dwell among the angels
as if we were living an angelic life;
in preaching
we must think, see, say and hear
human things,
adapting ourselves to them
as if we were living on a human level,
for men and among men.
But there is one thing to the contrary,
that seems to outweigh all these considerations
before God,
namely that the only begotten Son of God,
who is the highest wisdom,[4]
came down from *the bosom of the Father*[5]
for the sake of souls
in order to instruct the world with his example
and to speak the *word* of salvation to men,
whom he would redeem
with the price of his sacred blood,
cleanse with its *washing*[6]
and nourish with its draught,

---

2. Cf. *Regula I*, 23.
3. Cf. Luke 10:11.
4. Cf. 1 Cor. 1:24, 30.
5. John 1:18.
6. Eph. 5:26.

holding back for himself absolutely nothing
that he could freely give for our salvation.
And because we should do everything
according to the *pattern* shown to us in him
as *on the heights of the mountain*,[7]
it seems more pleasing to God
that I interrupt my quiet
and go out to labor."[8]
When he had mulled over these words
for many days with his friars,
he could not perceive with certainty
which of these he should choose
as more acceptable to Christ.
Although he understood extraordinary things
through the spirit of prophecy,
this question he could not resolve with certainty
on his own.
But God's providence had a better plan,
that the merit of preaching would be shown
by a revelation from heaven,
thus preserving the humility of Christ's servant.

2. He was not ashamed
to ask advice in small matters
from those under him,
true Friar Minor that he was,
though he had learned great things
from the supreme Teacher.
He was accustomed
to search out with special eagerness
how and in what way
he could serve God more perfectly
according to God's good pleasure.
As long as he lived

7. Exod. 25:40.
8. Cf. I C 35.

> this was his supreme philosophy,
> this his supreme desire,
> to inquire from the wise and the simple,
> the perfect and the imperfect,
> the young and the old,
> how he could more effectively reach
> the summit of perfection.[9]

Choosing, therefore, two of the friars, he sent them to Brother Silvester—who had seen the cross coming out from his mouth[10] and in those days spent his time in continuous prayer on the mountain above Assisi—that Silvester might ask God to resolve his doubt over this matter and send him the answer in God's name. He also asked the holy virgin Clare[11] to consult with the purest and simplest of the virgins living under her rule and to pray herself with the other sisters in order to seek *the Lord's will* (Luke 12:47) in this matter. Through the miraculous revelation of the Holy Spirit, the venerable priest and the virgin dedicated to God came to the same conclusion: that it was God's good pleasure that Francis should preach as the herald of Christ. When the two friars returned and told him God's will as they had received it, he at once rose, *girded himself* (John 21:7) and without the slightest delay took to the roads. He went with such fervor to carry out the divine command and he ran along so swiftly that *the hand of God* seemed to be *upon him* (4 Kings 3:15), giving him new strength from heaven.

3. When he was approaching Bevagna, he came to a spot where a large flock of birds of various kinds had come together. When God's saint saw them, he quickly ran to the spot and greeted them as if they were endowed with reason. They all became alert and turned toward him, and those perched in the

---

9. Major source: I C 91; the following incident and that described in no. 1 are not found in Celano or Julian, but appear in the *Fioretti*, 16.

10. Cf. III, 5, pp. 201-202.

11. Cf. IV, 6, p. 211.

trees bent their heads as he approached them and in an uncommon way directed their attention to him. He went right up to them and solicitously urged them to listen to the word of God, saying: "Oh birds, my brothers, you have a great obligation to praise your Creator, who clothed you in feathers and gave you wings to fly with, provided you with the pure air and cares for you without any worry on your part." While he was saying this and similar things to them, the birds showed their joy in a remarkable fashion: They began to stretch their necks, extend their wings, open their beaks and gaze at him attentively. He went through their midst with amazing fervor of spirit, brushing against them with his tunic. Yet none of them moved from the spot until the man of God made the sign of the cross and gave them his blessing and permission to leave; then they all flew away together. His companions waiting on the road saw all these things. When he returned to them, that pure and simple man began to accuse himself of negligence because he had not preached to the birds before.[12]

4. From there he went preaching through the neighboring districts and came to a village by the name of Alviano. When the people were gathered, he called for silence, but could scarcely be heard above the racket made by some swallows that were building nests there. In the hearing of all the people, the man of God addressed them and said: "My sister swallows, it is time now for me to speak because you have said enough already. Listen to the word of God and keep silence until his message is finished." As if they had been able to understand him, they suddenly became silent and did not move from that place until the whole sermon was finished. All who saw this were filled with amazement and glorified God. News of this miracle spread around everywhere, enkindling reverence for the saint and devotion for the faith.[13]

---

12. Major sources: III C 20; I C 58; minor source: Jul. 37.
13. Major source: III C 21; minor souce: I C 59.

5. In the city of Parma, a certain student, an excellent young man, was diligently studying with his companions when he was distracted by the troublesome chattering of a swallow. He began to say to his companions: "This must be one of those swallows that kept bothering the man of God Francis when he was once preaching, until he had to shut them up." He turned to the swallow and said confidently: "In the name of God's servant Francis I command you to come to me and to be silent at once." When it heard the name of Francis, it immediately became silent, as if it really had been trained by the teaching of the man of God, and entrusted itself to the student's hands as if to a safe refuge. The amazed student immediately set it free and never heard its chattering again.[14]

6. Another time when God's servant was preaching on the seashore at Gaeta, out of devotion crowds rushed upon him in order to touch him. Horrified at such popularity he jumped all alone into a small boat that was drawn up on the shore. The boat began to move as if it had both intellect and motion of itself and, without the help of any oars, glided away from the shore, to the wonderment of all who witnessed it. When it had gone out some distance into the deep water, it stood motionless on the waves, as long as the holy man preached to the attentive crowd on the shore. When, after hearing the sermon, seeing the miracle and receiving his blessing, the crowd went away and would no longer trouble him, the boat returned to land on its own power.

Who, then, would be
so obstinate and lacking in piety
as to look down upon the preaching of Francis?
By his remarkable power,
not only creatures lacking reason learned obedience
but even inanimate objects served him

---

14. Major source: III C 22.

when he preached,
as if they had life.[15]

7. *The Spirit of the Lord*
who had *anointed and sent*[16] him
and also *Christ,*
the power and the wisdom of God,[17]
were with their servant Francis
wherever he went[18]
so that he might abound
with words of sound teaching
and shine
with miracles of great power.
For his word
was like a burning fire
penetrating the innermost depths of the heart;
and it filled the minds of all
with admiration,
since it made no pretense
at the elegance of human composition
but exuded the perfume
of divine revelation.[19]

Once when he was to preach in the presence of the pope and cardinals at the suggestion of the lord cardinal of Ostia,[20] he memorized a sermon which he had carefully composed. When he stood in their midst to present his edifying words, he went completely blank and was unable to say anything at all. This he admitted to them in true humility and directed himself to invoke the grace of the Holy Spirit. Suddenly he began to over-

15. This incident is not found in Celano or Julian.
16. Isa. 61:1; Luke 4:18.
17. 1 Cor. 1:24.
18. Ruth 1:16.
19. Major source: I C 23; cf. also I C 72.
20. The pope was Honorius III; cf. IV, 11, pp. 216-217. The lord bishop of Ostia was Hugolino, the cardinal protector of the Friars Minor and later Gregory IX; cf. VI, 5, p. 233.

---

flow with such effective eloquence and to move the minds of those high-ranking men to compunction with such force and power that it was clearly evident it was not he, but the *Spirit* of the Lord who *was speaking* (Acts 6:10).[21]

8. Because he had first convinced himself by practice of what he persuaded others to do by his words, he did not fear reproof but preached the truth most confidently. He did not know how to touch the faults of others gingerly but only how to lance them; nor did he foster the habits of sinners but struck at them with harsh reproaches. He used to speak with the same firmness of mind to the great and the small and with the same joy of spirit to a few or to many. People of every age and sex hastened to see and hear this new man sent to the world by heaven.[22]

Traveling through various regions,
he preached the Gospel
with burning love,
as the Lord worked with him *and confirmed his preaching
with the signs that followed.*[23]
For in the power of the name of God,
Francis, the herald of truth,
cast out devils and healed the sick,[24]
and what is greater,
softened the obstinate hearts of sinners
and moved them to repentance,
restoring at the same time health
to their bodies and hearts,
as his miracles prove,
a few of which we will cite below as examples.

9. In the town of Toscanella he was warmly received and

---

21. Major source: 1 C 73; but Celano does not recount Francis's forgetting his sermon.
22. Major source: I C 36; minor source: Jul. 58.
23. Mark 16:20.
24. Luke 11:15, 9:2.

given hospitality by a certain knight whose only son had been crippled since birth. At the father's insistent pleading, Francis lifted the child up with his hand and cured him instantly, so that all the limbs of his body *at once got back their strength* (Acts 3:7) in view of all; and the boy became healthy and strong and immediately rose, *walking and leaping and praising God* (Acts 3:8).[25]

In the town of Narni, at the request of the bishop, Francis made the sign of the cross from head to foot over a paralytic who had lost the use of all his limbs, and restored him to perfect health.[26]

In the diocese of Rieti a boy was so swollen for four years that he could not see his own legs. When the boy was presented to Francis by his tearful mother, he was cured the moment the holy man touched him with his sacred hands.[27]

At the town of Orte a boy was so twisted that his head was bent down to his feet and some of his bones were broken. When Francis made the sign of the cross over him at the tearful entreaty of his parents, he was cured on the spot and stretched out immediately.[28]

10. There was a woman in the town of Gubbio whose hands were so withered and crippled that she could do nothing with them. When Francis made the sign of the cross over them in the name of the Lord, she was so perfectly cured that she immediately went home and prepared with her own hands food for him and for the poor, like Peter's mother-in-law (cf. Matt. 8:14-15).[29]

In the village of Bevagna he marked the eyes of a blind girl with his spittle three times in the name of the Trinity and restored the sight she longed for.[30]

---

25. Major sources: I C 65; III C 175.
26. Major sources: I C 66; III C 176; minor source: Jul. 48.
27. Major source: III C 174.
28. Major source: III C 178.
29. Major sources: III C 177; I C 67; minor source: Jul. 48.
30. Major source: III C 124.

A woman of the town of Narni who had been struck blind received from him the sign of the cross and recovered the sight she longed for.[31]

At Bologna a boy had one eye covered over with an opaque film so that he could see nothing at all with it nor could he be helped by any treatment. After God's servant had made the sign of the cross from his head to his feet, he recovered his sight so completely that, having later entered the Order of Friars Minor, he claimed that he could see far more clearly with the eye that had been previously ill than with the eye that had always been well.[32]

In the village of Sangemini God's servant was given hospitality by a devoted man whose wife was troubled by a devil. After praying, Francis commanded the devil to depart in virtue of obedience, and by God's power drove him out so suddenly that it became evident that the obstinacy of devils cannot resist the power of holy obedience.[33]

In Città di Castello an evil spirit which had taken possession of a woman departed full of indignation when commanded under obedience by the holy man, and left the woman who had been possessed free in body and mind.[34]

11. A friar was suffering from such a horrible illness that many were convinced it was more a case of possession by the devil than a natural sickness. For he was often cast down and rolled about foaming at the mouth, with his limbs now contracted, now stretched out, now folded, now twisted, now rigid and hard. Sometimes, when he was stretched out and rigid, he would be lifted into the air with his feet level with his head and then would fall down horribly. Christ's servant was full of pity for him in such a miserable and incurable illness, and he sent him a morsel of the bread he was eating. When he

31. Major sources: I C 67; III C 121.
32. This incident is not found in Celano or Julian. This is not the curing of Illuminato described in III C 123.
33. Major sources: I C 69; III C 155; minor source: Jul. 50.
34. Major sources: I C 70; III C 156.

tasted the bread, the sick man received such strength that he never suffered from that illness again.[35]

In the district of Arezzo a woman had been in labor for several days and was already near death; there was no cure left for her in her desperate state except from God. Christ's servant was passing through that region, riding on horseback because of physical illness. It happened that when the animal was being returned to its owner, it was led through the village where the woman was suffering. When the men of the place saw the horse on which the holy man had been mounted, they took off the reins and placed them on the woman. As soon as the reins touched her, all danger miraculously passed, and she gave birth safely.[36]

A man from Città della Pieve, who was religious and God-fearing, had in his possession a cord which our holy father had worn around his waist. Since many men and women in that town were suffering from various forms of illness, he went to the homes of the sick and gave the patients water to drink in which he had dipped the cord. In this way many were cured.[37]

Sick persons who ate bread touched by the man of God were quickly restored to health by divine power.[38]

12. Since the herald of Christ
in his preaching
brilliantly shone with these and many other miracles,
people paid attention to what he said
as if *an angel of the Lord were speaking.*[39]
His extraordinary achievement in virtue,[40]
his *spirit of prophecy,*[41]

---

35. Major sources: III C 195; I C 68; minor source: Jul. 49; in Celano and Julian, Francis prays and makes the sign of the cross over the friar but the detail of the bread is not mentioned.
36. Major sources: I C 63; III C 108; minor source: Jul. 51.
37. Major source: I C 64; minor source: Jul. 52.
38. Cf. I C 63; III C 19; Jul. 52.
39. Judges 2:4.
40. Beginning with this, Bonaventure lists ten items which he proposes as testimonies of the significance of Francis's preaching. For Francis's achievement in virtue, cf. V-X, pp. 218-279.
41. Apoc. 19:10; cf. XI, pp. 280- 290

the power of his miracles,[42]
his mission to preach conferred from heaven,[43]
the obedience paid him by creatures lacking reason,[44]
the powerful change of heart experienced
at the hearing of his words,[45]
his being instructed by the Holy Spirit
on a level beyond human teaching,[46]
his authorization to preach
granted by the Supreme Pontiff
who was guided by a revelation,[47]
the Rule, in which the manner of preaching is described,
confirmed by the same Vicar of Christ,[48]
and the marks of the Supreme King
imprinted on his body like a seal—[49]
these are like ten witnesses
which testify without any doubt to the whole world
that Francis, the herald of Christ,
is worthy of veneration because of his mission,
authoritative in his teaching,
admirable for his holiness,
and therefore he preached the Gospel of Christ
as a true messenger of God.

42. Cf. XII, 9-11, pp. 298-301.
43. Cf. XII, 2, p. 294.
44. Cf. XII, 3-6, pp. 294-297.
45. Cf. XI, 6; XII, 7-8, pp. 284, 297-298.
46. Cf. XI, 1-2; XII, 7, pp. 280-281, 297-298.
47. Cf. III, 8-10, pp. 203-206.
48. Cf. IV, 11, pp. 216-217; cf. *Regula II*, 9; also *Regula I*, 16-17, 43-48.
49. Cf. XIII, pp. 303-314.

CHAPTER THIRTEEN

ON
HIS SACRED STIGMATA

1. The angelic man Francis
had made it his habit
never to relax in his pursuit of the good.
Rather, like the heavenly spirits on *Jacob's ladder*
he either *ascended* to God
or *descended* to his neighbor.[1]
For he had wisely learned
so to divide the time given to him for merit
that he expended part of it in working for his neighbor's benefit
and devoted the other part
to the peaceful ecstasy of contemplation.
Therefore when in his compassion he had worked
for the salvation of others,
he would then leave behind the restlessness of the crowds
and seek out hidden places
of quiet and solitude,
where he could spend his time more freely
with the Lord
and cleanse himself of any dust
that might have adhered to him
from his involvement with men.[2]

Two years
before he gave his spirit back to heaven,
after many and varied labors,
he was *led apart* by divine providence
to a *high* place[3]

---

1. Gen. 28:12.
2. Major source: I C 91.
3. Matt. 17:1; by employing the Latin words *excelsum seorsum* from the above text in Matthew, Bonaventure is making an allusion to Mt. Tabor and Jesus' transfiguration.

which is called Mount La Verna.
When according to his usual custom
he had begun to fast there for forty days
in honor of St. Michael the Archangel,[4]
he experienced more abundantly than usual
an overflow of the sweetness of heavenly contemplation,
he burned with a stronger flame
of heavenly desires,
and he began to experience more fully
the gifts of heavenly grace.
He was borne aloft
not like one who out of curiosity
searches into the supreme majesty
only to be crushed by its glory,
but like *the faithful and prudent servant*[5]
searching out God's good pleasure,
to which he desires with the greatest ardor
to conform himself in every way.[6]

2. Through divine inspiration he had learned that if he opened the book of the Gospel, Christ would reveal to him what God considered most acceptable in him and from him. After praying with much devotion, he took the book of the Gospels from the altar and had his companion, a holy man dedicated to God, open it three times in the name of the Holy Trinity. When all three times the book was opened the Lord's passion always met his eyes, the man filled with God understood that just as he had imitated Christ in the actions of his life, so he should be conformed to him in the affliction and sorrow of his passion, before *he would pass out of this world* (John 13:1). And although his body was already weakened by the great austerity of his past life and his continual carrying of the

---

4. Cf. IX, 3, p. 264.
5. Prov. 25:27; Matt. 24:45.
6. Minor sources: I C 94; Jul. 61; cf. I C 91, 92.

Lord's cross, he was in no way terrified but was inspired even more vigorously to endure martyrdom. His unquenchable fire of love for the good Jesus had been fanned into such *a blaze of flames* that *many waters could not quench* so powerful a *love* (Cant. 8:6-7).

3. By the Seraphic ardor of his desires, he was being borne aloft into God; and by his sweet compassion he was being transformed into him who chose to be crucified because of *the excess of his love* (Eph. 2:4). On a certain morning about the feast of the Exaltation of the Cross,[7] while Francis was praying on the mountainside, he saw a Seraph with six fiery and shining wings descend from the height of heaven. And when in swift flight the Seraph had reached a spot in the air near the man of God, there appeared between the wings the figure of a man crucified, with his hands and feet extended in the form of a cross and fastened to a cross. Two of the wings were lifted above his head, two were extended for flight and two covered his whole body.[8] When Francis saw this, he was overwhelmed and his heart was flooded with a mixture of joy and sorrow. He rejoiced because of the gracious way Christ looked upon him under the appearance of the Seraph, but the fact that he was fastened to a cross *pierced his soul with a sword* of compassionate sorrow (Luke 2:35).[9]

He wondered exceedingly at the sight of so unfathomable a vision, realizing that the weakness of Christ's passion was in no way compatible with the immortality of the Seraph's spiritual nature. Eventually he understood by a revelation from the Lord that divine providence had shown him this vision so that,

---

7. September 14.

8. Cf. the vision of Isaiah (Isa. 6:1-13), where the Seraphim are described as follows: *I saw the Lord seated on a high and lofty throne, with the train of his garment filling the temple. Above him were stationed the Seraphim; each of them had six wings: with two they covered their faces, with two they covered their feet, and with two they hovered aloft. One called to the other: "Holy, holy, holy is the Lord of hosts! All the earth is filled with his glory!"* (1-3). Cf. Bonaventure's treatment of Francis's vision in *The Soul's Journey into God,* prol., 2-3, pp. 54-55.

9. Major sources: I C 94; III C 4; cf. Jul. 61.

as Christ's lover, he might learn in advance that he was to be totally transformed into the likeness of Christ crucified, not by the martyrdom of his flesh, but by the fire of his love consuming his soul.[10]

As the vision disappeared, it left in his heart a marvelous ardor and imprinted on his body markings that were no less marvelous. Immediately the marks of nails began to appear in his hands and feet just as he had seen a little before in the figure of the man crucified. His hands and feet seemed to be pierced through the center by nails, with the heads of the nails appearing on the inner side of the hands and the upper side of the feet and their points on the opposite sides. The heads of the nails in his hands and his feet were round and black; their points were oblong and bent as if driven back with a hammer, and they emerged from the flesh and stuck out beyond it. Also his right side, as if pierced with a lance, was marked with a red wound from which his sacred blood often flowed, moistening his tunic and underwear.[11]

4. When Christ's servant realized that he could not conceal from his intimate companions the stigmata that had been so visibly imprinted on his flesh, he feared to make public the Lord's *secret* (Tob. 12:7) and was thrown into an agony of doubt whether to tell what he had seen or to be silent about it. He called some of the friars and, speaking in general terms, presented his doubt to them and sought their advice. One of the friars, who was named Illuminato[12] and was illumined by grace, realized that Francis had had a miraculous vision because he seemed still completely dazed. He said to the holy man: "Brother, you should realize that at times divine secrets are revealed to you not for yourself alone but also for others.

---

10. Bonaventure uses the term *incendium mentis*, literally *the conflagration of his soul*. The term *incendium* appears in the alternate title of Bonaventure's treatise on the three stages of the spiritual life: *De triplici via seu Incendium amoris*, *On the Triple Way* or *The Fire of Love*. On Francis's desire for martyrdom, cf. C. IX, 5-9, pp. 266-271.

11. Major sources: III C 4; I C 95; minor sources: I C 94; Jul. 62.

12. Cf. IX, 8 and XI, 3, pp. 269, 282.

You have every reason to fear that if you hide what you have received for the profit of many, you will be blamed for *burying that talent*" (Matt. 25:25). Although the holy man used to say on other occasions: "*My secret is for myself*" (Isa. 24:16), he was moved by Illuminato's words and then with much fear recounted the vision in detail, adding that the one who had appeared to him had told him some things which he would never disclose to any man as long as he lived. We should believe, then, that those things he had been told by that sacred Seraph who had miraculously appeared to him on the cross were so *secret* that *men are not permitted to speak of them* (2 Cor. 12:4).[13]

5. When the true love of Christ
had transformed his lover *into his image*[14]
and the forty days were over
that he had planned to spend in solitude,
and the feast of St. Michael the Archangel
had also arrived,[15]
the angelic man Francis
came *down from the mountain*,[16]
bearing with him
the image of the Crucified,
which was depicted not on *tablets of stone*[17]
or on panels of wood
by the hands of a craftsman,
but engraved in the members of his body
by the finger of the living God.[18]
Because *it is good to keep hidden
the secret of the King*,[19]
Francis,

---

13. Cf. II C 135, 203; the incident of Brother Illuminato is not found in Celano or Julian.
14. 2 Cor. 3:18.
15. September 29.
16. Matt. 8:1; an allusion to Christ coming down the mountain after his transfiguration.
17. Exod. 31:18; an allusion to Moses coming down the mountain with the tablets of the Law.
18. Exod. 31:18; John 11:27.
19. Tob. 12:7.

aware that he had been given a royal secret,
to the best of his powers
kept the sacred stigmata hidden.
Since it is for God to reveal for his own glory
the wonders which he has performed,
the Lord himself,
who had secretly imprinted those marks on Francis,
publicly worked through them
a number of miracles
so that the miraculous though hidden
power of the stigmata
might be made manifest
by the brightness of divine signs.[20]

6. In the province of Rieti a very serious plague broke out and so cruelly took the lives of cattle and sheep that no remedy could be found. A certain God-fearing man was told in a vision at night to hurry to the hermitage of the friars and get the water in which God's servant Francis, who was staying there at that time, had washed his hands and feet and to sprinkle it on all the animals. He got up in the morning, came to the hermitage, secretly got the water from the companions of the holy man and sprinkled it on the sheep and cattle. Marvelous to say, the moment that water touched the animals, which were weak and lying on the ground, they immediately recovered their former vigor, stood up and, as if they had had nothing wrong with them, hurried off to pasture. Thus through the miraculous power of that water, which had touched his sacred wounds, the plague ceased and deadly disease fled from the flocks.[21]

7. Before the holy man stayed on Mount La Verna, clouds would often form over the mountain, and violent hailstorms would devastate the crops. But after his blessed

---

20. Minor source: II C 135; cf. II C 135-138; I C 95-96.
21. Major source III C 18.

vision the hail stopped permanently, to the amazement of the inhabitants, so that the unusually serene face of the sky proclaimed the extraordinary nature of his heavenly vision and the power of the stigmata that were imprinted on him there.

In wintertime because of his physical weakness and the rough roads Francis was once riding on a donkey belonging to a poor man. It happened that he spent the night at the base of an overhanging cliff to try to avoid the inconveniences of a snowfall and the darkness of night that prevented him from reaching his place of lodging. The saint heard his helper tossing and turning, grumbling and groaning, since, as he had only thin clothing, the biting cold would not let him sleep. Francis, burning with the fire of divine love, stretched out his hand and touched him. A marvelous thing happened! At the touch of his sacred hand, which bore the burning *coal of the Seraph* (Isa. 6:6-7),[22] immediately the cold fled altogether and the man felt great heat within and without, as if he had been hit by a fiery blast from the vent of a furnace. Comforted in mind and body, he slept until morning more soundly among the rocks and snow than he ever had in his own bed, as he used to say later.

Thus it is established by convincing evidence
that these sacred marks were imprinted on him
by the power of the One
who purifies, illumines and inflames[23]
through the action of the Seraphim.
With their miraculous power
these sacred marks,
in the external realm,
restored health by purifying from a pestilence,
produced serene skies,

---

22. In the vision of Isaiah (referred to in n. 8, above, p. 305), a Seraph carries in his hand live coal from the altar and touches the prophet's mouth with it.

23. A reference to the three hierarchical acts presented by the Pseudo-Dionysius, *De caelesti hierarchia*, III, 2; cf. n. 8, p. 90, and n. 20, p. 180.

and gave heat to the body.
After his death
this was demonstrated
by even more evident miracles
as we will record in the proper place later.[24]

8. Although he tried his best to hide the *treasure found in the field* (Matt. 13:44), he could not prevent at least some from seeing the stigmata in his hands and feet, although he always kept his hands covered and from that time on always wore shoes. A number of the friars saw them while he was still alive. Although they were men of outstanding holiness and so completely trustworthy, nevertheless to remove all doubt they confirmed under oath, touching the holy Gospels, that this was so and that they had seen it. Also some of the cardinals saw them because of their close friendship with the holy man; and they inserted praises of the sacred stigmata in the hymns, antiphons and sequences which they composed in his honor, and thus by their words and writings *gave testimony to the truth* (John 5:33).[25] Even the Supreme Pontiff Lord Alexander,[26] in a sermon preached to the people at which many of the friars and I myself were present, affirmed that he had seen the sacred stigmata with his own eyes while the saint was still alive. More than fifty friars with the virgin Clare, who was most devoted to God, and her sisters, as well as innumerable laymen saw them after his death. Many of them kissed the stigmata out of devotion and touched them with their own hands to strengthen

---

24. In his treatise on Francis's miracles, I, 2-6, which is not included in this present volume. The incident recorded in no. 7 is not found in Celano or Julian.

25. Gregory IX (Cardinal Hugolino) composed the hymn *Proles de caelo*, the response *De paupertatis horreo*, the antiphons *Sancte Francisce propere* and *Plange turba paupercula*, and the sequence *Caput draconis ultimum*; Cardinal Thomas of Capua, the hymns *Decus morum* and *In caelesti collegio*, the response *Carnis spicam*, the antiphon *Salve sancte Pater*, and the sequence *Laetabundus Francisco*; Cardinal Rainerio Capoci of Viterbo, the hymn *Plaude turba*; Cardinal Stefano di Casa Nova, the antiphon *Caelorum candor splenduit*. Most of these were incorporated into the rhymed office composed by Julian of Speyer.

26. Alexander IV, pope from 1254-1261, who made the same affirmation in his bulls: *Benigna operatio* (October 19, 1255) and *Quia longum esset* (June 28, 1259).

their testimony, as we will describe in the proper place.[27]

But the wound in his side he so cautiously concealed that as long as he was alive no one could see it except by stealth. One friar who used to zealously take care of him induced him with a pious strategem to take off his tunic to shake it out. Watching closely, he saw the wound, and he even quickly touched it with three of his fingers determining the size of the wound by both sight and touch. The friar who was his vicar at that time also managed to see it by a similar strategem.[28] A friar who was a companion of his, a man of marvelous simplicity,[29] when he was one day massaging Francis's shoulders that were weak from illness, put his hand under his hood and accidentally touched the sacred wound, causing him great pain. As a result, from that time on Francis always wore underclothes made so that they would reach up to his armpits to cover the wound on his side. Also the friars who washed these or shook out his tunic from time to time, since they found these stained with blood, were from this evident sign convinced without any doubt of the existence of the sacred wound, which after his death they along with many others contemplated and venerated *with unveiled face* (2 Cor. 3:18).[30]

9. Come now, knight of Christ,
vigorously bear the arms of your unconquerable Leader!
Visibly shielded with these,
you will overcome all adversaries.
Carry the standard of the Most High King,
and at its sight
let all who fight in God's army
be aroused to courage.

---

27. Cf. XV, 3-5, p. 323. Major source: III C 5; minor source: II C 135-136; cf. I C 95-96; 95-96; II C 135-138; II C 214; I C 116-117. Pope Alexander's sermon is not mentioned in Celano or Julian.
28. Brother Elias; cf. I C 95; II C 138.
29. Rufino; cf. I C 95.
30. Major sources: II C 138; I C 95; minor sources: II C 136; III C 5; cf. I C 102.

Carry the seal of Christ, the High Priest,
by which your words and deeds
will be rightly accepted by all
as authentic and *beyond reproach*.[31]
For now because of *the brand-marks of the Lord Jesus*
which you *carry* in your *body*,
no one should *trouble* you;[32]
rather every servant of Christ
should show them deep devotion.
Now through these most certain signs
(corroborated
not by the sufficient testimony
of two or three witnesses,[33]
but by the superabundant testimony
of a whole multitude)
God's *testimony* about you and through you
has been made overwhelmingly credible,[34]
removing completely from unbelievers
the veil of excuse,
while these signs confirm believers in faith,
raise them aloft with confident hope
and set them ablaze with the fire of charity.

10. Now *is fulfilled*
the first *vision which you saw*,[35]
namely, that you would be a captain
in the army of Christ
and bear the arms of heaven
emblazoned with the sign of the cross.[36]
Now is fulfilled
the vision of the Crucified

31. Titus 2:8.
32. Gal. 6:17.
33. Deut. 19:15.
34. Ps. 92:5.
35. Dan. 9:24; 4:6.
36. Cf. I, 3, p. 187.

at the beginning of your conversion
which *pierced* your soul
with a sword of compassionate sorrow.[37]
Now the voice that came from the cross
as if *from* the lofty throne and secret *mercy-seat*[38] of Christ,
as you have confirmed with your sacred words,
is believed as undoubtedly true.[39]
Now is fulfilled
the vision of the cross,
in the course of your conversion,
which Brother Silvester saw
marvelously coming from your mouth;[40]
and the vision which the holy Pacificus saw,
of the swords piercing your body
in the form of a cross;[41]
and the sight of you
lifted up in the air in the form of a cross,
which the angelic man Monaldus saw
when the holy Anthony was preaching
on the inscription on the cross—[42]
all of these
we now firmly believe
were not imaginary visions
but revelations from heaven.
Now, finally
toward the end of your life
you were shown at the same time
the sublime vision of the Seraph
and the humble figure of the Crucified,
inwardly inflaming you and outwardly marking you

---

37. Cf. I, 5, p. 189; Luke 2:35.
38. Num. 7:89.
39. Cf. II, 1, p. 191.
40. Cf. III, 5, pp. 201-202.
41. Cf. IV, 9, p. 214.
42. Cf. IV, 10, p. 215.

as the *second Angel*,
ascending from the rising of the sun
and *bearing* upon you *the sign of the living God.* [43]
This vision confirms the previous ones
and *receives* from them
the testimony of truth. [44]
Behold
these seven visions of the cross of Christ,
miraculously shown and manifested
to you or about you
at different stages of your life.
The first six were like steps
leading to the seventh
in which you have found your final rest. [45]
The cross of Christ
given to you and by you accepted
at the beginning of your conversion
and which from then on
you carried continuously
in the course of your most upright life,
giving an example to others,
shows that you have finally reached
the summit of Gospel perfection
with such clear certitude
that no truly devout person
can reject this proof of Christian wisdom
ploughed into the dust of your flesh.
No truly believing person can attack it,
no truly humble person can make little of it,
since it is truly the work of God
and *worthy of complete acceptance.* [46]

---

43. Apoc. 7:2; cf. prol., 1, p. 181.
44. John 5:33-34.
45. Note the similarity with the seven stages of *The Soul's Journey into God*, prol., 3; I, 1-7; VII, 1, pp. 54, 59-63, 110-111.
46. 1 Tim. 1:15, 4:9. Major source: III C 2-3; Celano lists Francis's visions of the cross, but without the rhetorical structure and spirited interpretation supplied by Bonaventure.

CHAPTER FOURTEEN

ON
HIS PATIENCE
AND
HIS PASSING IN DEATH

1. Now *fixed with Christ to the cross*,[1]
   in both body and spirit,
   Francis
   not only burned with a Seraphic love of God
   but also *thirsted*[2] with Christ crucified
   for the salvation of men.

Since he could not walk because of the nails protruding from his feet, he had his half-dead body carried through the towns and villages to arouse others to *carry the cross* of Christ (Luke 9:23). He used to say to the friars: "Let us begin, brothers, to serve the Lord our God, for up to now we have hardly progressed." He was ablaze with a great desire to return to the humility he practiced at the beginning; to nurse the lepers as he did at the outset and to treat like a slave once more his body that was already in a state of collapse from his work. With Christ as his leader, he proposed to do great things; and although his limbs were failing, he bravely and fervently hoped to conquer the enemy in a new combat. Laziness and idleness have no place where the goad of love never ceases to drive a person to greater things. His body was so much in harmony with his spirit and so ready to obey it that when he strove to attain complete holiness, his body not only did not resist, but even tried to run ahead.[3]

---

1. Gal. 2:19.
2. John 19:28.
3. Major source: I C 103; minor sources: I C 98; Jul. 64, 67; II C 209; I C 97.

2. In order that his merits might increase—for these are brought to perfection in patient suffering[4]—the man of God began to suffer from various illnesses, so seriously that scarcely any part of his body remained free from intense pain and suffering. Through varied, prolonged and continual illness he was brought to the point where his *flesh was* already *wasted away*, as if nothing but *skin clung to his bones* (Job 19:20; Lam. 4:8). But when he was tortured by harsh bodily suffering, he called his trials not by the name of torments but sisters.[5]

Once when he was suffering more intensely than usual, a certain friar in his simplicity told him: "Brother, *pray to the Lord* (Ecclus. 38:9) that he treat you more mildly, for he seems to *have laid* his *hand* on you more *heavily* than he should" (Ps. 31:4; 2 Cor. 1:8). At these words, the holy man wailed and cried out: "If I did not know your simplicity and sincerity, then I would from now on shrink from your company because you dared to call into judgment God's judgments upon me." Even though he was completely worn out by his prolonged and serious illness, he threw himself on the ground, bruising his weakened bones in the hard fall. Kissing the ground, he said: "*I thank you*, Lord *God* (Luke 18:11), for all these sufferings; and I ask you, my Lord, to increase them a hundredfold if it pleases you, for it will be most acceptable to me. *Afflict me with suffering and do not spare me* (Job 6:10), since to do your will is an overflowing consolation for me." So it seemed to the friars as if they were seeing another Job, whose vigor of soul increased with the increase of his bodily weariness.[6] He knew long in advance the time of his death, and as the day of his passing grew near, he told the friars that he should soon *lay aside the tent* of his body (2 Pet. 1:14), as it had been revealed to him by Christ.[7]

---

4. Cf. James 1:4.

5. Minor sources: I C 105, 107; II C 212.

6. Cf. Job 9:1ff.

7. Minor sources: II C 212-213; cf. I C 107. The incident of the simple friar's observation is not found in Celano or Julian.

3. For two years after the imprinting of the sacred stigmata—that is, in the twentieth year of his conversion—under the many blows of agonizing illness he was squared like a stone to be fitted into the construction of the heavenly Jerusalem[8] and like a work of wrought metal he was brought to perfection by the hammer of many tribulations. Then he asked to be carried to St. Mary of the Portiuncula so that he might yield up *the spirit of life* (Gen. 6:17) where he had received the *spirit of grace* (Heb. 10:29). When he had been brought there, in that last illness that was being concluded in a state of complete weakness, he wished to show by the example of Truth itself that he had nothing in common with the world. And so, in fervor of spirit, he threw himself totally naked on the naked ground so that in that final hour of death, when the enemy could still attack him violently, he would struggle naked with a naked enemy.[9] Lying like this on the ground stripped of his garments of sackcloth, he lifted his face to heaven in his accustomed way and gave his whole attention to its glory, covering the wound in his right side with his left hand lest it be seen. And he said to his friars: "*I have done my duty* (3 Kings 19:20); may *Christ teach you* (Eph. 4:21) yours."[10]

4. Pierced with the spear of compassion, the companions of the saint wept bitterly. The one among them whom the man of God used to call his guardian,[11] knowing his wish through divine inspiration, hurriedly arose, took a tunic along with a cord and underclothes, and offered them to the little poor man of Christ, saying: "I am lending these to you as to a beggar, and you are to accept them under the command of obedience." The holy man was happy at this and rejoiced in the gladness of his heart because he saw that he had been faithful to his Lady

---

8. An allusion to the hymn in the breviary *Urbs Jerusalem beata* for the feast of the dedication of a church.

9. That is, free from the encumbrances of earthly attachments; cf. Gregory the Great, *Homiliae in evangelia*, hom. 32, no. 2.

10. Major source: II C 214; minor sources: I C 109, 108, 106; Jul. 69; cf. I C 88.

11. Cf. n. 9, p. 232.

Poverty up to the end. Raising his hands to heaven, he glorified his Christ because he was going to him, free and unburdened by anything. He had done all this out of his zeal for poverty, for he did not even want to have a habit unless it were lent to him by another.

In all things
he wished to be conformed to Christ crucified,
who hung on the cross
poor, suffering and naked.
Therefore at the beginning of his conversion,
he stood naked before the bishop,[12]
and at the end of his life,
naked he wished to go out of this world.
He enjoined the friars assisting him,
under obedience and charity,
that when they saw he was dead,
they should allow
his body to lie naked on the ground
for the length of time
it takes to walk a leisurely mile.
O, he was truly the most Christian of men,
for he strove to conform himself to Christ
and to imitate him perfectly —
while living to imitate Christ living,
dying to imitate Christ dying,
and after death to imitate Christ after death —
and he merited to be honored
with the imprint of Christ's likeness![13]

5. When the hour of his passing was approaching, he had all the friars who were there called to him and, consoling them for his death with words of comfort, he exhorted them with

---

12. Cf. II, 4, pp. 193-194.
13. Major source: II C 215-217.

fatherly affection to love God. He long continued speaking about practicing poverty and patience and about keeping the faith of the Holy Roman Church, and he recommended the Gospel to them before any other rule of life. While all the friars were sitting around him, he extended his hands over them, crossing his arms in the form of a cross—for he always loved this sign[14]—and he blessed all the friars, both present and absent, in the name and power of Christ crucified. Then he added: "Fare well, all my sons, in the fear of the Lord; remain in it always! Temptation and tribulation are coming in the near future, but happy are they who will persevere in what they have begun. I am hastening to God, to whose grace I commend you all." When he finished this gentle admonition, the man beloved of God ordered the book of the Gospels to be brought to him and asked that the Gospel according to John be read to him from the place that begins: *Before the feast of Passover* (John 13:1). He himself, insofar as he was able, broke out with this psalm: *I have cried to the Lord with my voice, with my voice I have implored the Lord* (Ps. 141:2); and he finished it to the end: *The just will await me until you have rewarded me* (Ps. 141:8).[15]

6. At last, when all of God's mysteries were fulfilled in him and his most holy soul was freed from his body to be absorbed in the abyss of the divine light, the blessed man *fell asleep in the Lord* (Acts 7:60). One of his brothers and disciples saw his blessed soul under the appearance of a radiant star being carried aloft on a *shining cloud over many waters* (Apoc. 14:14; Ps. 28:3) on a direct path into heaven. It shone with the brightness of sublime sanctity and was full of the abundance of heavenly wisdom and grace by which the holy man had merited to enter the place of light and peace where forever he rests with Christ.

At that time the minister of the friars in Terra di Lavoro

---

14. Cf. XII, 9-10; XIII, 10, pp. 299-300, 312-314.
15. Major source: II C 216-217; minor source: I C 108-109.

was Brother Augustine, a holy and upright man, who was near death and had already for a long time lost his power of speech. Suddenly he cried out in the hearing of those who were standing about: "Wait for me, Father, wait for me. Wait, I am coming with you!" Amazed, the friars asked to whom he was speaking so boldly. He replied: "Don't you see our father Francis on his way to heaven?" And at once his holy soul left his body and followed his most holy father.

The bishop of Assisi was gone at that time on a pilgrimage to the shrine of St. Michael on Monte Gargano. Blessed Francis appeared to him on the night of his passing and said: "Behold, *I leave the world and go to* heaven" (John 16:28). Rising in the morning, the bishop told his companions what he had seen, and returning to Assisi, he carefully inquired and found out with certainty that the blessed father had departed this world at the very hour when he appeared to him in this vision.

Larks are birds
that love the light and dread the twilight darkness.
But at the hour of the holy man's passing,
although it was twilight and night was to follow,
they came in a great flock
over the roof of the house
and, whirling around for a long time
with unusual joy,
gave clear and evident *testimony*[16]
of the glory of the saint,
who so often had invited them
to praise God.[17]

---

16. John 1:7.
17. Major sources: I C 110; II C 218, 220; III C 32; minor source: Jul. 70. Cf. II C 217a.

CHAPTER FIFTEEN

ON
HIS CANONIZATION
AND
THE SOLEMN TRANSFERAL OF HIS BODY

1. Francis,
the servant and friend of the Most High,
the founder and leader of the Order of Friars Minor,
the practitioner of poverty, the model of penance,
the herald of truth, the mirror of holiness
and the exemplar of all Gospel perfection,
foreordained by grace from heaven,
in an ordered progression
from the lowest level reached the very heights.
This remarkable man —
rich in poverty, exalted in humility,
full of life in the midst of mortification,
wise in simplicity,
outstanding for the excellence of the total conduct of his life —
this remarkable man God made remarkably renowned
in his life
and incomparably more renowned
in his death.
When this blessed man
traveled away from this world,
his sacred spirit,
as it entered his *home of eternity*,[1]
was glorified by a full draught from *the fountain of life*[2]

1. Eccles. 12:5.
2. Ps. 35:10.

and left certain signs of *future glory*[3]
imprinted on his body,
so that his most holy flesh,
which had been *crucified along with its passions*[4]
and *transformed into a new creature*,[5]
might bear the image of Christ's passion
by a singular privilege
and prefigure the resurrection
by this unprecedented miracle.[6]

2. In his blessed hands and feet could be seen the nails that had been miraculously formed out of his flesh by divine power. They were so embedded in the flesh that when they were pressed on one side, they immediately stuck out the other, as if they were continuous hardened sinews. Also the wound in his side could be clearly seen, which was not inflicted on his body nor produced by human means; it was like the wound in the Savior's side,[7] which brought forth in our Redeemer the mystery of the redemption and regeneration of the human race. The nails were black like iron; the wound in his side was red, and because it was drawn into a kind of circle by the contraction of the flesh looked like a most beautiful rose. The rest of his skin, which before was inclined to be dark both naturally and from his illness, now shone with a dazzling whiteness, prefiguring the beauty of that glorious second stole.[8]

3. His limbs were so supple and soft to the touch that they seemed to have regained the tenderness of childhood and

---

3. Rom. 8:18.
4. Gal. 5:24.
5. 2 Cor. 5:17.
6. Minor sources: I C 95; II C 26, 161; I C 114, 112.
7. Cf. John 19:34.
8. That is, the glory of the body in heaven. Cf. Ecclus. 6:32; Apoc. 7:9; and *The Tree of Life*, 44, n. 16, p. 168. Cf. XIII, 3, 8, pp. 306, 311. Major sources: III C 5; I C 112; minor sources: IC 113; Jul. 71.

to be adorned with clear signs of his innocence. The nails appeared black against his shining skin, and the wound in his side was red *like a rose* in springtime (Ecclus. 50:8) so that it is no wonder the onlookers were amazed and overjoyed at the sight of such varied and miraculous beauty. His sons were weeping at the loss of so lovable a father but were filled with no little joy with they kissed on his body the seal-marks of the supreme King. This unprecedented miracle turned their grief into joy and transported into amazement their attempts at comprehending it. So unique and so remarkable was the sight to all who observed it that it confirmed their faith and incited their love. It was a matter of amazement to those who heard of it and aroused their desire to see it.[9]

4. When the people heard of the passing of our blessed father and news of the miracle had spread, they hurried to the place to see with their own eyes so that they could dispel all doubt and add joy to their love. A great number of the citizens of Assisi were admitted to see the sacred stigmata with their own eyes and to kiss them with their lips. One of them, a knight who was educated and prudent, Jerome by name, a distinguished and famous man, had doubts about these sacred signs and *was unbelieving* like Thomas (John 20:24ff.). Fervently and boldly, in the presence of the friars and the citizens, he did not hesitate to move the nails and to touch with his hands the saint's hands, feet and side. While he was examining with his hands these authentic signs of Christ's wounds, he completely healed the wound of doubt in his own heart and the hearts of others. As a result, later along with others he became a firm witness to this truth which he had come to know with such certainty; and he swore to it on the Gospel.[10]

---

9. Major sources: I C 112-113; minor source: Jul. 71; cf. I C 118, 114.

10. Cf. XIII, 8, pp. 310-311. Major source: I C 113. For this interpretation of the doubt of the knight Jerome, cf. Gregory the Great's treatment of the doubt of Thomas: *Homiliae in Evangelia* II, hom. 29, no. 1 The incident of Jerome is not found in Celano or Julian.

5. His brothers and sons who had been summoned to their father's passing, along with a great number of people spent that night, in which the blessed confessor of Christ departed, singing the divine praises in such a way that it seemed to be a vigil of angels and not a wake for the dead. *In the morning* (John 21:4), the *crowds that had assembled took branches from the trees* (John 12:13; Matt. 21:8) and with a blaze of many candles carried his sacred body to the town of Assisi, singing hymns and canticles. As they passed the church of San Damiano, where the noble virgin Clare, who is now glorious in heaven, lived at that time cloistered with her nuns, they stopped there for a short while so that those holy nuns could see and kiss his sacred body, adorned with its heavenly pearls. When they arrived at the city with great rejoicing, they reverently placed in the church of St. George the precious treasure they were carrying. It was there that he had gone to school as a little boy and there that he first preached and there, finally, that he found his first place of rest.[11]

6. Our venerable father left the shipwreck of this world in the year of the Lord's Incarnation 1226, on Saturday evening, October 3, and was buried on Sunday.

Immediately
the holy man began
to reflect the light radiating from the face of God
and to sparkle
with many great miracles
so that the sublimity of his holiness
which, while he was still in the flesh,
had been known to the world as a guide for conduct
through examples of perfect righteousness,
now that he is *reigning with Christ*[12]
was approved from heaven

---

11. Major source: I C 116; minor sources: I C 117, 118; Jul. 72.
12. Apoc. 20:4.

as a confirmation of faith
through miracles performed by the divine power.

In different parts of the world,
his glorious miracles
and the abundant blessings obtained through him
inflamed many to devotion to Christ
and incited them to reverence for his saint.
The *wonderful things*[13]
which God was working
through his servant Francis—
acclaimed by word of mouth
and testified to by facts—
came to the ears
of the Supreme Pontiff, Gregory IX.[14]

7. That shepherd of the Church was fully convinced of Francis's remarkable holiness, not only from the miracles he heard of after the saint's death, but also from his own experience during his life, having seen with his own eyes and touched with his own hands; consequently he had no doubt that Francis was glorified in heaven by the Lord. In order to act in conformity with Christ, whose vicar he was, after prayerful consideration he decided to glorify him on earth by proclaiming him worthy of all veneration. In order to certify to the whole world the glorification of this most holy man, he had the known miracles recorded and attested to by appropriate witness. These he submitted to the examination of those cardinals who seemed less favorable to his cause. This material was examined carefully and approved by all. With the unanimous advice and assent of his confreres[15] and of all the prelates who were then in the curia, he decreed that Francis should be canonized. He

---

13. Ps. 70:19.
14. Cardinal Hugolino, who became pope in 1227; cf. VI, 5, n. 16, p. 233. Major source: Jul. 73; minor sources: I C 88, 120-121.
15. That is, the cardinals.

came personally to Assisi in the year of the Lord's Incarnation 1228 on Sunday, July 16, and inscribed our blessed father in the catalog of the saints, in a great and solemn ceremony that would be too long to describe.[16]

8. In the year of Our Lord 1230, when the friars had assembled for a general chapter at Assisi, Francis's body, which had been so dedicated to God, was solemnly transferred on May 25 to the basilica constructed in his honor.

> While that sacred treasure was being carried,
> marked with the seal of the Most High King,
> he whose image Francis bore
> deigned to perform many miracles
> so that through his saving *fragrance*
> the faithful in their love
> might *be drawn to run after* Christ.[17]
> It was truly appropriate
> that he who was pleasing to God and beloved by him
> in his life;
> who, like Enoch,[18]
> had been borne into paradise
> by the grace of contemplation
> and carried off to heaven
> like Elijah *in a fiery chariot;*[19]
> now that his soul is blossoming
> in eternal springtime
> among the heavenly *flowers*[20]
> it was, indeed, truly appropriate
> that his blessed *bones* too
> should *sprout* with fragrant miracles
> *in their own place of rest.*[21]

16. Major source: Jul. 74; minor sources: I C 124, 126; cf. I C 121-126.
17. Cant. 1:3.
18. Gen. 5:24.
19. 4 Kings 2:11.
20. Ecclus. 50:8.
21. *Ibid.* 46:14. Minor source: Jul. 75-76.

9. Just as that blessed man
shone in his life
with the marvelous signs of virtue,
so from the day of his passing to the present,
in different parts of the world,
he radiated forth
with outstanding miracles
through the divine power that glorified him.
For the blind and the deaf,
the mute and the crippled,
paralytics and those suffering from dropsy,
lepers and those possessed by devils,
the shipwrecked and the captives—
all these were given relief
through his merits.
For every disease, every need, every danger,
he offered a remedy.
Many dead, even,
were miraculously brought back to life
through him.
Thus the magnificence
of the power of the Most High
doing wonders for his saint[22]
shines forth to the faithful.
To him be honor and glory
for endless ages of ages.[23]
Amen.

HERE ENDS THE LIFE OF BLESSED FRANCIS

22. Ps. 4:4.
23. Major source: Jul. 76.

SELECTED BIBLIOGRAPHY

Critical Texts

Bonaventure, Saint. *Doctoris Seraphici S. Bonaventurae opera omnia.* Edita studio et cura pp. Collegii a S. Bonaventura, ad plurimos codices mss. emendata, anecdotis aucta, prolegomenis scholiis notisque illustrata. X volumina. Quaracchi: Collegium S. Bonaventurae, 1882-1902.

_____. *Legenda maior*, in *Analecta Franciscana*. Vol. X: *Legendae S. Francisci Assisiensis saeculis XIII et XIV conscriptae*. Ad codicum fidem recensitae a patribus collegii, editae a patribus Collegii S. Bonaventurae, adiuvantibus aliis eruditis viris. Quaracchi: Collegium S. Bonaventurae, 1926-1946, pp. 555-652.

_____. *Collationes in Hexaemeron et Bonaventuriana quaedam selecta*. Ad fidem codicum mss. edita a F.M. Delorme, O.F.M. Quaracchi: Collegium S. Bonaventurae, 1934.

_____. *Sancti Bonaventurae sermones dominicales*. Ad fidem codicum nunc denuo editi studio et cura Iacobi Guidi Bougerol, O.F.M. Grottaferrata: Collegio S. Bonaventura, 1977.

Francis of Assisi, Saint. *Die Opuscula des Hl. Franziskus von Assisi: Neue textkritische Edition*. Edited by Kajetan Esser, O.F.M. *Spicilegium Bonaventurianm* cura pp. Collegii S. Bonaventurae. Vol. XIII. Grottaferrata: Collegium S. Bonaventurae, 1976.

Bibliographies

Bibliographia Bonaventuriana (c. 1850-1973). Cura Jacques Guy Bougerol, O.F.M. Vol. V of *S. Bonaventura 1274-1974*.

Edited by Jacques Guy Bougerol, O.F.M. Grottaferrata: Collegio S. Bonaventura, 1974.

"A Francis of Assisi Research Bibliography: Comprehensive for 1939-1963, Selective for Older Materials." Compiled by Raphael Brown. In Omer Englebert. *Saint Francis of Assisi: A Biography.* Translated by Eve Marie Cooper. Second English edition, revised and augmented by Ignatius Brady, O.F.M., and Raphael Brown. Chicago: Franciscan Herald Press, 1965, pp. 493-607. Also in *St. Francis of Assisi: Writings and Early Biographies, English Omnibus of the Sources for the Life of St. Francis.* Edited by Marion A. Habig, O.F.M. Chicago: Franciscan Herald Press, 1973, pp. 1667-1760.

Lexicon

Lexique saint Bonaventure. Published under the direction of Jacques Guy Bougerol, O.F.M. Paris: Editions Franciscaines, 1969.

English Translations

Saint Bonaventura: The Mind's Road to God. Translated with an introduction by George Boas. Indianapolis: Library of Liberal Arts, 1953.

Works of Saint Bonaventure. Vol. I: *De Reductione artium ad theologiam.* Translated with a commentary and introduction by Sr. Emma Thérèse Healy. Saint Bonaventure, N.Y.: The Franciscan Institute, 1955.

Works of Saint Bonaventure. Vol. II: *Itinerarium mentis in Deum.* With an introduction, translation and commentary by Philotheus Boehner, O.F.M. Saint Bonaventure, N.Y.: The Franciscan Institute, 1956.

The Works of Bonaventure, 5 vols. Translated by José de Vinck. Paterson, N.J.: St. Anthony Guild Press, 1960-1970.

Major and Minor Life of St. Francis, with excerpts from other works by St. Bonaventure. Translated by Benen Fahy, O.F.M. In *St. Francis of Assisi: Writings and Early Biographies, English Omnibus of the Sources for the Life of St. Francis.* Edited by Marion A. Habig, O.F.M. Chicago: Franciscan Herald Press, 1973, pp. 627-851.

What Manner of Man? Sermons on Christ by St. Bonaventure. Translated with introduction and commentary by Zachary Hayes, O.F.M. Chicago: Franciscan Herald Press, 1974.

Rooted in Faith: Homilies to a Contemporary World by St. Bonaventure. Translated with an introductory essay by Marigwen Schumacher. Chicago: Franciscan Herald Press, 1974.

Studies

The most important collection of recent studies is to be found in vols. II, III, and IV of the five-volume series entitled *S. Bonaventura 1274-1974*, edited by Jacques Guy Bougerol, O.F.M. (Grottaferrata: Collegio S. Bonaventura, 1972-1974).

Bettoni, Efrem, O.F.M. *St. Bonaventure.* Translated by Angelus Gambatese, O.F.M. Notre Dame: University of Notre Dame Press, 1964.

Bissen, Jean-Marie, O.F.M. *L'exemplarisme divin selon saint Bonaventure.* Paris: Vrin, 1929.

Boehner, Philotheus, O.F.M. *Works of Saint Bonaventure.* Vol. II. *Itinerarium mentis in Deum.* With an introduction, translation and commentary. Saint Bonaventure, N.Y.: Franciscan Institute, 1956.

Bonnefoy, Jean François, O.F.M. *Le Saint Esprit et ses dons selon saint Bonaventure*. Paris: Vrin, 1929.

_____. *Une somme bonaventurienne de théologie mystique: Le "De Triplici Via."* Paris: Vrin, 1949.

Bougerol, Jacques Guy, O.F.M. *Introduction to the Works of Bonaventure*. Translated by José de Vinck. Paterson, N.J.: St. Anthony Guild Press, 1964.

_____. *Saint Bonaventure: un maître de sagesse*. Paris: Editions Franciscaines, 1966.

Brooke, Rosalind B. *Early Franciscan Government: Elias to Bonaventure*. Cambridge: Cambridge University Press, 1959.

Fleming, John V. *An Introduction to the Franciscan Literature of the Middle Ages*. Chicago: Franciscan Herald Press, 1977.

Gilson, Etienne. *The Philosophy of St. Bonaventure*. Translated by Dom Illtyd Trethowan and Frank J. Sheed. Paterson, N.J.: St. Anthony Guild Press, 1965.

Gerken, Alexander, O.F.M. *Theologie des Wortes: Das Verhältnis von Schöpfung und Inkarnation bei Bonaventura*. Düsseldorf: Patmos, 1963.

Longpré, Ephrem, O.F.M. "Bonaventure, saint," *Dictionnaire de spiritualité* (Paris, 1937), Vol. 1, cc. 1768-1843.

Majchrzak, Colman J., O.F.M. *A Brief History of Bonaventurianism*. Pulaski, Wis.: Franciscan Publishers, 1957.

Moorman, John. *A History of the Franciscan Order: From Its Origins to the Year 1517*. Oxford: Clarendon Press, 1968.

Quinn, John, C.S.B. *The Historical Constitution of St. Bonaventure's Philosophy*. Toronto: Pontifical Institute of Mediaeval Studies, 1973.

Ratzinger, Joseph. *The Theology of History in St. Bonaventure.* Translated by Zachary Hayes, O.F.M. Chicago: Franciscan Herald Press, 1971.

de Régnon, Théodore, S.J. *Etudes de théologie positive sur la Sainte Trinité.* Vol. II: *Théories scolastiques.* Paris: Retaux, 1892, pp. 435-568.

Stohr, Albert, *Die Trinitätslehre des heiligen Bonaventura.* Münster in Westfalen: Aschendorff, 1923.

Szabó, Titus, O.F.M. *De SS. Trinitate in creaturis refulgente doctrina S. Bonaventurae.* Rome: Herder, 1955.

INDEX TO
PREFACE AND INTRODUCTION

power of, 29; reflections of, 30; return to, xvii, 34; and Trinity, 25, 33.

Fidanza, John di, 4.

Francis, cf. Stigmata; biographies of, 8, 9, 10, 13, 15, 16, 17, 22, 37, 38, 40, 41, 42; and Bonaventure, xiv, xv, 3, 4, 39; and Holy Spirit, xv, xvi; spirituality of, 1, 6, 7, 13, 14, 15, 17, 18, 19, 20, 21, 23, 24, 27, 42; vision of, xvii, 10, 18, 19, 20, 22, 33.

Franchi, Antonio, 8.

Franciscan Order, and Bonaventure, 1, 5, 10, 19, 38; growth, 2, 3, 7; intellectual tradition of, 5, 6, 7; rule of, 3; spirituality of, 1, 6, 7, 11, 12, 13, 14, 15, 22, 26, 36, 46.

Gerard of Abbeville, 11.

Gerlach, P., 12.

Gerson, John, xiii.

Giles, 39.

God, ascent to, xiii, xvii, 13, 17, 20, 21, 23, 24, 25, 30; as Being, 18, 21, 32, 33; dynamism of, 26; fecundity of, 46; as First Principle, 30, 33; as the Good, 20, 24, 25, 32; goodness of, 29; image of, 21, 31, 32, 34; knowledge of, 23, 26; and man, 34; plan of, xiii; praise to, 27, 28, 29, 30; presence of, 13, 31; reflections of, 13, 17, 20, 24, 26, 27, 29; as Source, 24; union with, 35.

The Good, xiii, 18, 20, 24, 25, 31, 32, 33.

Grace, xvi, 17, 20, 23, 27.

Greccio, 35.

Gregory IX, 3.

Gregory X, 8, 11.

Holy Land, 21.

Holy of holies, 17.

Holy Spirit, age of, 6, 7; fecundity of, 27; gift of, xvi; reflections of, 30, 31; and Trinity, 25, 33.

Ignatius of Loyola, 37.

Illumination, 32, 43, 44, 45.

Illuminato, 39.

Image, 25, 27, 31, 32; fallen, 32; of God, 21, 31, 32.

Incarnation, 13.

Innocent III, 3.

Intellect, 30, 31, 32.

Islam, 1, 44.

Joachim of Fiore, 6, 7.

John of La Rochelle, 5.

John of Parma, 7, 19.

John of St. Paul, 39.

John the Baptist, 45.

Journey, of Francis, xiv; spiritual, 14, 15, 17, 20, 21, 22, 35; stages of, 19, 23, 30, 32, 33.

Judaism, 1.

Julian of Speyer, 38, 39, 40.

La Verna, Mount of, xiv, xvii, 10, 12, 18, 19, 39, 40, 45.

Leo, xvii, 39.

Light, 30, 31, 32.

Little, A.G., 41.

Love, for the Crucified, xiv, xvi, 22.

Lyons, II Council of, 8.

Meditation, xiii, xvii, 20, 24, 30, 31, 32, 35, 37.

Masseo, 39.

Mats, Chapter of, 3.

Memory, 30, 31.

Mercy Seat, 7.

Michelangelo, 14.

Miracles, 16, 38, 39, 44.

Mirror, reflecting God, 13, 23, 24, 30.

Moorman, J.R.H., 7, 41, 42.

Morico, Fra, 39.

Mount Tabor, 45.

Mysticism, and Christ, xiii, 13, 14, 15, 21, 22, 35, 37; ecstasy, 20, 36.

Narbonne, Chapter of, xiv, 10, 37.
Neoplatonism, 33.
New Testament, 17, 35.
Old Testament, 17, 35.
Omega, 32.
Paris, Chapter of, 40, 41;
   University of, 1, 4, 5, 6, 7, 9,
   10, 11.
Pacificus, Brother, 5.
Papini, Francesco P., 12.
Perfection, xvi, 40, 43, 44.
Payne, Richard, 47.
Peter Lombard, 6.
Philip, 34.
Pisa, 40.
Poor Clares, xvii, 41.
Portiuncula, 3; Chapter of, 39.
Power, of Father, 29; of God, 29.
Purgation, 43, 44, 45.
Quaracchi, 8, 9.
Quinn, John, 2, 7.
Redemption, 13, 17.
Reeves, Marjorie, 7.
Richard of St. Victor, 2.
Ritello, Maria di, 4.
Rufino, 39.
Sabatier, xv, 41.
Salimbene, 7.
Salvation, history of, 17; and Lord,
   xiv; of man, 34.
Saint-Denis, 5.
Saint-Nazaire, xvii.
San Damiano, 3.
San Rufino, 39.
Saracens, 39.
Savior, freeing by, 34; suffering of,
   14, 35.
Scripture, 48; book of, 14.
Seraph, xvii, 10, 13, 18, 19, 20, 22,
   23, 34, 35.
Siena, 39.
Sin, 17, 34.
Sixtus IV, 3, 5, 8.
Sixtus V, 8.

Son, as Exemplar, 26; reflections
   of, 31; and Trinity, 25, 27, 33.
Soul, ascent of, 24, 25; book of, 14;
   and Christ, 13, 35; fallen, 31;
   goodness in, 31; as image, 31;
   journey of, 20, 22; nature of, 21,
   23; as mirror, 13; senses of, 32.
Spirituality, of Bonaventure, 1, 2,
   10, 11, 12, 13, 15, 16, 18, 22,
   27, 42, 46; Franciscan, 1, 6, 7,
   11, 12, 13, 14, 15, 22, 26, 34,
   35, 42, 46; Greek, 1, 24; of
   Middle Ages, 1, 2, 12, 14, 16,
   20, 21, 34, 42, 46.
Spirituals, 6, 7.
Stigmata, xv, 3, 14, 18, 35, 40, 44,
   45.
Sylvester, 39, 40.
Symbolism 44; Biblical, 2; in
   Bonaventure, 11, 20, 21, 47.
Tabernacle, 17.
Thomas Aquinas, 1, 2, 20.
Thomas of Celano, xiv, xvii, 38,
   39, 40, 41, 42.
Trinity, attributes of, 24;
   contemplation of, 33; doctrine of,
   1, 14, 16, 24, 25; fecundity of,
   25, 26, 27; and the Good, xiii,
   18; and man, xvii; processions of,
   33; reflections of, 24, 27, 30.
Truth, Eternal, 31, 32; in God, 31;
   and intellect, 31; and Son, 31.
Ubertino di Casale, 12.
Vestiges, 24, 26, 27, 30.
Victorines, xvii.
Virtues, 14, 15, 43, 44, 45; of
   Christ, 14, 34, 35, 36; of Francis,
   xvi, 39.
Vorreux, Damien, 37, 47.
Will, and Holy Spirit, 31.
William of Middleton, 5.
William of Saint-Amour, 6.
Wisdom, xiv, 29.
Word, 25.

INDEX

Abel, 127.

Acts, 1:1, 133; 1:9, 162; 1:9-11, 162; 1:14, 163; 1:15, 163; 2:1, 163; 2:4, 163; 2:11, 209; 2:17, 179; 3:7, 299; 3:8, 299; 4:12, 173; 4:13, 290; 6:10, 298; 7:60, 319; 9:6, 189; 10:44, 284; 13:9, 290; 20:28, 191.

Adam, 88, 122, 151.

Alan of Lille, 100.

Alexander IV, 310, 311.

Almohad, 268.

Alpha, Being as, 98; Christ as, 108, 172; God as, 61; Word as, 91.

Alviano, 295.

Ambrose, 215, 264.

Ancona, 267; Marches of, 241.

Angels, 70, 77, 92, 129, 145, 160, 162, 165, 196, 245, 246, 292, 301; choirs of, 90, 180; and Francis, 226, 264, 272; of peace, 180; and seal of God, 181, 314.

Animals, cf. Creatures; stories of, 225, 256, 257, 258, 260, 261.

Anna, 131.

Anselm, 102, 167.

Anselm, Psuedo, 162, 163, 171, 173.

Anthony of Padua, 215, 313.

Apocalypse, 1:8, 61, 91, 98, 108, 173; 2:10, 169; 2:17, 89, 112, 113; 2:23, 165; 5:1, 119; 5:5, 159; 5:9, 265; 5:12, 271; 6:12, 187; 6:16, 166; 7:2, 181, 217, 314; 7:9, 169, 218, 322; 12:7-9, 234; 14:11, 167; 14:14, 319; 19:7, 169; 19:10, 301; 19:16, 169, 240; 19:20, 167; 20:4, 324; 20:12, 165; 21:2, 90; 21:6, 91, 98, 108; 22:1-2, 120; 22:13, 91, 98, 108; 22:14, 53.

Apulia, 188, 242.

Arezzo, 236, 301.

Aristotle, 70, 96, 98.

Arles, Chapter of, 215, 289.

Ascension, 121.

Assisi, 185, 186, 188, 192, 196, 201, 208, 209, 213, 230, 246, 276, 287, 294, 320, 323, 324; Chapter of, 326.

Austerity, cf. Flesh; of Francis, 218-227.

Augustine, 66, 74, 75, 81, 83, 99.

Augustine, Brother, 320.

Baptism, 133.

Being, attributes of, 96-101, 107; and cause, 85, 98, 99, 100; divine, 96, 97, 107; Eternal, 82, 98, 100; and God, 95, 98, 102; knowledge of, 81; left behind, 115; and nonbeing, 96, 97.

Bernadone, Peter, 229.

Bernard, Brother, 200, 201.

Bernard of Clairvaux, 90, 167.

Bethlehem, 128, 130, 278.

Bevagna, 294, 299.

Birds, cf. Creatures; stories of, 257, 258, 259, 260, 294, 295, 296, 320.

Blessing, of Christ, 150; of Francis, 215, 252, 257, 258, 283, 284, 287, 288, 295, 296, 316.

Blood, of Christ, 55, 129, 140, 191, 250, 265, 292; of Lamb, 55, 159.

Boethius, 75, 100, 166.

Bologna, 300.

Bonaventure, and Francis, 182; and Friars, 54.

Borgo San Sepolcro, 274.

Brother Ass, 220, 222.

Caesar Augustus, 128.

Calvary, 148.

Canaan, 135.

Canticle of Brother Sun, 263.

Canticle of Canticles, 1:3, 326;

24:23, 210; 24:26, 63; 29:30, 212; 31:8, 186; 37:18, 282; 38:9, 316; 45:1, 185; 50:6, 180; 50:8, 323, 326.

Egypt, 63, 112, 132, 156, 161, 290; and Francis, 268.

Elias of Cortona, Brother, 216, 311.

Elijah, 135, 180, 181, 209, 285, 326.

Elisha, 209, 248, 285.

Emmaus, 160, 246.

Enoch, 326.

Ephesians, 1:18, 53; 2:4, 305; 2:19, 162; 3:9, 111; 3:10, 170; 3:17-18, 93; 4:11-12, 162; 4:21, 317; 5:26, 292; 6:10, 202.

Epiphany, 263, 264.

Esther, 10:6, 120.

Eternal Art, 61, 74, 83.

Eucharist, 139, 141, 264.

Eugene IV, 90.

Exaltation of the Cross, feast of, 305.

Exodus, 2:5, 162; 3:14, 95; 3:18, 61; 12:11, 114; 13:13ff, 63; 17:1-7, 248; 24:16, 62; 25:10-22, 94; 25:20, 106; 25:21, 111; 25:40, 293; 26:33-35, 80, 94; 27:9-18, 80; 29:18, 252; 30:1, 265; 30:27-28, 265; 31:18, 307; 32:12, 154; 33:19, 101; 33:20, 116; 37:17-24, 80; 38:9-20, 80.

Ezechiel, 182.

Ezechiel, 1:3, 187, 214; 2:9, 109; 9:4, 182, 214; 16:13, 168; 28:12, 182; 28:14, 16, 264.

Città della Pieve, 301.

Città di Castello, 300.

Faith, 312; in Christ, 89, 111, 112, 130, 173, 196; of Christ, 279, 282; and Church, 208, 319; and Holy Spirit, 93, 164; preaching of, 266-271; and prophecies, 127;

and providence, 64; and reason, 122; and Scripture, 91.

Father, cf. Power, Wisdom; and Christ, 126, 133, 135, 142, 150, 153, 154, 156, 161, 162; emanation of, 73; as First Principle, 85; as fountain-source, 73; and Francis, 275; gifts of, 53, 163; glory of, 154, 162, 175; prayer to, 114, 141, 174, 175; return to, 63, 72, 116, 246; sends Son, 108, 228, 292; and Trinity, 84, 95, 103.

Fear, of Christ, 122, 191; dispelled, 131, 266; of God, 267, 282, 301, 308; of Lord, 60, 319.

Flesh, cf. Austerity; drives of, 185, 283; mortification of, 190, 202, 218, 221, 222, 322; and stigmata, 271.

Foligno, 192.

Forgiveness, cf. sin; 137, 143, 157, 164, 220, 237, 254, 284, 286, 289.

Francis, cf. Martyrdom, Miracles, Stigmata, Vision; blessings of, 215, 252, 257, 258, 283, 284, 287, 288, 295, 296, 319; compassion of, 186, 187, 190, 196, 225, 250, 253, 255, 300, 303, 305; conversion of, 313, 314, 317, 318; as father, 53, 54, 182, 200, 213, 254, 255, 257, 259, 285, 286, 287, 289, 319, 320, 323, 324; fervor of, 139, 194, 269, 277, 295, 316, 317; humility of, 189, 195, 224, 228-238, 293, 297, 315, 321; imitation of, 181, 182, 238, 266, 279; joy of, 189, 192, 195, 199, 243, 252, 278, 298; kindness of, 253, 265; and lepers, 188, 189, 190, 195, 274, 315; as man of God, *passim* 189-327; obedience

304; and God, 179, 319; guiding, 210; and Holy Spirit, 122, 163, 164, 174, 286, 297; law of, 64, 91, 126; and prayer, 273, 276, 291; reforming, 62; restoring, 63, 90; strengthening, 207; and union, 72.

Greccio, 257, 260, 278, 288.

Gregory IX, cf. Hugolino; 233, 297, 310, 325.

Gregory the Great, 317, 323.

Gubbio, 195, 255, 299.

Heart, ardor of, 306; ascent of, 59, 90, 116, 120; and faith, 127, 173, 179; and Francis, 186, 200, 250, 271, 281, 297; hardness of, 137, 141, 147, 154, 241, 282, 298; and Holy Spirit, 122; and judgment, 165; and love, 155, 173; and peace, 179; rejoicing of, 60, 171, 172.

Heaven, 160; ascension to, 162.

Hebrews, 63, 246.

Hebrews, 1:2, 126, 179; 1:3, 72, 89; 1:4, 162; 1:14, 70; 3:1, 200; 4:15, 134; 5:7, 137, 153; 6:1, 228; 6:6, 148; 7:26, 162; 9:2-5, 94; 9:24, 162; 10:29, 317; 11:3, 64; 12:2, 157.

Hell, 159.

Henry VI, 214.

Herod, 130, 132, 146.

Holiness, of Francis, 228, 229, 244, 259, 271, 277, 281, 283, 285, 286, 287, 288, 302, 304, 307, 310, 316, 319, 321, 324; of Friars, 212, 252, 310; and obedience, 232; and rule of Francis, 207.

Holy Land, 268.

Holy of Holies, 94.

Holy Spirit, charity of, 122; and Christ, 133, 134, 135, 163; and Francis, 187, 192, 200, 201, 216,

264, 273, 281, 291, 297; is gift, 93, 113; gifts of, 85, 113, 163, 164, 174, 286; and incarnation, 127, 157; and inspiration, 205, 206, 213, 216, 273, 291; joy of, 202; prayer to, 114, 191; presence of, 274, 284; and revelation, 294; is sent, 108, 113; and spiration, 103; teaching of 290, 302; and Trinity, 95, 103.

Honorius III, 216-217, 297.

Hope, 312; in Christ, 111, 142; and desire, 89; in Father, 194; for forgiveness, 143; and Holy Spirit, 93; of pardon, 150; for reward, 135, 173; and scripture, 91.

Hugolino, Cardinal, cf. Gregory IX; 233, 245, 297, 310, 325.

Humility, of Christ, 129-133, 134, 138, 139, 140, 148, 196, 228, 233; of Francis, 189, 195, 224, 228-238, 293, 297, 315, 321; of Friars, 235, 236, 246, 289; and honors, 233; and obedience, 231, 232; and poverty, 240; of Virgin, 131; and virtues, 129, 132, 228, 238.

Illumination, 309; and grace, 306; and Holy Spirit, 163; and meditation, 63, 275; and mind, 85, 93, 97, 108, 110, 280; and scripture, 91; and soul, 89, 90, 91, 92; source of, 53; stages of, 54, 55, 61, 90, 109.

Illuminato, Brother, 269, 270, 300, 306, 307.

Image, cf. mirror, vestige; of Christ, 206, 254, 306, 307, 322; in creation, 60, 92, 111; generation of, 73; of God, 60, 72, 73, 77, 79, 81, 84, 87, 92, 94, 108, 265; man as, 80; in mind, 79, 111; reformation of, 90; Son

as, 85; of Trinity, 79.
Imola, 235.
Incarnation, 160.
Innocent III, 182, 204-206, 216.
Intellect, cf. mind, soul, spirit, understanding; blindness of, 96; and contemplation, 119; function of, 81-83, 84; and illumination, 93, 163, 280; and laws, 73, 74; left behind, 111, 113, 114; and memory, 80; and senses, 63, 83.
Isaiah, 61; 1:6, 149; 6:1-13, 305, 309; 6:2, 54, 62, 75, 91; 6:6-7, 309; 9:2, 159; 11:1, 160; 11:2, 210; 12:3, 155; 14:9-15, 234; 20:3, 230; 21:8, 220; 22:12, 181; 24:16, 307; 24:20, 87; 28:19, 187; 30:26, 168; 31:9, 115; 32:18, 168; 33:7, 180; 38:1, 283; 38:15, 202; 40:3, 180; 40:11, 136; 49:6, 179; 52:7, 200; 53:3, 148, 190; 53:4, 142, 148; 53:7, 145, 255; 61:1, 297; 63:2, 156; 66:2, 179; 66:24, 167.
Israel, 112, 203; people of, 209.
Jacob, 63, 112; ladder of, 303.
Jacoba of Setesoli, Lady, 256.
James, 135.
James, 1:4, 316; 1:17, 53, 170.
Jerome, 323.
Jeremiah, 6:26, 138; 31:3, 239; 48:28, 155.
Jerome of Ascoli, 204.
Jerusalem, City of, 132, 138; heavenly, 54, 55, 89, 90, 93, 168, 317; interior, 110.
Jews, 145, 146, 155.
Job, 316.
Job, 1:1, 185; 6:4, 151; 6:8, 149; 6:10, 316; 7:15, 115; 9:1ff, 316; 19:20, 316; 23:11, 263; 28:11, 280, 281; 29:16, 246; 31:18, 186; 36:22, 171; 40:25, 159; 41:12, 220.

John, 55, 90, 135, 139, 151, 181.
John, 1:1, 53, 55, 82, 89; 1:7, 179, 215, 320; 1:9, 82; 1:14, 62, 199; 1:16, 173; 1:18, 292; 1:29, 129, 139; 1:47, 209; 3:29, 181; 4:14, 155; 4:42, 270; 5:33, 310; 5:33-34, 314; 6:12, 39, 183; 8:3-11, 136; 8:10-11, 137; 9:32, 150, 209; 10:7, 110; 10:9, 55, 88; 10:11, 136; 11:27, 307; 11:35, 137; 12:3, 252; 12:6, 241; 12:12-26, 138; 12:13, 324; 13:1, 63, 115, 139, 246, 304, 319; 13:29, 241; 13-17, 139; 14:6, 89, 110; 14:8, 34, 115; 16:11, 290; 16:28, 320; 17:3, 105, 270; 18:1, 141; 18:2-11, 142; 18:4, 141; 18:12-27, 144; 18:13, 19-24, 145; 18:28-19:16, 145; 18:23, 145; 19:1-16, 146, 147; 19:15, 146; 19:17, 148; 19:17-24, 148; 19:19, 215; 19:26, 153; 19:28, 151, 315; 19:28-30, 151; 19:30, 151, 153; 19:31-37, 154; 19:34, 322; 19:37, 155; 19:38-42, 157; 20:1, 157; 20:1-31, 159; 20:24ff, 323; 20:28, 160; 21:1-25, 159; 21:4, 188, 324; 21:7, 294; 21:15, 290; 21:17, 268.
1 John, 2:1, 163; 2:20, 281; 3:29, 262; 4:18, 266.
John of Greccio, 278.
John of St. Paul, 205.
John the Baptist, 127, 133, 180, 219.
John Damascene, 95.
Jordan, 133.
Joseph (husband of Mary), 128.
Joseph (son of Jacob), 156, 161.
Joseph of Arimathea, 157.
Josiah, 22:18, 260.
Judah, 130, 132, 159.
Judas, 139, 143.
Judges, 2:4, 301; 16:30, 159.
Judgment, and Christ, 165-167;

day of, 164, 165, 166, 167, 252;
divine, 289; of God, 283, 284,
316.
Julian of Speyer, *passim* 186-327.
Justice, 63, 193; and Christ, 129,
133, 153, 165-168; ordering of,
126; and Pilate, 146; and reason,
64; and rule of Francis, 207; time
of, 284.
Kingdom, of Christ, 132, 162, 169;
eternal, 203, 206; of Father, 160;
glory of, 169; of God, 136, 169,
170, 202, 210; of heaven, 193,
245, 262.
1 Kings, 2:5, 203, 252; 2:8, 179;
16:11-12, 290; 19:10, 155; 30:6,
269.
2 Kings, 5:2, 290.
3 Kings, 4:7, 212; 10:19, 61; 10:24,
169; 19:20, 317.
4 Kings, 2:9ff, 285; 2:11, 180, 209,
326; 2:12, 209; 3:15, 294; 4:1ff,
248; 6:17, 209.
Knowledge, 61, 63, 88; cf. God.
Lago Trasimeno, 257.
Lamb, blood of, 55, 271; innocence
of, 129, 139, 147, 150, 153, 159,
225, 255, 264; marriage of, 168;
meekness of, 140, 141, 143,
145-46, 150, 255, 256; paschal,
139; as victorious, 167; wrath of,
166.
Lamentations, 1:13, 151; 2:18, 138;
3:1, 151; 3:15, 144, 146; 4:8, 316.
Lateran, 204, 206; Fourth Council
of, 182.
La Verna, Mount of, 54, 259, 286,
304, 308.
Law, 61; of certitude, 73, 74, 83; of
charity, 64, 91; of Christ, 131,
135, 253; eternal, 169; given, 92;
of God, 261; of grace, 91; and
Moses, 307; of nature, 64, 91; of
scripture, 64, 67, 91, 95.

Lazarus, 137, 138.
Lent, 279; of the Assumption, 264;
of Epiphany, 263-264; of Peter
and Paul, 265; of St. Michael,
259, 264, 304.
Leo, Brother, 287.
Leo, Lord, 236.
Leonard, Brother, 285.
Life, book of, 165, 170.
Light, and Christ, 171, 319; and
Father, 126, 170; and Francis,
179, 180, 197, 224, 275, 319;
God as, 72, 76, 77, 78, 82, 85,
324; and mind, 55, 79, 82, 94,
98, 111, 163, 204, 280, 288; and
reason, 63; source of, 53; in
visions, 209.
Lombardy, 226.
Lord, 106; cf. Christ; covenant of,
180; of creation, 145; and
Francis, 195, 210, 231, 269, 272,
298, 315; glory of, 231; as God,
60, 131, 140; of heaven, 138; as
mediator, 53; name of, 277, 278,
299; passion of, 119; rejoicing in,
202; works of, 68, 240, 262, 267,
298.
Love, for Christ, 88, 93, 111, 121,
131, 135, 142, 144, 160, 173,
196, 231, 252, 264, 265, 270,
272, 278, 305, 306, 307; of
Christ, 119, 121, 135, 137, 140,
150, 155, 181, 187, 264, 275;
divine, 157, 262; and Francis, 55,
187, 250, 280; and Holy Spirit,
163; for God, 61, 77, 186, 212,
246, 266; of God, 234, 246, 247,
262, 273, 326; for Gospel, 212;
and Mary, 157, 196, 264; of soul,
79; and spiration, 84; in Trinity,
104; and Word, 89.
Luke, 1:17, 181; 1:26-38, 127; 1:35,
127; 1:46, 128; 1:52, 234; 1:67,
180; 1:68, 226; 1:75, 207; 1:76,

160; 28:16-20, 161; 28:19, 95.
Meditation, cf. Contemplation.
Memory, 74; and contemplation, 119; function of, 80-81, 84; as image, 81; and soul, 80.
Mercy, of Christ, 136, 137, 143, 144, 234, 255; divine, 155, 215, 275; of Father, 251, 252; of God, 126, 179, 220, 252, 253, 284; and Mary, 199, 264; ordering of, 126; of self, 260.
Mercy Seat, 94, 106, 107, 108, 111, 313.
Micah, 2:13, 162.
Michael the Archangel, 259, 164, 304, 307.
Mind, cf. intellect, soul, spirit; changeable, 82; and desire, 87, 173; and divine image, 79; and God, 110; illumination of, 55, 85, 93, 97, 108, 111; knowledge of, 61; as mirror, 78; and senses, 69, 74, 75, 87; and truth, 94.
Miracles, 214; of Christ, 134-35, 143; of Church, 163; and followers of Francis, 210, 294; and Francis, 184, 195, 196, 225, 235, 237, 238, 247, 248, 249, 267, 277, 279, 281, 285, 287, 289, 295, 296, 297, 298, 299, 300, 301, 302, 308, 309, 322, 323, 324, 325, 326, 327; of Seraph, 54, 306, 307, 310.
Miramamolin, 268.
Mirror, Francis as, 228, 321; mind as, 78, 288; self as, 79, 80; soul as, 56, 84; world as, 56, 63, 69, 92; and Word, 170.
Monaldus, 215, 313.
Monte Casale, 234.
Morico, 213.
Morocco, 267, 268.
Moses, 62, 91, 95, 101, 135, 161, 248, 307.

Mount of Olives, 141, 162.
Mount Tabor, 303.
Mystical Theology, 60.
Mysticism, 244; communication of, 114; ecstasy of, 55, 60, 63, 89, 90, 91, 92, 109, 113, 115, 201, 202, 234, 277.
Narbonne, Chapter of, 182.
Narni, 299, 300.
Nature, cf. Christ; creation, 126; divine, 108; human, 90, 142, 187; law of, 64, 91, 126; rational, 72; and sin, 63; and Son, 127; stages of, 62.
New Testament, 95.
Nicholas IV, 204.
Nicodemus, 157.
Nocera, 246.
Numbers, 74-75.
Numbers, 6:24-26, 287; 7:89, 313.
Obedience, 132, 244, 296; of devil, 300; of Francis, 196, 219, 228-238, 317; of Friars, 203, 211, 215, 235, 243, 288, 318; and humility, 231, 232.
Old Testament, 95.
Omega, Being as, 98; Christ as, 108, 172; God as, 61; Word as, 91.
Order of the Brothers of Penance, 210.
Order of the Crosiers, 213.
Order of Friars Minor, 192; cf. Chapters; beginning of, 197, 210; belief in Francis, 210; and Bonaventure, 54; as Christ's little poor, 207, 213; and Gospel, 241; growth of, 201-202, 210, 216; name of, 233, 245; and Rome, 204; rule of, 201, 203, 206, 207, 208, 216, 217, 302; visions of, 209, 210; and work, 222.
Orte, 299.
Ostia, Cardinal of, 233, 245, 297; cf. Hugolino.

Providence, divine, 128, 203, 235, 249, 269, 303; and Francis, 197, 226; of God, 64, 132, 207, 237, 293.

Psalms, 4:4, 327; 4:7, 79, 94; 4:9, 92; 5:12, 173; 15:11, 160; 16:4, 266; 16:8-9, 274; 17:11, 162; 18:6, 128; 18:15, 211; 20:4, 187; 22:4, 269; 28:3, 319; 30:13, 230; 30:16, 192; 31:4, 316; 35:9, 172; 35:10, 172, 321; 36:4, 88; 37:9, 55; 40:9, 87; 40:10, 141; 41:2, 139; 41:4, 158; 41:5, 172; 44:3, 154; 44:8, 56, 171; 44:15, 163; 45:5, 171; 50:8, 275; 54:13, 141; 54:14-15, 141; 54:23, 203, 273; 54:24, 142; 56:2, 151; 56:5, 253; 57:11, 167; 61:10, 185; 61:13, 165; 62:10-11, 167; 67:19, 162; 67:34, 162; 68:2, 149; 68:5, 147; 70:15-16, 240; 70:19, 325; 71:18, 134; 72:26, 115; 75:3, 54; 75:5-6, 86; 76:10, 143; 76:11, 187; 77:16, 248; 77:25, 245; 77:54, 215; 79:6, 208; 83:4, 155; 83:6-7, 59, 60; 83:8, 63; 83:10, 154; 84:4, 154; 85:11, 60; 91:5, 262; 91:5-6, 68; 92:5, 312; 94:2, 236; 96:3, 165; 102:22, 161; 103:24, 68; 105:48, 116; 106:24, 267; 108:31, 192; 109:1, 167; 109:3, 92; 118:37, 221; 119:7, 54; 121:6, 54; 129:7, 156; 141:2, 319; 141:7, 192; 141:8, 319; 142:1-2, 167; 146:2, 203; 148, 29; 148:1-14, 263.

Purity, 309; of Francis, 220, 225, 227.

Rainerio Capoci of Viterbo, Cardinal, 310.

Reason, and faith, 122; and grace, 63; and judgment, 72, 73; and justice, 64; and memory, 80; and truth, 83.

Red Sea, 112.

Redemption, cf. Christ; through Christ, 62, 131, 139, 154, 173, 250, 265, 292, 322; day of, 128; and God, 156.

Regeneration, 133, 322.

Remorse, 143, 144.

Repentance, 136, 151, 237, 283, 298; preaching of, 180, 203, 260.

Resurrection, of Christ, 121, 322.

Revelation, cf. Vision; and Francis, 200, 208, 216, 241, 271, 286, 293, 297, 302, 304, 305, 308, 313, 316; and Friars, 197, 208; illumining, 91, 92, 106; and rule, 216, 217.

Riccardo degli Annibaldi, Cardinal, 204.

Rieti, 247, 283, 299, 308; Lake of, 257.

Rivo Torto, 208.

Romans, 1:16, 120; 1:20, 76, 77; 2:6, 165; 5:8, 93; 8:3, 129, 156; 8:18, 322; 8:21, 131; 8:26, 189; 8:32, 163; 9:5, 149; 10:15, 180; 11:36, 101; 12:1, 266; 12:19, 192; 13:10, 91; 14:10, 165.

Rome, 204, 256.

Rufino, Brother, 311.

Ruth, 1:16, 297.

Sacraments, 133, 264; and Church, 155; and God's goodness, 67; and Holy Spirit, 164; and symbol, 77.

Sacrifice, Christ as, 142; to Christ, 277; of martyr, 266, 271.

St. Anthony, hospice of, 204.

St. George, church of, 324.

St. Mary of the Angels, 196; cf. Portiuncula.

St. Mary of the Portiuncula, cf. Portiuncula.

St. Martin of Tours, 215, 271.

St. Nicholas, Church of, 200.

Salvation, 222; of all, 264, 267,

303; of believers, 120, 161, 170;
and Christ, 129, 130, 133, 151,
155, 173, 194, 292, 293; and
Friars, 251, 252; and Gospel,
180; and poverty, 240; and
preaching, 200, 251, 269, 292;
promise of, 126; of souls, 251,
252, 265, 270.
Samson, 159.
Sanctuary, 79, 94.
San Damiano, 189, 191, 196, 324.
San Severino, 214.
Sangemini, 300.
Sant' Urbano, 225.
Saracen, 212, 213, 267, 268, 269.
Satan, 163.
Satriano, 246.
Saul, 155.
Savior, cf. Christ; Christ is, 120,
121, 129, 130, 137, 138, 160,
161, 173, 269; Crucifixion of,
147; as grace, 179; presence of,
264; promised, 126.
Scripture, book of, 77; and Francis,
280, 281, 185; law of, 64, 67, 91;
levels of, 91, 92; and reparation,
91; symbolism of, 255; testimony
of, 130, 151, 155.
Self, First Principle in, 87; as
mirror, 79, 111; transcendence
of, 111, 115; victory over, 188.
Seraph, 260; ardor of, 305, 309;
and Crucified, 54, 112, 305; and
illumination, 55, 75, 92, 110;
vision of, 305-309, 312-314.
Seraphim, 61, 305, 309.
Siena, 243, 254, 256, 259, 281,
285.
Silvester, Brother, 201, 202, 236,
294, 313.
Sin, 253; avoidance of, 63; and
Christ, 129, 135, 153; confession
of, 283; deforming of, 62, 251;
expiation of, 137; forgiveness of,

202, 203; and Holy Spirit, 164;
and judgment, 166; original, 62.
Sinner, 130, 150, 162, 166, 167,
220, 231, 251, 253, 255, 275,
276, 298; Francis as, 228, 234,
270.
Sion, 54, 63.
Soldan of Babylon, 268-270.
Solomon, 54, 61, 110.
Son, as Eternal Art, 61; and Father,
161, 170, 228, 292; generation of,
73, 103; humiliation of, 148, 239;
hypostatic union of, 127; as
Image, 85, 108, 170; as incarnate,
133; and judgment, 166; and
man, 265, 292; as mediator, 53,
174; prayer to, 114; relatedness
of, 85; sent, 108, 126, 156, 163;
and Trinity, 95, 103.
Soul, ascent of, 54, 90, 139; and
Christ, 129, 134, 135, 145, 147,
148, 171, 194, 208; of Christ,
149, 159; enlightenment of, 53,
89, 90, 92, 224, 232, 313; and
God, 87, 92, 139, 151, 171; and
God's image, 60, 81, 84; as
mirror, 56; needs help, 88; and
peace, 150, 277; persecution of,
192, 253; powers of, 62, 80, 84,
92; salvation of, 251, 252, 265,
284; and self-knowledge, 80; and
self-love, 70; and senses, 69, 70,
71, 72, 221; Spouse of, 89, 90,
91, 92; stages of, 180.
Spain, 268.
Spirit, 70; ardor of, 139, 194, 269,
277, 295, 316, 317; ascent of, 90;
and body, 55, 224, 225, 315; and
hope, 135; of Jesus, 142, 153;
and mind, 61; peace of, 54, 173;
seeing in, 288, 289.
Spoleto, 195, 207, 208.
Stefano di Casa Nova, Cardinal,
310.

351

63; 14:1-7, 194; 16:20, 120, 139; 16:24, 225; 18:14, 129.

Word, 91, 199; as creator, 64, 91, 173; generation of, 73, 84; as incarnate, 62, 89, 91, 170, 173; and Light, 82; and wisdom, 85, 170.

World, calling of, 203; contempt for, 188, 190, 194, 200, 202, 214, 270; honors of, 190, 212, 229, 230, 237; renunciation of, 240, 274.

Zacchaeus, 136, 137.

Zachariah, 9:11, 159; 12:10, 155.